1989

THE POLITICAL ECONOMY OF
CHINESE
SOCIALISM

★ *The Political Economy of Socialism* ★

THE POLITICAL ECONOMY OF
CHINESE
SOCIALISM

MARK SELDEN

An East Gate Book

M. E. SHARPE, INC.
Armonk, New York
London, England

Grateful acknowledgment is made to the following for permission to reprint previously published material:

Pergamon Journal Ltd., Oxford, United Kingdom: "Original Accumulation, Equity and Late Industrialization: The Cases of Socialist China and Capitalist Taiwan," in *World Development* 14, 10/11 (October 1986). Reprinted by permission of Pergamon Press.

Peasant Studies: "The Reform of Land Ownership and the Political Economy of Contemporary China," in *Peasant Studies* 14, 4 (summer 1987). Reprinted by permission of *Peasant Studies*.

Sage Publications: "Imposed Collectivization and the Crisis of Agrarian Development in the Socialist States," in *Crises in the World-System*, ed. Albert Bergesen, 1983. Reprinted by permission of Sage Publications.

M. E. Sharpe, Inc.: "Income Inequality and the State," in *Rural Development in China*, ed. William Parish, 1985. Reprinted by permission of M. E. Sharpe, Inc.

"Cooperation and Conflict: Cooperative and Collective Formation in China's Countryside," in *The Transition to Socialism in China*, ed. Mark Selden and Victor Lippit, 1982. Reprinted by permission of M. E. Sharpe, Inc.

An East Gate Book

Library of Congress Cataloging-in-Publication Data

Selden, Mark.
  The political economy of contemporary China.

  Bibliography: p.
  Includes index.
    1. China—Economic policy—1949-   . 2. Agriculture and state—China.
3. Land reform—China. 4. Rural development—China. 5. Industry and state—China.
I. Title.
HC427.9.S415   1988   338.951   88–4666
ISBN 0–87332–426–9
ISBN 0–87332–504–4 (pbk.)

Printed in the United States of America

For Edward Friedman

CONTENTS

LIST OF TABLES

ACKNOWLEDGMENTS

This book is dedicated to Edward Friedman, whose scholarship and probing questioning over the last twenty-five years have forced me, again and again, to rethink parameters of the theory and practice of revolutionary change and development . . . particularly many of my own earlier judgments.

I have been fortunate to have the benefit of suggestions and comments of numerous friends and specialists on China, on development, and on socialist revolutions, including colleagues in China, Japan, and the United States, and particularly those of my students in the sociology department at the State University of New York at Binghamton. I especially wish to thank Chih-ming Ka and Aiguo Lu for their contributions as co-authors of two chapters in this volume. Many people have read and criticized portions of this manuscript in draft form and provided valuable information and suggestions for its improvement. For this I thank Anthony Barnet, Frederick Buttel, Tiejun Cheng, Chengchang Chiu, Deborah Davis, Charles Geisler, Thomas Gold, Ishikawa Shigeru, Kay Johnson, Kojima Reiitsu, Nicholas Lardy, Elisabeth Lasek, Victor Lippit, Thomas Lyons, Ramkrishna Mukherjee, Muto Ichiyo, Victor Nee, Peter Nolan, Paul Pickowicz, Thomas Rawski, William Parish, Vivienne Shue, Benedict Stavis, David Stark, Tang Tsou, Immanuel Wallerstein, Andrew Watson, and Martin Whyte, and above all Marc Blecher, Edward Friedman, Terence Hopkins, and Carl Riskin. I regret that I could not fully pursue some of their most intriguing and demanding suggestions.

I acknowledge with appreciation support for the research and writing of this volume provided by National Endowment for the Humanities Research Grants RO-20611 and RO-20903.

Once again Douglas Merwin of M. E. Sharpe has supported this project with intelligence, acumen, and enthusiasm. The manuscript has benefited from the professional editing of Anita O'Brien. I also wish to thank Nancy Hall for skilled preparation of portions of the manuscript. Kyoko, Lili, Ken, and Yumi wondered, and occasionally inquired delicately, but with the passage of time more pointedly, whether this manuscript would ever see the light of day. Now is the time to say "It's finished" . . . for the moment.

Ithaca, New York
January 1, 1988

THE POLITICAL ECONOMY OF

CHINESE

SOCIALISM

1

RETHINKING CHINA'S SOCIALIST ECONOMIC DEVELOPMENT

This volume is the product of three decades of reflection building on archival, documentary, and field research on the revolutionary transformation of Chinese political economy and society, noting both its achievements and its limits. The focus is the interrelationship—at times reciprocal but often conflictual, even explosive—between state and society and between city and countryside, with particular reference to patterns of economic development and class transformation.

China's development trajectory[1] remains a conundrum, comprising contradictory, even dialectical, elements as large and complex as that continental, multi-ethnic nation itself.

China has experienced four decades of rapid, but highly uneven, industrialization, and its urban population is the world's largest; yet in no other major industrializing nation does the specific gravity of agriculture and the countryside loom so large.

Similarly, no other country with such high, sustained national income growth rates (averaging approximately 7 percent annually in the thirty-five years from 1952 through 1986) has such low per capita income, U.S.$310 in 1985 according to World Bank calculations, $340 by U.S. Central Intelligence Agency estimate (World Bank 1987: 202; Directorate of Intelligence U.S. C.I.A. 1986: 25).

More than any other nation, China has experimented with a range of policies from radical mobilizational collectivism and self-reliant development to far-reaching reformist attempts to build the household sector and the market and to induce foreign investment—and it has swung repeatedly between policy poles in the search for a viable development path.

This volume inquires into the results of China's socialist development with particular reference to the social consequences and costs of alternative strategies. From this perspective it probes the continuing tensions between city and countryside, between growth-oriented and equity-oriented initiatives, between the state's voracious demand for accumulation, investment, and centralization of power and pressures from below for greater autonomy, to boost consumption and expand the scope of household and market activity. All these become manifest in policy and resource conflicts and changing institutional configurations. The attempt is made to compare the developmental outcomes from multiple perspectives, including those of China's earlier development performance, of other state socialist societies, of the newly industrializing nations of East Asia, and of other large agrarian developing nations such as India. But the primary focus is on the consequences of alternative development strategies pursued at critical junctures within China.

More than 80 percent of China's one billion people live in the countryside where more than 70 percent of the nation's labor force is employed in agriculture. The most distinctive and controversial policies associated with the Chinese revolution in general and the leadership of Mao Zedong in particular have been set in, or have special significance for, the rural areas. These include the constellation of strategies associated with people's war, nationwide land reform, cooperative formation, collectivization, communization, and local, regional, and national self-reliance. They also include far-reaching changes associated with household contracts, the resurgence of markets, rural industrialization, and myriad other reforms enacted in the 1980s under the leadership of Deng Xiaoping. While formidable obstacles confront the reform program in the state sector, in industry and the cities, and in international economic relations, through the first decade of reform the countryside and the peasantry have been the locus of the most far-reaching changes taking place in Chinese society. Indeed, where industrial and urban institutions have been remarkably stable since the early 1950s (a minor exception being the incorporation of rural temporary and contract laborers in the urban labor force), the countryside has been rocked by each of the major policy shifts and popular upheavals that have punctuated Chinese political economy. The reemergence in the 1980s of the household and the market as dynamic forces makes clear that no understanding of Chinese political economy and society that slights the values and goals of China's 800 million peasants or that misreads the complex interaction of state and rural society will suffice to capture China's volatile course. The results of the modernization strategy hinge in large part on rural outcomes, or, more precisely, on the interrelationship between an overwhelmingly rural population and a party-state elite whose core, throughout the period of the People's Republic, has been ever more firmly rooted in the cities.

Chinese Model or Models?

In the 1960s and 1970s international scholarly and political attention centered on the "Chinese model" or the "Chinese road to socialism." Discussion pinpointed the commune system, class struggle, uninterrupted revolution, egalitarian distribution, and self-reliance as the hallmarks of a revolutionary development strategy whose most distinctive features—and for some, China's finest achievements—centered in the rural areas and represented fundamental departures from Soviet approaches to development since Stalin. In the late 1960s and throughout the 1970s, despite, or perhaps because of, the paucity of economic data and direct observation, perceptions of China's achievements figured prominently in the global critique of developmentalist strategies that neglected rural welfare while pursuing the historically familiar (and World Bank-supported) urban-centered industrialization strategies; relied heavily on foreign capital and technology and hewed to export-oriented industrialization at the sacrifice of autonomous development and popular welfare; and exacerbated urban-rural and class cleavages. Some saw in the Chinese model of that era a dynamic and egalitarian way forward for poverty-stricken, stagnant, and polarized Third World nations (Gurley 1976; Eckstein 1978).[2] Critics on the other hand, maintained that the commune was a coercive institution that presided over shared poverty and that the claims of high growth and popular participation were at best unsubstantiated and at worst fraudulent (Liu and Yeh 1965; Joint Economic Committee 1967; London and London 1970).

These conflicting perspectives, in which both proponents and critics agreed on the essential features of "the Chinese model," however profound their disagreements in evaluating its results, must and can now be transcended. The long trajectory of revolutionary strategies, and particularly party-peasant relations, from the 1920s to the 1980s reveals no single model for development and social change but persistent unresolved conflicts that gave rise to drastic policy shifts, repeated assaults on institutional structures, social relations and social values, and a pattern of uneven development, both temporally and spatially. The notion of a unitary "Chinese model" fails to capture the deep and unresolved conflicts and tensions within Chinese society, the fact that Mao Zedong, whose pronouncements constituted the principal basis for world understanding of that model, frequently occupied a minority (if supremely powerful) position in Chinese politics during the tumultuous final decades of his career, and above all the large swings that have distinguished rural policy and practice over the last six decades.[3] It is tempting to suggest that if there was a single development model, its most salient feature was the large and frequent oscillation among the different policy poles marking the clock-face of alternative emphases.

The present study seeks to clarify and reassess two deeply rooted tendencies within Chinese policy and practice in light of insights derived from analysis of changing urban-rural relations and state-society conflicts. The first of these approaches, emphasizing class struggle, mass mobilization, high rates of state-centered accumulation,[4] egalitarian distribution, collective and communal production, and elimination of the market, the household economy, and traditional values, is well known: While some of its distinctive features can be traced back to the revolutionary base areas in the years 1928–1935, and others emerged briefly in the most violent phase of land reform in 1947-1948, their quintessential crystallization was in the nationwide collectivization drive of 1955-1956 and the communization at the heart of the Great Leap Forward of 1958-1960, with the Dazhai movement of the Cultural Revolution decade exhibiting certain common features in more muted form.

To categorize this mobilizational collectivism emphasized by Mao in the years 1955-1976 as "*the* Chinese model," however, distorts the twists and turns of rural policy and party-peasant relations and obfuscates some of the party's signal achievements from the Anti-Japanese resistance forward. These include gradual but far-reaching wartime economic and social reforms predicated on broad popular support, mutual aid and gradual, voluntary cooperation in the early 1950s, and the reopening of the household sector and the market in the early 1960s. The salient alternative to mobilizational collectivism was not the "capitalist road" but an innovative approach to socialist development in a poor agrarian society that had virtually none of the material preconditions for socialism which even Marx in the nineteenth century had taken for granted. From the 1940s forward, the predominant alternative to mobilizational collectivism within the Chinese Communist movement emphasized the broad unity of a coalition of social forces, assuring welfare and consumption gains for the peasant majority; gradual, voluntary processes of cooperation; tolerance toward heterodox peasant cultural, religious, and economic values; astute balancing of market and plan and of state and household interests; and attempts to integrate planned changes in relations of production with realized advances in agricultural technology and infrastructure.

A monolithic, and in my view misleading, perspective on a unitary Chinese model, drawn principally from the priorities and the historical reinterpretations advanced during the Great Leap Forward and the Cultural Revolution, leads ineluctably to the view that the contractual and market-oriented reforms of the 1980s constitute a reversal, even a betrayal, of China's finest traditions of rural revolution and development, and the restoration of capitalism (Chossudovsky 1986). The reforms introduce a mixed system of collective, cooperative, and household-based agriculture, complementary roles of plan and market, and of foodgrain, sideline, and industrial activity. The 1980s reforms do indeed break with central premises of the agrarian program of the collectivization and communization drives of 1955–56 and 1958. They similarly challenge premises of the Cultural Revolution and of Mao's priorities in the final decades of his career. There is, moreover, much that is new in the reforms, particularly the central role accorded rural household production and marketing. On the other hand, they also resonate with innovative and successful approaches implemented in the wartime base areas, in the early 1950s cooperative movement, and in the resurgence of household and market activities in the short-lived rural reforms of the early 1960s. The reforms ultimately will have to be judged not by their congruence with late Maoist blueprints or Stalinist orthodoxy but on their consequences for the nation and its component groups from the perspective of development and socio-political change. In ranging widely over the long history of Marxist, Leninist, Stalinist, and Maoist approaches to the theory and practice of development, this volume provides a basis for assessing the contemporary reform agenda.

The reformist rural policies implemented in the base areas during the Anti-Japanese resistance of 1937–1945 rested on consensus of a broad class coalition of forces and acceptance of limits on the scope of changes possible and appropriate to foster national unity in the face of the Japanese enemy. Their implications, however, were profoundly revolutionary. The wartime program undermined the economic and political position of the landlord class, strengthened the poorest rural strata, expanded the ranks of an independent cultivator majority, and so established a firm rural base for a rising Communist Party. While the Guomindang-Communist united front quickly dissolved in mutual recrimination and armed conflict, throughout the war years the Communist Party in base areas behind Japanese lines wooed and worked with a broad spectrum of rural social classes and forces including those from among the landlords and rich peasants who rallied to the resistance. Poor and marginal farmers constituted fertile ground for recruitment to the Red Army, as they did for all Chinese armies, but sons of owner-cultivators and of the local notables also enlisted in the course of the resistance and the civil war, and many subsequently rose through the ranks of the military, party, and government as these organizations grew.

The reformist programs in the Communist-led base areas sustained a broad coalition of forces essential to the resistance while aiding the poor through progressive tax reform, rent and interest reduction, small-scale mutual aid and cooperation, and expanded access to education and welfare services. These policies, which preserved essential foundations of the peasant household economy, rural market structures, lineage relations, and cultural forms, were broadly consistent with peasant values and goals. Cumulatively, however, they initiated a quiet revolution in the rural base areas: In gradually undermining the economic and political monopoly on power of landlords and merchants, in advancing the economic interests and landed stake of the poor, in strengthening the independent cultivator foundations of rural society, in promoting modest but effective cooperative solutions to shortages of labor and investment, in strengthening the party's position within the village, and in expanding the ranks of politically relevant strata, the political economy of people's war interwove growing ties of reciprocity between the Communist Party and broad strata of the peasantry.

The restraint, responsiveness, and receptivity to peasant values and culture, and the party's leadership of a broad coalition of anti-Japanese forces unified on the basis of wartime nationalism and the legitimacy of the reform program, formed the dominant face of party leadership at this time. At critical junctures in the resistance, however, as in the 1942 party rectification movement, and particularly during the extreme radical phase of the 1947 land reform, the emerging socialist party-state, at times with the enthusiastic support of segments of the peasantry and local cadres, carried to destructive extremes class-struggle, antimarket, and rigidly authoritarian policies. In such cases the result was to weaken or split the revolutionary coalition, undermine the economy of the base areas, and threaten not only the prosperous but also the growing independent cultivator center and the poor. Nevertheless, striving to win popular support in the face of powerful foreign and domestic forces, the Communists repeatedly checked these divisive tendencies and drove the Japanese and then the U.S.-backed Guomindang from the mainland.[5] Land reform broke the economic and political power of the landlord and rich peasant classes, consolidated the position of the Communist Party in the rural areas, and won broadly based popular support. Between the 1930s and 1952, as a result of redistribution of approximately 40 percent of the land and progressive tax measures, the poorest 20 percent of the peasantry nearly doubled its income share (Roll 1980).

With the establishment of the People's Republic, the focus of the party's development policy and priorities shifted from the countryside to the city and from agriculture to industry. Observing this shift as well as the primacy of capital-intensive, nationalized heavy industry and the substantial Soviet contribution in charting the First Five-Year Plan (1953–57), many dubbed this the Soviet model. In the early 1950s China's leaders called on the people to "Be Modern and Soviet," and the foundations of China's industrialization rested heavily on Soviet aid, technology, and organization as a U.S.-led blockade ruptured China's ties to its prewar trading partners. With Soviet aid and advice in the First Five-Year Plan, the Chinese state led the way in transforming the ownership structure, class relations, and the investment climate and initiated accelerated development.

In the early 1930s China's ratio of gross investment to gross domestic product was 7.5 percent and machinery and equipment accounted for just 5 to 7 percent of total imports. In the mid-50s, gross capital formation reached 24 percent of gross domestic product, and between 1952 and 1957 the share of machinery and equipment in China's imports soared from 20 to 40 percent (Chen 1975: 621). The core of China's industrialization during the First Five-Year Plan period was the 156 large projects designed by and built with Soviet technical assistance. These projects, predominantly large, capital-intensive producer goods complexes, accounted for nearly half of all industrial investment and shifted the locus of industrialization from treaty port coastal cities inland. Imports of machinery and equipment for these and other projects accounted for 30 percent of China's industrial investment during the plan period (Lardy 1987: 177). The ability to sustain high rates of accumulation and investment would characterize China's political economy throughout the People's Republic with significant fluctuations between high and extremely high accumulation.

At the same time, from the completion of land reform at least until the summer of 1955, China charted a distinctive rural course that built on earlier successes and owed little to Soviet aid, inspiration, or direction. The ultimate goal was, to be sure, large-scale, mechanized collective agriculture along the lines of Stalin's collectives. Yet from the perspective of socialist development strategies, the effort to promote gains in rural incomes, the "rich peasant" policy of the early 1950s, and the program of gradual voluntary cooperation implemented between 1951 and 1955 all contrast sharply (and in my view positively) with Lenin's War Communism and even his New Economic Policy[6] and with Stalin's forced march to collectivization. In contrast to the Bolsheviks, who came to power with no significant rural experience or popular base, and who faced powerful peasant-based opposition, China's new leaders founded the People's Republic after twenty years' experience in the countryside. In the early 1950s, when the party set about charting socialist development, it drew on insights and practices from policies implemented in rural base areas during the earlier people's war and civil war phases as well as the lessons gleaned from the study of Soviet development experience.

Neither in earlier periods of reform nor in the 1980s, when reformers sought to build on the strengths of the household economy, have the dominant groups in the leadership abandoned their convictions about the ultimate superiority of large-scale, mechanized collective agriculture. This is manifest in the continued active discussion in the mid-1980s of reviving cooperative forms of agricultural production and permitting the exchange and sale of land rights in order to raise productivity through land consolidation and specialization. In the 1980s, however, there is clear leadership recognition of the ability of the household, at present low levels of technology, to out-produce the collective and to free labor for a wide range of industrial, sideline, commercial, and other productive and income-generating activity. Party General Secretary Zhao Ziyang's report at the 13th Party Congress in October 1987 not only observed that China is at present in the primary stage of socialism "in which the productive forces are to be highly developed,'' but emphasized that it would require at least a century from the socialist transformation of ownership in the 1950s basically to complete socialist modernization and to move to an advanced stage of socialism (Zhao 1987: 26, 27; cf. Su 1988). In important respects, the 1980s reforms represent a shift in the leadership consensus toward the more sober views of the early 1950s, prior to collectivization, when the party projected a long-term transition to higher forms of cooperation in step with the mechanization, electrification, and general technological advance of the rural economy, when it linked social transformation to peasant acceptance of more socialized forms of farming, and when it recognized *in practice* that the success of the development project hinged on concurrent income gains for the worker and peasant populations.[7]

The Political Economy of Mobilizational Collectivism

For reasons explored below, in 1955 China's leaders abandoned this reformist and gradualist approach to rural social change that projected eventual collective formation in tandem with mechanization and growing household prosperity. The new course of mobilizational collectivism promised instant results in laying the foundations of an advanced socialist economy and society and bringing prosperity to all. The term mobilizational collectivism is introduced for purposes of contrast with the early 1950s' strategy of gradual, voluntary cooperation, on the one hand, and with Stalin's bloody collectivization from above in the Soviet Union on the other. The near universal collectivization that China completed in less than one year between the fall of 1955 and summer of 1956 represented the abandonment of the party's attempt to effect a gradual, long-term shift from household agriculture to large-scale, mechanized collective agriculture by laying the material, organizational, and motivational foundations for such an advance.

The 1955-56 collectivization was completed in the absence of the bloodshed and armed conflict that characterized Soviet collectivization. The mobilizational politics that precipitated collectivization, and which remained an essential characteristic of Chinese political economy for the next twenty-five years, nevertheless rested on powerful, if more subtle, mechanisms of coercion and control of the household sector and the market. Following nationwide collectivization in 1956, the leadership carried the themes of egalitarian, antimarket collectivism to what proved to be disastrous extremes during the Great Leap Forward and Cultural Revolution.

The policy constellation that came to be known as the Chinese model drew in part on mobilizational elements perfected during previous periods. While avoiding the massive bloodshed of Soviet collectivization, China's collectivization drive nevertheless constituted a decisive break with initiatives resting on the essential harmony of interests of the peasant majority and the party. When Mao forced the pace of collectivization, particularly when the party in the Great Leap Forward and Cultural Revolution pressed extreme egalitarian, antimarket policies and attacked core peasant values and precepts as feudal (or, sometimes in the same breath, as capitalist), and when the party in the 1960s and 1970s continued to press rural "class struggle" and sharply to restrict household enterprise and consumption, the relationship between the party-state and the peasantry was strained to the breaking point.

The depth of state-society tensions is well illustrated by the fact that, following collectivization, the state erected, and has subsequently maintained, an elaborate administrative structure that binds the peasantry to the land by means of a household registration (*hukou*) mechanism that is the centerpiece of a system of universal population, employment, rationing, residential, and mobility controls. From its inception in 1955, the household registration system, backed by the power of the army, public security forces, and militia, has regulated most long-term and even short-term entry into the cities as well as intrarural movement. When the state sought to eliminate most household sideline production and private marketing activity, activities which had long spelled the difference between subsistence and starvation for many rural households, and as control over economic and cultural activities passed from households, lineages, and the market into the hands of collectives and local cadres, many villagers experienced both impoverishment and alienation.[8] The fratricidal and frequently incomprehensible political scapegoating and ideological manipulation of the Cultural Revolution compounded the anxiety and frustration of the collectivized peasantry.

Two points bear emphasis. First, the consequences of imposed collectivization included depriving early smaller, voluntary, fragile, and struggling cooperatives of their legitimacy—the sense of popular legitimacy resting on shared labor and decisions as well as the ability of successful units to deliver higher incomes and a measure of security for

Table 1.1

China: Major Income and Industrial Indicators, 1949–1985

	(1) National income index (1952 = 100)	(2) National income increase %	(3) Per capita national income increase %	(4) Steel output (million tons)	(5) Coal output (million tons)	(6) Oil output (thousand barrels)
1949	n.a.	n.a.	n.a.	0.2	32	2
1950	n.a.	n.a.	n.a.	0.6	43	4
1951	n.a.	n.a.	n.a.	0.9	53	6
1952	100.0	n.a.	n.a.	1.4	67	3
1953	114.0	14.0	11.7	1.8	70	12
1954	120.6	5.8	3.5	2.2	84	16
1955	128.3	6.4	4.2	2.9	98	19
1956	146.4	14.1	12.0	4.5	110	23
1957	153.0	4.5	1.5	5.4	131	29
1958	186.7	22.0	20.0	11.1	230	15
1959	202.1	8.2	6.4	13.9	300	74
1960	199.2	− 1.5	0.0	18.7	280	100
1961	140.0	− 42.3	− 41.9	8	170	110
1962	130.9	− 7.0	− 9.1	8	n.a.	120
1963	144.9	7.0	4.2	8	n.a.	130
1964	168.8	6.5	4.6	10	214	180
1965	197.5	7.0	4.2	12	232	230
1966	231.0	7.0	4.2	15	271	290
1967	214.3	− 7.8	− 10.4	10	190	260
1968	200.4	− 6.9	− 9.6	9	235	300
1969	239.1	19.3	16.5	16	282	430
1970	294.7	23.3	20.4	18	327	600
1971	315.3	7.0	4.3	21	354	770
1972	324.5	2.9	0.6	23	377	900
1973	351.4	8.3	6.0	25	398	1,140
1974	355.2	1.1	− 0.8	21	407	1,360
1975	384.7	8.3	6.6	24	478	1,540
1976	374.4	− 2.7	− 3.7	21	483	1,740
1977	403.6	7.8	6.1	24	550	1,870
1978	453.2	12.3	10.9	32	618	2,080
1979	484.9	7.0	5.8	35	635	2,120
1980	515.9	6.4	5.2	37	620	2,120
1981	541.2	4.9	3.5	36	622	2,020
1982	586.1	8.3	6.9	37	666	2,040
1983	643.5	9.8	8.8	40	715	2,120
1984	730.4	13.4	12.4	44	789	2,280
1985	820.2	12.3	11.3	47	872	2,500

Sources: Columns 1-3 calculated from State Statistical Bureau, *Statistical Yearbook of China 1986*, 41 and 71. Columns 4-6 for the years 1949-1980 are from Arthur Ashbrook, "China: Economic Modernization and Long-term Performance," in Joint Economic Committee of Congress, *China Under the Four Modernizations*, 104; for 1981–85 data are drawn from Rock Creek Research, *1987 China Statistical Handbook*, 2, 9–10.

Note: Chinese national income is given here at "comparable prices," that is, linked 1952, 1957, 1970, and 1980 constant prices. National income (net material product) excludes the (small and, until the 1980s, diminishing) service sector.

their members. Second, while collectivization was the centerpiece, it was only one of a series of state policies that proved detrimental to agriculture and the peasantry from the mid–1950s to the late 1970s. These included compulsory marketing of crops at low state prices (that is, prices far below those that had prevailed in the now proscribed market), high crop-sale quotas, low state investment in agriculture, sustained high collective accumulation rates, the decimation of the service sector and private markets, and enforced low levels of consumption.

Table 1.1 reveals the economic setbacks suffered in periods of extreme mobilizational collectivism in contrast to the gains registered in other periods: the economic collapse of the Great Leap Forward when national income declined by 50 percent over a three-year period (1960-1962) and the Cultural Revolution (1966-68) when political turmoil lay behind two consecutive years of decline on a smaller scale. The economic gains, measured in national income and industrial and agricultural production, peaked during the First Five-Year Plan period (1952-1957), the post-Leap recovery (1962-1966), and the post-Mao reforms (1978–1985).

I document here ways in which the Communist Party, which had effected the elimination of major property-based inequalities through land reform and nationalization of industry and commerce, and which continued to proclaim the goal of eradicating differences in well-being between city and countryside and in conditions of work between industry and agriculture, in the years after 1955 actually presided over a substantial widening of urban-rural and intrarural inequalities in income, social conditions, and cultural opportunities. Too much of the debate over Chinese inequality has been structured by Mao's distinctive pronouncements on the issues of inequality and empowerment; it is essential to transcend theoretical and strategic pronouncements and explore the abundant evidence of a range of stratifying processes. The evidence shows that important dimensions of inequality and stratification were exacerbated—or newly created—in precisely the periods of fundamentalist mobilization that targeted for elimination inequality and privilege of all kinds. The peasantry, particularly poorer rural communities and strata, bore the brunt of state policies in the peak periods of mobilizational collectivism. The gap between word and deed among Maoists on issues of rural and urban-rural inequalities and stratification was enormous and growing in the decades following land reform.

This volume explores the consequences—for the countryside, for city-country relations, and for sectoral and class relations—of the developmental policies of the People's Republic over forty years. It reveals important developmental achievements in the three decades prior to Mao's death:

• elimination of all major property-based inequalities and substantial reductions in intravillage and intraurban inequality;

• substantial increases in the rate of accumulation and investment leading to rapid and sustained industrial growth, in particular laying further foundations for heavy industry;

• elimination of foreign control of core elements of modern industry, trade, and finance;

• gains in agricultural output (slightly) outpacing China's growing population;

• gains for the industrial working class including lifetime job security, generous pension and welfare benefits, heightened social status as well as modest gains in per capita household incomes;

• significant national gains in nutrition and life expectancy and rising basic levels of education and health care.

These achievements in the world's most populous country, and, despite four decades of relatively rapid growth, still one of the poorest, by means of changes strikingly different from those employed in most postcolonial societies, properly captured world attention. Close examination of China's performance in the years after the promising beginnings of the late 1940s and early 1950s reveals, however, that economic and social progress in some respects was achieved at heavy costs in other respects. China is hardly unique in finding the initial period of modern industrialization and accelerated development a painful passage; but insufficient attention has been paid by observers to the fact that the weightiest burdens were long borne disproportionately by the peasantry, above all during periods of extreme collective mobilization, particularly the Great Leap Forward and the Cultural Revolution. The other side of the coin of Chinese developmental achievements, then, in the era of Mao's leadership and Maoist strength in the party, particularly in the two decades following collectivization, is this:

• deep imbalance between high industrial growth rates and stagnation at low levels (even for China) of rural incomes and subsistence consumption;

• substantial widening of urban-rural and intrarural differentials in income, opportunity, and consumption;

Table 1.2

Foodgrain Production and Consumption and Nutrient Availability, 1952–1985

	(1) Foodgrain output (million tons)	(2) Population (millions at year end)	(3) Per capita foodgrain output (kg)	(4) Per capita grain consumption (kg)	(5) Per capita nutrient avail- ability from all sources (k cal)
1952	164	575	285	198	2,083
1953	167	588	284	197	2,048
1954	170	602	282	197	2,041
1955	184	615	299	199	2,232
1956	193	628	307	204	2,326
1957	195	647	301	203	2,217
1958	200	660	303	198	2,248
1959	170	672	253	187	1,854
1960	144	662	218	164	1,578
1961	148	659	225	159	1,763
1962	160	673	238	165	1,867
1963	170	692	246	165	1,857
1964	188	705	267	182	2,037
1965	195	725	269	183	2,021
1966	214	745	287	190	2,154
1967	218	764	285	186	2,118
1968	209	785	266	174	1,979
1969	211	807	261	174	1,950
1970	240	830	289	187	2,192
1971	250	852	293	188	2,138
1973	240	872	275	173	1,972
1974	274	909	301	188	2,264
1975	285	924	308	191	2,266
1976	286	934	306	190	2,235
1977	283	950	298	192	2,233
1978	305	963	317	195	2,413
1979	332	975	341	207	2,592
1980	321	987	325	214	2,473
1981	325	1,001	325	219	2,511
1982	355	1,015	350	225	2,725
1983	387	1,025	378	232	n.a.
1984	407	1,035	393	252	n.a.
1985	379	1,045	363	n.a.	n.a

Sources: Columns 1, 2, 3: State Statistical Bureau (1986: 71, 143); *Guanghui de 35 nian 1949-1984* (1984). Output and per capita output are measured in unprocessed form. Foodgrain is a composite figure including grains, tubers, soybeans, peas, and beans, the latter calculated at grain equivalent weight. For slightly different figures for columns 1 and 3 see Alan Piazza (1986: 36, 77).

Column 4: Taylor and Hardee (1986: 110). Grain consumption figures are measured in trade grain calculated on the basis of processed rice and millet with other grains, tubers, soybeans, peas, and beans in unprocessed form at equivalent weight.

Column 5: Piazza (1986: 77). Nutrient availability is calculated as the difference between domestic food supply (domestic production net of foreign trade) and the sum of all nonhuman food end uses such as seed, livestock fodder, and manufactures. Piazza (1986: 73).

• long-term stagnation in productivity and income for many poorer and marginal rural localities and widening income gaps between dynamic and declining regions;

• stagnant or declining labor productivity in industry and agriculture, particularly as measured by return on investment and on labor;

• long-term decline of the service sector.

One vital indicator of the kind of fundamental problem that deepened throughout the period of collective mobilization is given by aggregate information about foodgrain output and consumption (table 1.2). As the table reveals, per capita foodgrain production and nutrient availability peaked in 1955-1956, then dropped sharply after 1958. This was principally the result of monumental leadership blunders in the Great Leap Forward, compounded by flood, drought, and cold weather. Despite substantial famine-induced deaths, beginning in 1959 and continuing for three years, per capita food production did not regain precollectivization levels until the mid-1970s, and it was not until 1980 that nutrient availability slightly surpassed mid-1950s' levels. In those same years the party-state dramatically heightened requirements for productive labor; indeed, during the Leap, leaders frequently treated collective labor as a limitless free good. Simultaneously the state prodded collectives to cut back on foodgrain acreage and forced accumulation rates to extraordinary levels: Annual accumulation rates averaged 39 percent in the years 1958-1960, further driving down consumption at the very moment when China entered a period of acute famine (*Statistical Yearbook of China 1986:* 49). Between 1958 and 1960 China's per capita grain production and consumption plummeted to famine levels. The 1960 death rates of 25.4 per thousand compared with 10.8 per thousand in 1957 on the eve of the Leap. In the single year 1960 China experienced a net population decline of 10 million people (ibid. 1986: 72, 73). In all four years 1958–1961, mortality rates exceeded those of 1957, the year prior to the Leap. With a death rate of 68 per thousand, Anhui, the hardest hit province, experienced population loss exceeding 2 million (Bernstein 1984: 344). The deaths were in part the product of the fact that in 1958 and 1959 China increased net grain *exports*, reaching 4 million tons in the latter year. Not until the worst of the famine had passed, in 1961, did significant foodgrain imports begin (Taylor and Hardee 1986: 188). What some have taken as the apotheosis of the Chinese model, the Great Leap Forward, precipitated the most devastating famine in China's modern history and the collapse of the economy. Moreover, at the most basic

Table 1.3

Urban and Rural Per Capita Food Consumption, 1952–1986
(Kg per person per year)

	Foodgrain		Edible oil		Pork	
	Urban	Rural	Urban	Rural	Urban	Rural
1952	241	192	5.1	1.7	8.9	5.5
1953	242	190	5.4	1.5	10.1	5.5
1954	236	190	4.7	1.4	10.1	5.4
1955	214	196	5.2	1.7	9.7	4.2
1956	200	205	5.1	2.1	8.4	4.0
1957	196	205	5.2	1.9	9.0	4.4
1958	186	201	4.5	1.9	8.1	4.6
1959	201	183	4.0	1.8	5.0	2.6
1960	193	156	3.5	1.4	2.7	1.2
1961	180	154	2.7	1.1	1.8	1.3
1962	184	161	2.5	0.8	3.8	1.9
1963	190	160	3.6	0.7	8.3	2.0
1964	200	178	3.7	0.9	10.8	4.6
1965	211	177	4.8	1.6	10.4	5.4
1966	206	186	5.3	1.1	12.8	5.9
1967	200	184	4.9	1.1	11.9	5.8
1968	189	171	4.5	1.1	11.7	5.6
1969	192	171	4.5	1.0	10.5	5.0
1970	202	185	4.2	1.1	10.8	5.2
1971	199	186	4.2	1.1	11.2	6.2
1972	206	166	4.4	1.1	12.5	6.6
1973	208	188	4.4	1.1	13.5	6.5
1974	205	184	4.5	1.2	14.3	6.4
1975	210	187	4.7	1.2	14.9	6.3
1976	212	186	4.6	1.0	13.9	6.1
1977	210	188	4.1	1.0	12.9	6.1
1978	205	193	4.1	1.1	13.7	6.4
1979	211	206	5.0	1.3	17.4	8.0
1980	214	214	5.5	1.6	19.0	9.4
1981	216	220	6.9	2.0	17.0	9.7
1982	217	227	8.9	2.3	17.6	10.4
1983	222	235	10.0	2.6	18.0	11.0
1984	239	254	11.1	3.2	18.7	11.7
1985	239	258	12.3	3.4	19.7	12.6
1986	242	259	12.4	3.5	20.3	12.9

Source: Taylor and Hardee (1986: 110–12); State Statistical Bureau, *China, Trade and Price Statistics in 1987* (1987: 5–7).
Note: For other dietary items not included in this table, vegetables, eggs, fish, sugar, beef, mutton, and salt, see Taylor and Hardee, pp. 108–109, 113–15; State Statistical Bureau (1987: 8–11, 22–23).

level of food consumption, twenty-five years of collective agriculture brought no gain.

City Versus Countryside?

In the early 1960s the state cushioned urban residents from the worst manifestations of famine, leaving the countryside to bear the brunt of starvation. As shown in table 1.3, at the height of the famine, in 1960, urban per capita foodgrain consumption dipped slightly below the 1957 figure of 196 kilograms to 193 kilograms while rural consumption plummeted from 205 kilograms to starvation levels of just 156 kilograms (or less than a pound per day per person on the average). The precipitous drop in edible oil and pork, critical supplements to the basic grain diet, was felt even more strongly in the countryside, not only in the immediate aftermath of the Great Leap but, in edible oil consumption, for virtually two decades.

Urban people shared in the belt tightening that all Chinese experienced during the Great Leap disasters, but almost all of the 15-30 million famine deaths took place in the countryside (Riskin 1987: 136-38; Ashton et al. 1984). China's per capita foodgrain, oil, and pork consumption did not consistently surpass precollectivization levels until at least the late 1970s. In later years there was no repetition of the manmade famine of the Great Leap as the state backed away from the most disastrous economic and distributive policies associated with mobilizational collectivism. The problems of the countryside nevertheless remained acute, and at the height of the Cultural Revolution in the late 1960s grain output again stagnated and oil and pork consumption declined from already low levels. A survey of twenty-three provinces shows that in the years 1965-1977, while grain yields rose by 36 percent, agricultural costs increased 54 percent and the average value of the labor day for peasants dropped from .70 yuan to .56 yuan (Watson forthcoming). For substantial numbers of peasants, particularly those in chronic poverty regions, two decades of collective agriculture brought no discernible gains in income or consumption and in some years a real worsening of their conditions of work and living.

The roots of rural stagnation did not lie exclusively in the institutional fabric of collective life. With rural population virtually doubling in the absence of an effective national birth control policy from the 1950s to the early 1970s—despite the famine-years deaths—with villagers barred from migrating or turning to the market and enjoined to rely on collective self-reliance; with the state consistently extracting more than it invested in the countryside in the form of grain procurements at low prices and the provision of fertilizer and other modern inputs at high prices; and with China cut off from international markets and advanced technology, many poor, marginal, and peripheral rural communities experienced long-term income stagnation at bare subsistence levels. This volume brings out myriad dimensions of the subordinate position of agriculture and the countryside to industry and the cities, and it explores growing intrarural and urban-rural regional inequalities, which left hundreds of millions of the collective rural poor with scant prospect of improvement of their livelihood or their conditions of work.

The problems were not, of course, confined to the countryside or to the realms of production and consumption. Observing the characteristic pattern of lifetime employment at a single industrial enterprise for state-sector employees and the pervasive character of the enterprise in all facets of working-class life, Andrew Walder (1986: 14–17) has underscored the heavy dependence of Chinese workers on their enterprises. Walder defines dependence in terms of the high proportion of the workers' needs satisfied (or intended to be satisfied) through the workplace, including money wages, health care, housing, pensions, entertainment, and education and the low availability of alternative outlets or autonomous resources to satisfy these needs. The Chinese industrial enterprise does exercise pervasive, even ubiquitous, powers compared with its American, European, or even Japanese counterpart. Dependence, however, is a feature characteristic not of the industrial enterprise per se, but of Chinese socialist society in general.

Indeed, its purest expression is found not in the industrial enterprise but in the collective-village during the era of mobilizational collectivism from 1955 to the early 1980s. This is in part because small rural communities are far more tightly knit and offer less scope for autonomy than large cities. It is also a product of the unitary character of village life in which work and living arrangements are closely integrated and in which there is virtually no alternative to brigade-assigned and directed employment. In an urban household, by contrast, husband and wife and working children frequently work in different units and their apartment may be located far from the work unit of any or all members of the household. Workers in both the state and collective sectors faced constricted mobility in the years after 1958. Urban industrial employees in state enterprises nevertheless enjoyed substantial gains in income, security, benefits, services, and prestige compared both to opportunities offered them during the Republican period and, particularly, to those available to the peasantry.

Throughout the People's Republic, peasants have aspired to urban and industrial jobs in the state sector—aspirations which were virtually unattainable after the economic crash of 1960 and the imposition of tight state controls on work and residence—while urban state-sector workers strongly resisted official pressures both to go to the countryside and to increase the intensity of industrial labor. Following the economic collapse in the wake of the Great Leap, twenty million industrial workers were laid off and sent to the countryside, virtually the only breach in the lifetime job guarantee enjoyed by state-sector workers in the People's Republic. State-sector workers could not, moreover, prevent the permanent transfer of their children to the countryside; in the years after 1966 some sixteen million junior and senior high school graduates were dispatched to work in the rural areas. The term *xiafang* or downward transfer, which is applied to urban workers, intellectuals, and students sent to live and work (usually permanently) in the countryside, unerringly captures the gulf between city and countryside by underlining the universal valuation of the superior position and benefits of urban life and employment in state-sector industry over the countryside and collective agriculture.

In another important respect, the sense of loss, of dependence, alienation, and anomie experienced by substantial segments of the peasantry as a result of collectivization and subsequent extremes of mobilizational collectivism, as well as state pricing, procurement, and cropping policies, have no real counterpart among industrial workers. In 1955 Chinese farmers, many of whom had so recently won access to land and enjoyed rising incomes in the honeymoon years immediately after the land reform, lost control over both land and labor to collective institutions and officials. The new collectives inevitably lacked legitimacy. When collectivization and communization were coupled with attacks on peasant culture, religion, and values, and when collectivization and communization were followed shortly by devastating famine, frustration and passivity reached extreme levels in many communities.[9] When subsequent decades brought no improvement in per capita income for most communities and households despite rising grain yields (if not gains in labor productivity), anomie, alienation, and resignation deepened.

Urban industrial workers, by contrast, experienced no comparable loss of status, power, or welfare in the nationalization of their industries, which took place over the years 1946–1956. For most industrial workers, nationalization and socialism brought gains including lifetime job security, higher prestige than as workers they had previously enjoyed, and, in some cases, rising per capita household incomes, particularly when the value of state subsidies is included. These gains, both real and relative (vis-à-vis the peasants and prerevolutionary elites), were threatened neither by nationalization of industry nor by the Great Leap Forward. Many industrial workers did, however, experience a loss of power and authority in the workplace during the Cultural Revolution when labor unions were eliminated, as the army exercised controls that in time also grew more arbitrary, and when workers' wages were unilaterally frozen. The structural loss was of course amplified in consciousness given the gap between the language of a Great (socialist) *Proletarian* Cultural Revolution and the transparent experienced decline in their powers and rights at points of production (Walder 1986; Andors 1977 provides an alternative view).

In the early years of the People's Republic the countryside provided the surplus that made possible the surge in heavy industry that has long been a hallmark of Chinese socialist development. With state investment targeted overwhelmingly to urban industry, with state and collective sharply restricting rural consumption, and with the continued rapid growth of a rural population essentially confined to growing grain, by the late 1970s the poverty, low and stagnant rural labor productivity, and large and growing labor surplus in the countryside constituted heavy constraints on continued development of the Chinese economy and society.

Concealed behind the high growth rates, analogous problems plagued Chinese industry. The heart of the problem lay in the fact that, in contrast to most industrializing countries, China's growth was fueled by heavy investment in machinery and equipment with virtually no increase provided by gains in labor productivity within given technologies. According to a 1985 World Bank study, "in China's state-owned industry, total factor productivity apparently increased in 1952–57, then stagnated or declined in 1957–82," where an increase in total factor productivity means that output grows faster than the total of all inputs (Lim and Wood 1985: 110). These findings are consistent with my analysis of the impact of mobilizational collectivism in the decades after 1956. Similarly, while the index of output per industrial worker in state enterprises increased from 159 in 1957 to 277 in 1978 (1952 = 100), in the same years the index of the value of fixed structures and working equipment increased nearly tenfold from 226 to 2,222. In short, the gains in industrial output were overwhelmingly a product of labor-saving machinery and equipment; there was little increase from a more adept or more disciplined labor force (Field 1982: Riskin 1987: 263–71).[10] Moreover, while investment grew from approximately one-fourth of national output in the mid-1950s to one-third or higher in the 1970s, annual industrial growth rates declined from 15.8 percent in the First Five-Year Plan to 9.7 percent in the years 1970–77. Stated differently, during the First Five-Year Plan it required an investment of $1.53 to produce each new dollar of output; by the years 1970–77, a $3.26 investment was required to produce each additional dollar of industrial output (Selden and Lippit 1982: 20–21; Harding 1987: 31).

The Political Economy of Reform

This was the context in which, following Mao's death, a coalition of forces embracing market-oriented reformers at the state center and substantial segments of the peasantry at the rural periphery pressed the program of household-based and market-oriented reforms that has swept the countryside in the 1980s, contributing to the invigoration of the rural economy and rising consumption. The discussion below of the contractual and market-oriented reforms assesses these gains against a range of social, economic, and demographic problems and conflicts, including both those flowing directly from the reforms and others springing from the disjunctures between partially realized reforms, remaining elements of prereform policies, and long-term continuities.

China's reforms constitute perhaps the most far-reaching reform agenda implemented in any state socialist society. Before considering their content, it is important to underline the overriding structural continuities: the new role of the market and the private sector take place in an economy in which state enterprises remain dominant and the Communist Party continues to exercise tight control over the political process.

For all its problems, including cross-nationally low per capita incomes and GNP, China's development performance over nearly forty years has surpassed that of many other poor agrarian nations. From the First Five-Year Plan forward the Chinese state has succeeded in capturing a substantial, and a substantially increased, portion of the surplus, channeling it to industry, and gaining access to foreign (initially Soviet, later Western and Japanese) technology, which together provided the bases for long-term rapid industrialization centered on heavy industry. Moreover, as a result of the land reform of the 1940s, the distributive consequences of Chinese development for the millions of landless and land-poor peasants living at the edge of hunger have been relatively favorable. India, with its continental size, predominantly agrarian population, and roughly comparable levels of development and income at the time of independence in the late 1940s, provides the most salient comparison, although comparisons with the development performances of predominantly agrarian Pakistan, Bangladesh, Indonesia, and the Philippines are also suggestive.

In 1957, as China ended the First Five-Year Plan period, Mao contrasted India's lagging industrialization to China's rapid advance as proof of the efficacy of China's socialist planning: "India undertook a five-year plan and increased its steel output by 300,000 tons. We raised our steel output by 4 million tons. Our system does not impede the development of the productive forces" (Mao 1957: 75).

Between 1965 and 1985, according to World Bank estimates, China's gross domestic product increased at a rate more than 40 percent higher than did India's: and in the years 1980–85, increases of 9.8 percent per year in China were nearly twice India's 5.2 percent. Similarly, China's annual industrial growth rates have consistently surpassed India's over the last forty years (World Bank 1987: 202, 204). By the early 1980s China's grain yields per land unit were nearly double those of India: 4,245 kilograms per hectare of rice paddy in China in 1979 compared with 2,049 per hectare of rice paddy in India in 1980; 2,138 kilograms per hectare versus 1,437 kilograms per hectare in wheat; 2,985 kilograms per hectare versus 1,103 kilograms per hectare in corn.[11]

China has not only sustained substantially higher rates of accumulation and industrial and agricultural growth since the 1950s, it also has outpaced India and most postcolonial societies in major quality of life indicators. By 1985, China's reported life expectancy was 69 years versus 56 for India; per capita nutrition stood at 2,602 calories for China versus 2,189 for India; infant mortality, 35 per thousand for China versus 89 for India; and so forth (World Bank 1987: 202, 258, 260). Indeed, by these latter indicators, each of which reflected rapidly improving conditions in the course of the reforms of the 1980s, China compares favorably not only with the poor but with many middle- and even some upper-income industrialized countries with per capita GNPs ten or more times higher than China's.

It is necessary, however, to insert at least one important caveat in comparing the Indian and Chinese performances. The loss of life in China's Great Leap famine of the early 1960s dwarfs the Chinese famines of the early twentieth century and even the great famines in colonial India. And for all the misery experienced by India's poor, there have been no mass famines in postindependence India. As Amartya Sen has observed, the Indian system "permits endemic malnutrition and hunger that is not acute; it does not permit a famine both because it would be too acute and because it cannot happen quietly" (Sen 1986: 41; see also Rubin 1986). Viewing the recent performance of the Chinese state, not only its economic policies but particularly its response to famine conditions in Hebei and Hubei provinces in the early 1980s, including its use of United Nations disaster relief, there is reason to believe that it will take energetic measures to prevent a major famine from taking place and will use substantial state resources to alleviate hunger in the event of local and regional natural disaster.

China's overall economic performance compares favorably with that of India and other large, postcolonial agrarian nations, but in important respects it lags behind the performances of the rapidly industrializing East Asian nations and city-states: Taiwan, Hong Kong, the Republic of Korea, and Singapore. This group has sustained long-term growth rates approximately 50 percent higher than China's, avoided the extreme fluctuations experienced by the Chinese economy, and achieved per capita income levels many times higher than China's ($1,700 for Korea and $2,577 for Taiwan in 1981).[12] These countries, moreover, score relatively well, though not as high as China, on indexes of income equality (Myers 1987: 136, 155; Chen 1985: 133, 151). It remains, however, to develop appropriate yardsticks for comparing giant agrarian states such as China with the ministates that comprise the East Asian NICs, unless one is content with existing GNP measures to capture the essential elements of developmental reality. All the NICs, moreover, began their postwar industrializing drives from positions far higher on the scale of development and per capita incomes.

The primary focus of this study is not on international comparisons but on patterns of alternating periods of mobilization, reform, and consolidation, that is, on diverse developmental approaches and their consequences for different strata and sectors of the Chinese economy and society. Chinese economic and social performance in periods characterized by leadership commitment to building socialism on the foundations of popular support, hence accepting gradual, voluntary processes of social change, a role for the market and the household sector, and assuring rising popular consumption levels, contrasts favorably with the heavy economic and social costs and the political catastrophes marking periods of extreme mobilizational collectivism. The former periods, in the early years of the People's Republic, in stepping back (briefly) from the disasters of the Leap in the early 1960s, and in the contractual and market-oriented reforms of the 1980s, produced rapid advances in industrial and agricultural output and consumption. The latter periods, notably in the Great Leap and at the height of the Cultural Revolution in the late 1960s, wrought stagnation or disaster. I simply can find no evidence in support of the view that radical mobilizational collectivism served any of the interests of the poorest classes or regions. Because their margin for survival was so slender, it was they who most acutely felt the shortages and administered inequities that accompanied the state's insistence on monopolizing processes of circulation; and it was they for whom the general economic setbacks, which policies in these periods generated, lost marginally most, because they started with so little margin of survival to begin with. The period of reform since 1978 has ushered in the longest era of rapid and sustained growth of the four decades of the People's Republic, a performance particularly notable for gains in the countryside and including agriculture, industry, and commerce, and for the gains accompanying advances in output (table 1.4).

The startling growth of foreign trade and the induction of foreign—particularly Japanese and American—technology and capital since 1970, and wider infusions of foreign capital in the 1980s, have been vital to China's new course. In 1955 trade with the socialist nations peaked at 74 percent of China's total trade, coinciding with the high point of their aid and economic integration and the demise of trade with China's principal trade partners as a result of the U.S.-led embargo associated with the Korean War. This pattern would come full circle by the 1970s as Japan, the United States, and Western Europe resumed their positions of trade and investment primacy in the China market.

In the 1950s China's trade with, and technical assistance from, the Soviet Union and East European nations were critical to laying the foundations of industrialization. By the mid-1970s, trade with socialist nations accounted for less than 20 percent of the total, and a broad range of trade, financial, investment, technical, and educational ex-

Table 1.4

National Income, Growth, and Foreign Capital Absorption, 1979–1986

Output: Billions of 1980 yuan [real annual growth rate in brackets];
Capital: Million U.S.$.

	1979	1980	1981	1982	1983	1984	1985	1986	Average annual growth, 1979–1986
National income	347	369	387	419	460	522	586	630	
		[6.3]	[4.9]	[8.3]	[9.8]	[13.5]	[12.3]	[7.5]	[8.9]
Gross value rural output	214	222	237	263	288	339	387	429	
		[3.9]	[6.6]	[11.1]	[9.6]	[17.6]	[14.2]	[10.8]	[10.5]
Nonindustrial rural output	193	196	209	233	251	282	291	301	
		[1.9]	[6.5]	[11.3]	[7.7]	[12.3]	[3.4]	[3.5]	[6.7]
Rural industrial output	21	26	28	30	38	58	96	128	
		[21.6]	[7.3]	[9.4]	[23.7]	[52.9]	[67.1]	[33.1]	[30.7]
Gross value industrial output	457	497	518	558	616	703	830	903	
		[8.7]	[4.1]	[7.7]	[10.5]	[14.0]	[18.0]	[8.8]	[10.3]

Sources of foreign capital								Total 1979–1986
Loans	3,030		1,783	1,065	1,286	2,506	5,015	20,745
Direct foreign investment	380		649	916	1,418	1,956	2,155	8,215
Total	3,410		2,432	1,981	2,704	4,462	6,985	28,960

Sources: Compiled from Harry Harding (1987: 106, 154); Rock Creek Research (1987: 1, 2).
Note: The term "national income" is used here for the Chinese term "net material product." Gross value of rural output includes the value of industry at the village but not the township level. Nonindustrial rural output includes the value of farming, forestry, animal husbandry, fisheries, and sideline production. Gross value of industrial output includes the value of township but not village industry. Figures for foreign capital listed under 1980 represent the average annual figures for 1979–1981.

changes linked China's economy and society with Japan, the United States, and Western Europe. The rapid and sustained growth in China's foreign trade, the purchase of important turnkey plants in fertilizer, metallurgy, and petrochemicals, the substantial reduction in military spending, and the growing role of manufactures and raw materials in China's exports, all sustained since the early 1970s, have stimulated the economy. China's foreign trade, which accounted for $4.6 billion, less than 3 percent of national output in 1970, by 1979 had increased to $20.6 billion and by 1986 reached $73.8 billion, accounting for 13.9 percent of national output (Harding 1987: 131, 139). In the years 1979–1986 China absorbed some $30 billion in foreign capital, much of it invested in new plants and equipment. This was the basis for a substantial infusion of advanced technology (Geraedts 1983: 49–91; Harding 1987: 154).

These and other rapid changes have, however, also posed formidable economic, political, and cultural challenges to reform proponents of the outward-looking policies. Among the most severe of these directly related to the reform agenda are balance-of-payments and foreign-exchange crises in the mid–1980s; new forms of social polarization (the issues are multifaceted and the outcomes include reduced urban-rural inequality); the most severe inflation since the late 1940s, a product of initial efforts to reform an archaic price system and the overheating of the economy as consumption far outstripped increases in national output; rapid decline of "productive investment," and myriad forms of social dislocation associated with the influx of foreign capital, goods, and personnel and the relaxation of China's rigid system of population control (Reynolds 1987; Harding 1987).

Other problems of the reform era reflect policy priorities that have persisted through the many swings of the policy pendulum. The household contract system, diversification of crops and a renaissance of household sidelines, the resurgence of open markets, and substantial increases in state purchasing prices produced rapid, sustained gains in agricultural productivity and rural incomes between 1978 and 1984. But the reforms have been accompanied by a sharp drop in the already low levels of state investment in agriculture from 10.6 percent of state investment in 1978 to 3.3 percent in 1986. Overall, state investment in agriculture during the Sixth Five-Year Plan (1981–85) fell by 30 percent from the level of the previous plan and is projected to fall by an additional 15 percent in the Seventh Plan period (Harding 108). And there has been no followup on increased state purchasing prices in agriculture since the early 1980s.

Coupled with the collapse of collective investment in agriculture, and with peasants investing heavily in private housing as well as in trade, in household sidelines, in small industries, in anything but agriculture, tendencies toward agricultural stagnation reemerged in the mid-1980s. An internal report on economic restructuring, for example, noted that China's irrigated area actually declined by 15 percent in the course of the Sixth Five-Year Plan. In the years 1985–87 China was unable to reach the levels of production achieved in the bumper harvest of 1984, prompting demands for radical market-oriented restructuring of ownership and production relations in agriculture and calls for increased state investment to reverse the decline in productivity. In agriculture as well as in industry and international economic relations, pressures continue to stimulate the economy and redefine state-household-market relations through further reform of the institutions of socialism in China.

The far-reaching contractual and market-oriented reforms have led some to conclude that capitalism has been restored in agriculture. It is true that the household has replaced the collective as the primary locus of agricultural production, and the overall scope of household economic activity in crop and sideline production, small industry, and commerce has grown substantially and rapidly in the 1980s. It would be a mistake, however, to underestimate the continued capacity of the state and collective units to set much of the direction and tone of rural development. Not only do the state and the collectives retain residual landownership rights and set many of the terms of the contracts that shape agricultural production, but village and state units continue to control the lion's share of assets in rural industrial and sideline production, exercise the rights to assign corvée labor, determine the financial obligations of households to the village and the state, and, in the absence of a firm legal structure or the institutionalization of a broad range of democratic rights, play a decisive role in determining whether the present system continues or is substantially altered. In short, the present system, for all its changes, represents a new mix of state, collective, and household power and authority, not the unalloyed triumph of household and market in China's countryside. At the same time, the state retains its tight grip on the core of the economy: large modern industry, banking, and foreign trade.

Many of the watchwords of the Mao period are no longer to be heard in China: Instead of mobilization, the commune, class struggle, cultural revolution, equality, and self-reliance, China's reform leaders, while attempting to further state control of the core industrial economy, emphasize the dynamic effects of commodification and markets; the international and national division of labor; the expanded roles of the household, of intellectuals and technical personnel, growing foreign trade, technology, and investment; the necessity for some to "get rich first"; the call to end the "iron rice bowl" of lifetime job security and low production incentives; and reduction of the monopoly power of state and collective in production-circulation-distribution. Marxist democrats, moreover, contine to insist on the centrality of democratizing reforms (Su 1988). The reform policy mix has contributed to accelerated growth and diversification as growth rates in sidelines and rural industry have outpaced those of grain; it has made possible the first surge in peasant incomes since the 1950s. But it has also raised questions about whether growth can be sustained, particularly in the agrarian sector; whether major problems left unresolved, such as price reform, and the state's monopoly position on a range of issues, can be resolved; and whether a modernizing and developing China can carry forward the best elements of the socialist course while overcoming the anachronisms remaining from mobilizational collectivism in nodes and interstices of the centralized party-state.

2

MARXISM AND THE PEASANTRY: COLLECTIVIZATION AND STRATEGIES OF SOCIALIST AGRARIAN DEVELOPMENT

At the center of the 1970 and 1980 eruptions of strike activity culminating in independent worker and peasant movements and the formation of Solidarnosc in Poland was widespread resentment over the acute shortage and skyrocketing prices of food. The Polish case exemplifies in concentrated form aspects of the long-term systemic crisis of agrarian development that socialist states have confronted and most continue to confront. The Soviet Union, China, Yugoslavia, and Poland, all substantial food exporters prior to revolution, became food importers. Following collectivization and the crushing of the household economy and the market, the Soviet Union and China became two of the world's largest grain importers. In recent years, moreover, collective agriculture has come under severe scrutiny as reformers embarked on a search for viable agrarian institutions, incentive practices, and marketing relationships. The Soviet Union has been among the most resistant to market-oriented reforms and enlargement of the scope of the household economy. Nevertheless, since the 1960s, the Soviet *kolkhoz* (collective farm) has declined in importance, particularly vis-à-vis the expanding *sovkhoz* (state farm) and a slightly growing private sector (Kerblay 1983: 77, 78, 83–88). Yugoslavia and Poland years ago acknowledged the failure of collectivization and restored private agriculture to a position of dominance, albeit within a system of restrictive marketing and purchase practices. China, which until the late 1970s was widely regarded as the most successful practitioner of collective agriculture, in the 1980s carried out the most far-reaching reform of collective and communal agriculture since the formation of the communes in 1958.

Sustained and growing food imports by socialist states to combat food shortages are simply the most visible signs of the heavy costs of and conflicts endemic to collectivization and the range of socialist agrarian strategies. The unresolved agrarian question constitutes perhaps the central dilemma of the political economy of the socialist transition.

With the proliferation of socialist states following World War II as a result in part of the expansion of Soviet military power in much of Eastern Europe, and with autonomously generated socialist states in Yugoslavia, China, Vietnam, and Korea, the Soviet Union vigorously pressed collectivization as *the* universal model, the path for agrarian development combining the class struggle and high accumulation to generate rapid industrialization. In the late 1940s and early 1950s each new self-proclaimed socialist state, with certain interesting variations, followed the sequence of land revolution leading to imposed collectivization. Three decades later, despite widespread criticism of the Stalinist agrarian strategy, state-imposed collectivization continues to be regarded as the sine qua non of socialist rural development. And, for all the human costs, the setbacks dealt to agrarian development, and its bleak implications for socialist democracy, collectivization is still widely viewed as the basis for Soviet achievements of high accumulation and rapid industrialization.

This chapter addresses three issues:

• The origins of cooperative and collective approaches to the "agrarian question" in Marxist and Leninist thought and early Soviet practice.

• The formative experience of the Soviet Union in the Stalin era culminating in "the great turn" in the 1928–1933 period and its consequences for Soviet socialism.

• Contradictions of collectivization and the search for alternative strategies, with examples drawn from Yugoslavia and China at the critical juncture of collectivization in the 1950s.

In this survey I seek to discover the most promising elements of theory and praxis toward the creation of a socialist agrarian strategy, to explore the problems and limits of previous approaches, and to suggest some of the reasons why solutions to the agrarian question continue to elude socialist societies, whatever their commitment to the full development of the productive forces and to the flowering of socially rooted democratic cooperative institutions.

The "Agrarian Question": From Marx and Engels to Lenin

If the writings of the mature Marx reflect a preoccupation with the proletariat and capitalist development, he also wrote extensively on important aspects of what would come to be called the "agrarian question." In Marx's view, the "dwarf-like prosperity" of the peasantry in its numerous forms was doomed by the advance of bourgeois civilization (Draper 1978: 344–45). In an important passage in the section on "So-Called Primitive Accumulation" in *Capital* I, Marx (1977: 927–28) summed up the shared limitations of precapitalist, small-scale peasant agriculture and artisanal industry. "This mode of production presupposes the fragmentation of holdings and the dispersal of other means of production. As it excludes the concentration of these means of production, so it also excludes cooperation, division of labor within each separate process of production, and the social control and regulation of the forces of society."

For Marx, peasant agriculture, characterized by fragmented private landholding and individual cultivation, was a barrier to cooperation, to the division of labor, and to the rapid development of the productive forces. As in industry, concentration and division of labor held the keys for advance in agriculture. At the moment "it brings into the world the material means of its own destruction," Marx observed,

> new forces and new passions spring up in the bosom of society, forces and passions which feel themselves to be fettered by that society. It has to be annihilated; it is annihilated. Its annihilation, the transformation of the individualized and scattered means of production into socially concentrated means of production, the transformation, therefore, of the dwarf-like property of the many into the giant property of the few, and the expropriation of the great mass of the people from the soil, this terrible and arduously accomplished expropriation of the mass of the people forms the pre-history of capital. (Marx 1977: 928)

Marx assumed, quite reasonably and quite incorrectly, that capitalist development on a world scale would sweep away all vestiges of such a fragmented "mode of production." Quite incorrectly because, as Kautsky, Chayanov, and others have stressed, while capitalism has fostered large-scale concentrated agricultural formations, the family farm has shown extraordinary vigor and resilience, but also because it has been left not to capitalism but to socialism to provide the most vigorous challenge to peasant agriculture. Moreover, as the cases of Yugoslavia, Poland, and, most dramatically, China in the 1980s well show, the family farm continues to survive and challenge large-scale, socialized farms under socialism.

If Marx in most of his work perceived fragmented peasant agriculture as a barrier to cooperative production, the division of labor, and the development of the productive forces, he did not rely on the objective workings of capital and the market to solve the agrarian question. One finds in Marx the origins of the concept of the worker-peasant alliance as the bulwark of proletarian revolution. While viewing the rural proletariat as the most important ally of the industrial proletariat in the countryside, Marx insisted that it was possible and necessary to win over to the revolutionary camp at least a portion of the peasantry. Marx never unequivocally ruled out land redistributive strategies, but his approach to the agrarian question generally centered on the elimination of private landownership and the socialization of agricultural production. This perspective was mediated by a clear awareness of the necessity for revolutionaries to develop a rural strategy based on the protection of peasant interests and capable of winning peasant support. Marx's notes on a polemic of Bakunin make the point well. The proletariat, he insisted, must "take measures whereby the peasant sees his situation immediately improved and which therefore win him over to the revolution—measures, however, which in embryo facilitate the transition from private property in land to collective property, so that the peasant comes to it by himself, for economic reasons" (Draper 1978: 409). Here Marx touched on one of the most difficult short-run and long-run challenges that socialist revolutionaries, sharing Marx's belief in the superiority of collective agriculture, would everywhere confront in the twentieth century.

Late in life Marx developed a quite different perspective on the question of the peasant and the transition to socialism. In the 1870s and 1880s, on the basis of study of Russian rural society, particularly the mir, Marx concluded that the communal foundations of rural Russia, if spared destruction by the advance of capitalism, could provide a basis for socialism. As he observed in his 1881 letter to Vera Zasulich, "the commune is the fulcrum for social regeneration in Russia" (Shanin 1983: 124). Marx thus opened the possibility of a second road: not only could socialism be created on the basis of advanced capitalist development, but also, building on precapitalist communal foundations, areas peripheral or marginal to capitalist development might, under certain conditions, approach socialism from another direction.

In his final work addressed to the peasant question, Friedrich Engels envisaged that large landed estates would be "organized into cooperatives . . . under the control of the community." "The example of these agricultural cooperatives," he held, "would convince also the last of the still resistant small-holding peasants, and surely also many big peasants, of the advantages of cooperative, large-scale production." The peasantry would be won to the virtues of large-scale cooperative agriculture by the power of example, certainly not, as all agreed, by coercion. "We foresee the inevitable doom of the small peasant," Engels observed, but "we shall not even think of forcibly expropriating the small peasants . . . as we shall have to do in the case of the big landowners" (Engels 1969; Draper 1978: 412–13, 417).

Lenin and the Bolsheviks came to power sharing many of the proclivities on the agrarian question of Marx and Engels after having vacillated and shifted course on all major agrarian issues for two decades. One stage or two; immediate advance to a socialist agriculture or the thorough destruction of remnants of serfdom; nationalization and cooperative agriculture or redistribution of the land; the resurrection or the destruction of the commune; alliance with the peasantry as a group or a focus on the demands of its poorest sectors, particularly the rural proletariat: The answers to these questions had changed repeatedly in the course of the search to frame a winning rural policy. In 1903, in one of his earliest attempts to frame a program, Lenin proposed confiscation and redistribution of the large estates and the formation of cooperative farming: "When the working class has defeated the entire bourgeoisie, it will take the land away from the big proprietors and introduce cooperative farming on the big estates, so that the workers will farm the land together, in common, and freely elect trustworthy men to manage the farms." In this vision Lenin proposed to reserve a place for the small peasant in a milieu free from the despotism of money and the market: "Then, the small peasant who prefers to carry on his farm in the old way on individual lines will not produce for the market, to sell for the first comer, but for the workers' cooperatives; the small peasant will supply the workers' cooperatives with grain, meat, vegetables, and the workers in return will, without money, provide him with machines, livestock, fertilizers, clothes, and everything else he needs" (Lenin 1959a: 70).[1] In 1907, to clear the land "of all medieval lumber," Lenin had urged "the nationalization of the land, the abolition of the private ownership of land, and transfer of *all* the land to the state, which will mark a complete break with feudal relations in the countryside'' (1959d: 169).

In his April 1917 Theses and then in the Bolshevik Party's resolution on the agrarian question, however, Lenin combined the principle of land nationalization with ''the immediate transfer of all lands to the peasantry organized in Soviets of Peasants' Deputies, or in other organs of local self-government elected in a really democratic way and entirely independent of the landlords and the officials.'' In short, the Bolsheviks proposed to vest the right to cultivation of the nationalized land ''in local democratic institutions'' (Lenin 1959g: 190). In 1917, confronting a peasantry vociferously demanding land, Lenin and the Bolsheviks sought to frame a policy acceptable to the majority. It is unclear whether the power of ''organs of local self-govenment'' indicated Bolshevik intention to shift from household-centered to cooperative-centered agriculture or whether the slogan simply masked provisional acceptance of household-based agricultural production. What is clear is that in 1917 the desperate attempt to win the support of the peasantry at a moment of extreme vulnerability, coupled with the absence of any significant Bolshevik organizational presence in the rural areas, resulted in the abandonment of the nationalization program in favor of one long advocated by the Social Revolutionaries in which land-hungry peasants were permitted and encouraged to seize and subdivide the large estates into family-cultivated microholdings (Hussain and Tribe 1981: 80–99). Land parcelization and redistribution thus entered the Bolshevik arsenal as a tactical weapon that stood in direct conflict with the principal goals of nationalization of land and large-scale socialized agriculture advanced earlier by Marx, Engels, and Lenin himself. The course of land redistribution as a first stage would be followed in virtually all subsequent revolutions with the exception of Cuba and Laos.

It is customary to pass quickly over the policies of the War Communism period (1917–1920) as a set of exceptional emergency measures whose excesses were rapidly corrected by the New Economic Policy. But as the Hungarian economist Laszlo Szamuely (1974: 10–44) has convincingly demonstrated, whatever the impact of wartime necessity, the creation of a centralized subsistence economy, abolition of money and commodity relations, heavy reliance on compulsory labor mobilization, and egalitarian distribution of the War Communism period were not ephemeral. They embodied strongly held concepts of the transition period shared by leading Bolsheviks from Bukharin and Trotsky to Preobrazhensky, Lenin, and Stalin.

In the War Communism period, the Soviet state and the peasantry clashed head on as a result of state-imposed grain sales and outright confiscation. When the proposal to exchange commodities for grain produced insufficient supplies to feed the cities, a May 9, 1918, decree set compulsory sales quotas for peasants and even called on urban workers and poor peasants to confiscate "surplus" grain. The free market in grain was thus formally abolished, though it continued to exist illicitly (Szamuely 1974: 16–17).

The failure of compulsion associated with War Communism to solve the supply crisis led Lenin to initiate the New Economic Policy. Lenin had long been acutely aware of the dual character of the peasant as a laborer and a petty commodity producer (Lenin 1977). In 1919 he declared that it is necessary

> to abolish the difference between working man and peasant, *to make them all workers*. It is not a problem that can be solved by overthrowing a class; it can be solved only by the organizational reconstruction of the whole social economy, by a transition from individual, disunited, petty commodity production to large-scale social production. This transition must of necessity be extremely protracted. It may only be delayed and complicated by hasty and incautious administrative and legislative measures. It can be accelerated only by affording such assistance to the peasant as will enable him immensely to improve his whole agricultural technique, to reform it radically. (Lenin 1959f: 318)

For Lenin, the goal was clear: the transformation of the peasant into a laborer, the elimination of the family farm, and universal wage labor in large socialized production. Equally clear were the strictures against hasty measures that could damage the rural economy, peasant livelihood, and the worker-peasant alliance. Under NEP the state refrained from pressing its cooperative goals. The dominant rural reality was one of household-based agriculture within the framework of a resurgent mir.

In 1923, in the final year of his life, Lenin began to focus on the importance of cooperatives as the heart of state policy during the transition to socialism in the countryside. He had in mind not the peasant communes (*kommuna*) of 1918–19, which organized production and consumption on a basis of equal sharing, but trading cooperatives, which left intact household-organized agricultural production.

With this as a modest first step toward winning peasant support for proto-socialist institutions, and after the technological revolution (tractors, electricity, chemical fertilizer) made possible an appropriate material basis, collectivization of agriculture would then become feasible (Lenin 1975: 708).

Neither Lenin nor other Bolshevik leaders perceived in the peasantry the revolutionary or creative impulses they attributed to the proletariat or to revolutionary intellectuals, bases on which to construct the foundations of socialist society in the vast countryside of a predominantly peasant nation. But the peasant could be led to socialism by power of cooperative example, strengthened by the technical-material support of the state. State policies would ensure that the peasantry would gradually come to recognize that its material interest lay in large-scale collective agriculture. Collectivization, mechanization, and education could gradually narrow the urban-rural gap.

The core of NEP practice was not gradual cooperation, however, but the attempt to win peasant support and to obtain much-needed grain through the revival of market mechanisms including free markets and the payment of higher state purchasing prices designed to stimulate household production and sales. Yet as the 1920s advanced, conflict between the peasantry and the Soviet state over the grain issue deepened, calling into question fundamental principles of the NEP and the future of Soviet socialism.

The Great Turn: Imposed Collectivization as "Socialist Agrarian Policy"

"When the Petrograd proletariat and the soldiers of the Petrograd garrison took power," says Lenin, "they fully realised that our constructive work in the countryside would encounter great difficulties; that there it was necessary to proceed more gradually; that to attempt to introduce collective cultivation of the land by decrees, by legislation, would be the height of folly; that an insignificant number of enlightened peasants might agree to this, but that the vast majority of the peasants had no such object in view. We, therefore, confined ourselves to what was absolutely essential in the interests of the development of the revolution; in no case to run ahead of the development of the masses, but to wait until, as a result of their own experience and their own struggle, a progressive movement grew up."

The reason why the Party achieved a great victory on the front of collective-farm development is that it exactly carried out this tactical directive of Lenin's. (Stalin 1929a: 133–34)

Imposed collectivization, the centerpiece of Soviet agrarian policy, indeed of the entire Stalinist political economy, was the product of no articulated conception of socialism or rural development. Inflicted by the Soviet state over the opposition of *all* rural classes, and at immense human and material cost for the long-term prospects of the countryside and agrarian development, collectivization negated the soundest and most humane elements of the Marxist and Leninist visions of socialist transformation, and particularly of the processes of gradual, voluntary cooperation which Lenin had articulated but had done little to implement. The fact that these principles of voluntary participation and gradual reform were fervently invoked by the Soviet leadership at the very moment they were being desecrated—and indeed ever since— draws our attention to a constellation of problems of agrarian policy in the socialist states, one that is by no means restricted to the Soviet case.

Collectivization was the most far-reaching institutional restructuring attempted in the entire history of the Soviet Union and of other socialist countries. In no other sector have the relations of production, including ownership, labor process, and remuneration, been so fundamentally transformed or the changes so jarring. Yet imposed collectivization was essentially an afterthought, a reflexive response to the grain crisis and the challenge it posed to super-industrialization goals, rather than of any articulated rural development strategy. Because of its decisive influence on all subsequent socialist attempts to forge an agrarian policy, I will attempt to reconstruct the origins of the Soviet collectivization drive and to assess the consequences of collectivization within the larger parameters of Soviet socialist development.

The agrarian crisis that erupted in 1927 on the eve of the ambitious First Five-Year Plan charting rapid industrialization was the product, above all, of the failure of state policy. Without minimizing either the extraordinary economic and political challenges that the first socialist state confronted or the achievements of the NEP, it must be emphasized that the heart of the problem of the grain shortages of the late 1920s lay in state pricing and marketing policies which wreaked havoc with the entire peasantry. The NEP did at first stimulate the household-based agrarian economy: by 1926 agriculture had regained, and livestock exceeded, prewar production levels, although grain production was still just 92 percent of the prewar high (Lewin 1968: 172; Davies 1980a: 3). In the years 1925, 1926, and the first three quarters of 1927, Soviet harvests, marketing, and state collections of grain all exceeded official expectations (Cohen 1980: 250). Nevertheless, in 1926 *market-ed* grain was approximately 10 million tons compared with 18.8 million tons in the 1913 record year. In 1926 the state slashed purchasing prices for grain by 20–25 percent, attacked peasant private trade, and cut back sharply on the provision of industrial goods to the rural areas. The inevitable results of this onslaught against the peasantry included desperate peasant efforts to shift from grain to the production of other crops; to channel larger quantities of grain toward livestock rather than the market; and to sell the maximum possible in private markets, which offered substantially higher prices than those offered by the state (Nove 1971: 70–71). The crisis was the product not of kulak sabotage but of an inevitable reaction by all strata of the peasantry against the onslaught of the state. Bukharin, the most sensitive of Bolshevik leaders to the peasant's plight, continued to stress the need for wooing the peasantry, but the 1926 policies marked the victory of Preobrazhensky and others who called for the use of price and sale quota mechanisms to siphon resources from the peasantry as the foundation for primitive socialist accumulation and industrialization (Preobrazhensky 1926: 30, 84, 88; Nove 1965: xi-xii).

This strategy aggravated the very problem it was designed to solve. In 1928 grain procurements had fallen to barely half those of the peak prewar year, and the Soviet Union had ceased to be a grain exporter. At precisely this moment, as Soviet planners launched their ambitious First Five-Year Plan with its focus on heavy industry and the necessity to secure foreign exchange, the grain shortage assumed crisis dimensions (Lewin 1968: 172; Cohen 1980: 282–86).

In 1928 forced draft collectivization was on the lips of no leading Soviet officials; the order of the day was the extraction of grain from a reluctant peasantry. Stalin personally led the procurement drive, pinpointing "kulak sabotage" as the heart of the problem and pioneering in imposing coercive approaches to grain extraction that struck at *all* rural classes (Lewin 1968: 214–44; Davies 1980a: 56–97). The militarized language and methods of the drive recreated the atmosphere of War Communism throughout the countryside, pitting the state against the peasantry. The result, as Valentinov commented of Stalin, was "primitive socialist accumulation by the methods of Tamerlane" (Nove 1965: xiv). State violence replaced the market as the primary vehicle for state grain purchase and accumulation from the agrarian sector.

Was there in fact a kulak problem and, if so, in what did it consist?

Policies associated with NEP had made possible, even encouraged, a degree of rural class differentiation; a small number of middle peasants prospered while others declined to the ranks of poor and landless peasants. The central fact, however, is that state extraction and controls on marketing checked tendencies for the emergence of a kulak class. The most important tendency of the preceding years was the strengthening of the ranks of the *serednyaks*, middle peasants who produced a modest surplus and who, according to Strumilin and the Central Statistical Board, in 1926–27 accounted for 68 percent of the rural population compared with 3 percent for kulaks (Bettelheim 1978: 87–88). Estimates of the kulak population vary between 2 and 5 percent, and Kritsman observed that only 1 percent of the farms hired more than one laborer. In the agitprop of the grain confiscation drive, the kulak was portrayed as the enemy and target, but most of the grain was actually requisitioned from the ranks of the much larger serednyak group (Lewin 1968: 69–78). The small kulak group neither controlled the lion's share of grain surplus nor distinguished itself in sabotaging state procurement plans. But like the bednyaks and serednyaks, when procurement policies were tantamount to a declaration of war on the peasantry, kulaks used the slender means at their disposal to attempt to circumvent measures that would destroy them. As Carr (1964: 99) aptly observed, "It was no longer true that class analysis determined policy. Policy determined what form of class analysis was appropriate to the given situation."

In April–May 1929, at the height of the grain crisis, the Soviet Union's hastily drafted First Five-Year Plan projected grandiose targets, including a 2.5-fold increase in investment and an annual industrial growth rate of 21.5 percent. The goal was a 135 percent increase in industrial output and an 81.6 percent rise in national income. On the basis of the projected leap forward, real industrial wages were slated to rise by 58 percent and agricultural wages by 30 percent (Lewin 1968: 344–45).

The vast majority of the peasantry was to be linked to the state plan as drafted in 1928 and early 1929 not by the immediate transformation of production relations but through contracts committing peasants to the sale of fixed quantities of grain to the state. The state would gradually encourage and support kolkhoz formation over a five-year period to include 4.5 million households. By the end of the plan period, the kolkhoz and sovkhoz sector was to account for 13 percent of grain acreage. The concentration of all available tractors in the kolkhozes and sovkhozes would provide a dramatic demonstration effect of the merits of large-scale collective farming. Meanwhile, industrial growth would make possible substantial increases in the production of tractors, agricultural machinery, and chemical fertilizer, the material base for an industrialized collective agriculture. As Lewin (1968: 354–57) has observed, "The question of mass collectivization affecting the majority of the peasantry was one that had not even arisen. . . . There was general acceptance of the principle that both large-scale agricultural production and collectivization could only be introduced gradually, as material circumstances permitted." The experiments with mechanized collectives would provide the experience, and accelerated tractor production, while stimulating the material foundations, would encourage the majority of peasants voluntarily to join large-scale collectives. The peasantry would be won to mechanized collectives by their demonstrated superiority in securing peasant interests.

This approach was obliterated in Stalin's "Great Turn" of 1929. In the summer of 1929, the high five-year plan goals were hiked, making optimal goals minimal and raising annual industrial growth targets from 22.5 to an extraordinary 32.5 percent. By fall, plan targets were ordered to be fulfilled and surpassed in just four years (Cohen 1980: 330). The 1929 grain procurement drive swiftly turned into a savage onslaught against the "kulaks," which in turn gave way to universal command collectivization. Within a matter of weeks millions were forced to give up their land and join collectives whose methods of operation and remuneration remained unknown but which provided the state tighter control over the fruits of the land.

In 1929, having eliminated Bukharin and other critics of forced collectivization, and proclaiming that millions of peasants favored collectivization ("the serednyak has moved toward the kolkhozes"), Stalin suddenly, with no warning or organizational preparation, demanded the formation of giant multivillage kolkhozes of up to ten thousand hectares (Lewin 1968: 428, 456; Cohen 1980: 330–34). The drive for instant transformation swept aside earlier painstaking discussions of technical and political preconditions. Until the summer of 1929 the notion that "millions of *sokhi* (wooden ploughs) all added together would make an imposing sum" was a matter of ridicule. Now it suddenly became reality (Lewin 1968: 460). Not only land but, at the height of the collectivization madness, livestock and household plots were also collectivized, that is, confiscated. A wage system was to provide remuneration (Davies 1980b: 172). The break with household-based agriculture was virtually complete. With just eighteen thousand tractors available in the entire country, the combination of accelerated collectivization and the elimination of the kulaks resulted in "a new form of agrarian socialism . . . before even capitalism had had time to develop a production and marketing organization appropriate to the needs of the countryside" (Kerblay 1983: 93, 97).

The liquidation of the kulaks—some 1.3–1.5 million households were deprived of their land and property and many were killed, deported, imprisoned, or forced to flee—provided grim testimony to hesitant bednyaks and serednyaks of their real options as they weighed the pressures to join the collectives. At the end of September 1929, 7 percent of rural households were collectivized; this figure doubled in the next three months and by March 1930, 59 percent of peasant households were formally enrolled in kolkhozes. Eleven million households were forced to join in the course of just two months (Lewin 1968: 506–507, 514).

In his March 1930 statement, "Dizzy With Success," noting that 50 percent of the peasants had already joined collectives, Stalin proclaimed that "a radical turn of the countryside towards socialism may be considered as already achieved" (Stalin 1930: 197). Stalin's speech, notable primarily for its utter cynicism,[2] signaled the start of a period of consolidation and temporary retreat from some of the most extreme and unworkable features of the kolkhozes (p. 199). Between March and June the number of peasant households who were kolkhoz members dropped from 58 percent to 24 percent; that is, more than half the reported members defected, and in areas like the Central Black region membership plummeted within three months from 82 to less than 16 percent of the rural population (Nove 1971: 89; Cohen 1980: 339). Several more years would be required to complete collectivization throughout the countryside by methods including state-imposed famine (Lewin 1985: 151–56). But by 1930, the dye was already cast. As Stalin put it, "Anyone who does not join the collective farm is an enemy of the Soviet regime" (Cohen 1980: 336). The synthesis that emerged at this time as 250,000 collectives replaced 25 million family farms would long characterize Soviet agriculture.

The essential elements of the Stalinist agricultural synthesis were these (Davies 1980b; Lewin 1968; Cohen 1980):

• *State-imposed collectivization.* The large kolkhoz became the norm of Soviet agriculture, institutionalizing the preference for giantism which finds its parallel in the structure of Soviet industry. In return for the loss of private lands, the kolkhoz member received income not in the form of wages, as originally proposed, but as a share of collective production with payment in cash and kind based on the number of labor days.

• *The private plot and the right to maintain livestock.* The private sector, eliminated during kolkhoz formation, was restored as a crucial element in the uneasy quid pro quo between the collectivized peasantry and the state, and between central plan and market. The contribution of collective labor was the precondition for access to the private plot and to private raising of livestock, pigs, and so forth. Since the 1930s, the private sector has produced a significant portion of Soviet meat, vegetables, and fruit, contributed a substantial share of rural income, and preserved the household-based structure of rural life.

• *The centralized command procurement structure.* This provided the regime the principal channel for ensuring supplies of marketed grain, other foods, and commercial crops for the cities, for industry, and as a source of foreign exchange. State prices and fixed quotas (with above-quota bonuses) provided the structure that regulated agricultural sales and integrated agriculture within state plans.

• *Private plots and controlled access to private markets.* This limited access to private markets, after fulfillment of state quotas, paralleled and was functionally integrated with the private plots. Household plots and private markets were essential elements of the uneasy compromise erected following collectivization.

• *Machine tractor stations* (MTS). For most peasants, collectivization was completed prior to mechanization of any kind. Eventually the MTS became the technological link between state and collective, the channel for disseminating tractors, fertilizer, and machinery as well as an important outlet for extracting the produce of the countryside. Through the MTS, the kolkhoz was firmly lashed to the state.

The consequences of violent collectivization included the peasants' masochistic revenge in the form of the slaughter of more than half of the 33 million horses, 70 million cattle, 26 million pigs, and two-thirds of the 146 million sheep and goats (Cohen 1980: 339; Lewin 1985: 148, 156), and subsequent problems of collective organizations and motivation which contributed to chronic low productivity and food shortages. The view nevertheless remains widespread, particularly in parts of the Third World, that whatever the human costs and errors associated with collectivization, and regardless of the long-range setback to agricultural production and peasant interests, collectivization was a necessary, indeed inevitable, precondition for the crowning achievement of the Soviet regime (Carr 1964). On foundations of collectivization rose the industrial structure that enabled the Soviet Union to survive the Nazi onslaught in World War II and subsequently to emerge as a major industrial power. For many, the "Soviet model" consists precisely of rapid industrialization made possible by accumulation that inevitably followed the path of forced collectivization.

Issues of human cost aside, the research of A. A. Barsov and others has cut the economic ground out from under this argument. On the basis of urban-rural and state-collective capital flows, he has shown that in the 1930s the state was forced to subsidize agriculture heavily, both directly in the form of substantial allocations to the MTS and sovkhozes, and indirectly through improved terms of trade for the countryside. The state did squeeze the countryside of the agricultural surplus, but costly and inefficient collective agriculture required substantial state subsidies in both the short and long run (Millar 1970; 1974; cf. Ellman 1975). Far from providing the surplus that fueled Soviet industrialization, following collectivization the net resource flow was *to* the countryside. The case that imposed collectivization is an indispensable measure for rapid industrialization can no longer withstand scrutiny.

Michael Ellman (1979: 81) has summed up the case for collectivized agriculture as follows: First, it prevents rural exploitation, that is, the emergence of a rural proletariat side by side with an agrarian capitalist class. Second, it allows the rational use of the available resources. Third, it ensures a rapid growth of the marketed output of agriculture. Fourth, it provides a large source of accumulation.

To the above one may add the Marxist conviction that the superior productivity of large-scale collective agriculture is its ability to provide higher and more equal incomes for all rural producers, and to place control over the land and its product in the hands of the immediate producers.

These assertions of the superiority of collective agriculture, both economically and socially, must be tested empirically. Soviet approaches to collectivization from the 1930s to the 1950s constituted a declaration of war on the peasantry, what Cohen (1980: 340) has aptly labeled "military-feudal exploitation." The result was to set back agrarian development and achieve none of these goals. Soviet collectivization provided the crucible within which many of the most anachronistic elements of state socialism took shape, including the institutionalization of an antagonistic relationship between the state and the peasantry, the emergence of the Stalinist cult of personality, and foreclosure of possibilities for the development of cooperative and democratic processes. Nevertheless, Stalinist collectivization has had profound direct and indirect impact on subsequent agrarian strategies in the socialist states.

Comparative Reflections on Collectivization: The Yugoslav and Chinese Cases

Unlike the Bolshevik regime, which came to power with no significant roots in the countryside, Communist movements in Yugoslavia and China were tempered in the course of protracted guerrilla struggles in the rural areas. Both parties had substantial peasant party membership and abundant experience in dealing with complex rural issues and the politics of multiclass united fronts. And both had the benefit of hindsight in assessing the results of two decades of collectivization in the Soviet Union. Against this background may be charted the formation of agrarian policies, with particular attention to the influence of Soviet-style strategies of imposed collectivization.

With the 1948 eruption of Yugoslav-Soviet conflict, the Soviets singled out Yugoslav agrarian policy as a litmus test of loyalty to the Soviet Union and of a "correct line" in domestic policy. Stalin castigated the Yugoslav leadership for avoiding the question of the class struggle and the checking of the capitalist elements in the village. He went on to charge that the Yugoslav leaders view the peasantry "as an organic whole, and the party does not mobilize its forces in an effort to overcome the differences arising from the increase of the exploiting elements in the village" (Clissold 1975: 190). The Cominform resolution of June 28, 1948, which expelled Yugoslavia from the Cominform, condemned Yugoslav failure to attack the kulaks and collectivize: "The experience of the Communist Party of the Soviet Union (B) shows that the elimination of the last and biggest exploiting class—the kulak class—is possible only on the basis of the mass collectivization of agriculture, that the elimination of the kulaks as a class is an organic and integral part of the collectivization of agriculture" (Clissold 1975: 205).

In 1945 Yugoslavia had carried out a land reform, confiscating estates larger than 35 hectares (much of it land abandoned by collaborators) and distributing 745,000 hectares of land to 330,000 households

(Horvat 1976: 80–81). The available evidence suggests that the Yugoslav leadership, in the land-to-the-tiller program and subsequent campaigns for cooperative and collective formation, downplayed class struggle themes while attempting to formulate fiscal and other policies to reduce inequality and differentiation. There is nothing to suggest that the leadership saw a significant threat from a Yugoslav kulak class.

And yet, within months *after* the break with the Soviet Union and its expulsion from the Cominform, Yugoslavia embarked on a program of imposed collectivization that bore many—though certainly not all—of the features of the earlier Soviet drive. Having defied the Soviet Union, and facing economic and political crisis of epic proportions with its major lines of trade and aid cut off, the Yugoslav leadership initiated a collectivization drive along with its First Five-Year Plan. As Branko Horvat (1976: 88) later summed up this period of what he styled etatist collectivization, "Agriculture was treated as a source of capital accumulation and the peasants as a social group of small property and (potentially) capitalist elements" to be incorporated in the socialized sector.

To be clear, the Yugoslav state initiated no violent uprooting and slaughter of a rich peasant class on a scale comparable to that carried out earlier by the Bolsheviks. But the combination of direct and indirect pressures on all rural classes, and particularly the imposition of high procurement and tax quotas on private farmers, produced the rapid expansion of peasant work cooperatives directly modeled on the Soviet kolkhoz.

In 1948, just months before Yugoslavia's own "Great Turn," Eduard Kardelj lucidly presented to the Fifth Party Congress the case for gradual, voluntary cooperation. The basic organizational form for the peasant en route to socialist agriculture was not the collective of the Soviet type, he explained, but more elementary cooperative forms familiar to the peasant, built on democratic principles and above all providing the peasant "a guarantee that the progress of agriculture will not proceed in ways that are unacceptable to him" (Horvat 1976: 89). Kardelj thus returned to that wisdom of the precollectivization Marxist-Leninist tradition and NEP. But in January 1949 it was Kardelj himself whose address emphasizing the role of collectives initiated Yugoslavia's accelerated collectivization. (Participation, he said, was of course "strictly voluntary.")

In one year, the number of collectives had increased sixfold to incorporate one-fifth of all agricultural land, including much of the richest. Collectives had been initiated on a trial basis as early as 1946, apparently on confiscated land owned by the state. Their numbers gradually increased to 1,318 with 286,234 members in 1948. Suddenly in the critical 1949 campaign they grew to 6,626, with 1,707,073 members and 1,838,613 hectares (Popovic 1964: 14). With this wave of collectivization, the state tightened compulsory sales quotas, set up a Soviet-type network of machine tractor stations concentrating control over modern machinery, and reformed the tax structure to the detriment of private agriculture (Horvat 1976: 90; Popovic 1964: 14). The Yugoslav state thus entered on a collision course with a substantial portion of its peasant majority as a result of the 1949 decision to impose collectivization.

As in the Soviet Union, collectivization appealed to the beleaguered Yugoslav leadership not primarily as a vehicle for agrarian development but as a vehicle that promised both to avert the prospect of the imminent collapse of its industrial program and to strengthen the control and penetration of the state at a time of external challenge. The key lay in the idea that collectivization could produce immediate state control of a substantially larger share of the agricultural surplus. Abandoning the implicit critique of Soviet collectivization developed in its earlier statements on agrarian policy, the Yugoslav leadership attempted to solve at a stroke both the agrarian question and the problem of centralized accumulation by imposition of collectives.

In the face of fierce peasant resistance, however, the Yugoslav leadership recognized the failure of imposed collectivization. In 1953, when the state offered peasants the option of continued collective membership or private farming, the collectives collapsed virtually overnight. Yugoslavia, followed by Poland three years later, became one of the two socialist states to abandon imposed collectivization.

Yugoslavia subsequently developed a dual agriculture in which privileged state farms and the remaining collectives enjoyed a monopoly on modern equipment while the majority of peasants clung to private agriculture on microholdings limited to ten hectares and denied access to tractors. In 1965 this course was carried further with the elimination of most crop and purchasing quotas on the private sector and predominant reliance on the role of the market in setting prices, a policy which produced substantial price increases advantageous to agricultural producers. At the same time, discriminatory policies that barred access of private farms to tractors and advanced technology were eliminated (Horvat 1976: 110–55). Yugoslav agriculture came to pivot on the family farm. As Horvat observes (pp. 149–50), throughout the entire postwar period, the party and state strongly resisted "the self-initiated association of peasants in traditional cooperatives. Such cooperatives were termed wild, and their formation was prevented." Yet no one ever tried to explain "why plots would have to remain small, why the rise in productivity and the standard of living on the individual holding would be an illusion, why the experiences of pre-war Yugoslavia would have to be repeated, and why the basic social transformations—which consist of the elimination of exploitation and the establishment of self-management—would not be possible."

Yugoslav Communists, preoccupied with the goals of rapid industrialization, initially embarked on the Soviet path of imposed collectivization. As in the Soviet Union, collectivization precipitated fierce peasant resistance. Yugoslavia, however, avoided the worst elements of the reign of terror set in motion by Stalin in the Soviet Union in 1929. In the face of costly agricultural failures associated with inefficient collectives, the Yugoslav state quickly abandoned forced collectivization and permitted the resurrection of the family farm but continued restrictive and discriminatory policies that held back the development of private agriculture. As in the Soviet case, the choice seemed to be imposed collectives or the family farm; the attempt to promote and support voluntary cooperatives was abortive.

After more than two decades of building rural base areas, leading a national liberation movement, and carrying out a successful agrarian reform, the Chinese Communist Party came to power with deep roots in the countryside. In the early 1950s, the socialist state encouraged rural prosperity through the family farm and promoted a nationwide movement gradually to form mutual-aid teams and small-scale cooperatives attuned to local conditions and peasant tradition and experience. It provided technical, administrative, and financial support to promising units and widely publicized them as a spur to rural cooperation. A leadership consensus projected the socialist transformation of the countryside proceeding gradually by stages from household-based agriculture through more advanced cooperative forms, eventually culminating in large-scale mechanized collectives directly inspired by the Soviet kolkhoz but avoiding the disastrous antipeasant extremes of Stalin's forced collectivization. The institutional goals of large-scale mechanized collective agriculture were strikingly similar; the methods for attaining them profoundly differentiated Chinese theory and practice from Soviet-type forced collectivization. China would realize mechanized collectivization through voluntary participation by peasant households based on the recognition of the superiority of collectives to produce and to reward their members. In 1955, Mao Zedong affirmed the leadership consensus that it would require three five-year plans before industrialization and mechanization could provide the technical foundations for large-scale collective agriculture (Mao 1978: 199). It is widely but incorrectly believed that China followed this path of voluntary, staged transition from small-scale mutual aid and coopera-tion to large-scale collectivization and mechanization. China not only embarked on such a path but achieved impressive results in implement-ing it in the early 1950s. Nevertheless, like the Soviet Union and Yugoslavia, China abruptly abandoned this constellation of policies in favor of instant imposed collectivization.

Mao's speech of July 31, 1955, "On the Cooperative Transforma-tion of Agriculture," while ostensibly reaffirming the course of gradu-al, voluntary cooperation, actually touched off the "Great Turn" in Chinese rural strategy (Mao 1978: particularly 211–25). China virtual-ly completed nationwide collectivization in a single year. The logic of the new strategy mirrored the concerns that lay behind Soviet collec-tivization. In the absence of drastic action, Mao insisted, the ambitious industrializing goals of the First Five-Year Plan were doomed as a result of the substantial shortfall of marketed grain and agricultural commodities. Moreover, class polarization—the emergence of a new rich peasantry or kulak class—constituted a grave threat to socialist development in the countryside. Only accelerated collectivization, Mao held, could stimulate productive energies, making possible plan fulfillment and the promise implicit in the land revolution by eliminat-ing class exploitation and all existing extremes of wealth. Just as Stalin had raised the spectre of a kulak stranglehold on the Soviet countryside, in 1955 Mao posed the issues of collectivization in terms of a class struggle to block rich-peasant domination of China's countryside.

The collectivization campaign from the fall of 1955 to the spring of 1956 overturned central premises of the earlier strategy of co-operative development. By June 1955, 14 percent of China's rural households had pooled resources in small elementary cooperatives averaging approximately ten households, nearly all of them in older liberated areas in the North. By the end of 1956, 88 percent of China's rural households had been swept into large, Soviet-style collectives organized on a village or even a multivillage scale. The vast majority of communities completed the leap from household farming to collectivization in less than one year.

China did not experience the massive resistance put up by the Soviet peasantry; there was no uprooting of a section of the peasantry, little state violence, and the slaughter of draught animals took place on a far smaller scale than in the Soviet case. China's agriculture did not collapse immediately with forced collectivization.

Bigger, faster, more egalitarian, more collective may express aspirations and goals for the formation of socialist communities. But goals and results are not necessarily identical. Mao himself, following in the steps of Marx, Engels, Lenin, and Bukharin, had well articulated the case for proceeding by stages, gradually, in order to construct firm foundations of organizational experience, cooperative values, appropriate technology, capital accumulation, economic growth, and popular consensus and support in the course of a transition from small-scale private agriculture to large-scale, socialized, mechanized agriculture. He also had done more: He had led China in initiating such a course from land revolution through 1955. In retrospect it is clear that the abandonment of this strategy exacted a heavy price on the future course of China's socialist development.

Here I would like to consider that price from two perspectives. One is the problem of socialist democracy, particularly the process by which the forms of state or cooperative ownership become invested with the substance of mastery by the immediate producers, or, more accurately, by the new class of rural cooperants. This goal, which ultimately requires mastery by the producers of the highest technological processes as well as of institutions of popular expression, cannot of course be achieved rapidly, much less instantly, with the change from private to public ownership systems. At best, formal ownership changes create the preconditions for and the full realization of socialism's cooperative, democratic, and egalitarian promise. The process of transition is critical in determining whether the outcome strengthens tendencies toward state despotism or reinforces cooperative forms resting on the support of their members and responsive to their needs. China's imposed collectivization reinforced those manipulative tendencies of the Leninist party and state and undermined the democratic possibilities inherent in the cooperative form.

The long-term viability of cooperatives must hinge on the active support of their members. From this perspective, coerced collectivization created long-term structural and incentive problems. Many came to associate cooperation and particularly collectivization not with mutual prosperity—their original promise—but with permanent sacrifice, belt-tightening, and control, with the priorities of the state and industry over the countryside and rural producers.

The second and related issue concerns the viability of cooperatives and collectives as economic institutions. If collectives are to win the loyalty of their members, they must prove their worth both in terms of social justice and equity criteria and superior performance measured in productivity, personal income, accumulation, and security. Viewed from the perspective of the peasantry, by the late 1970s per capita income and living standards in the countryside had not exceeded levels attained in the mid-1950s prior to collectivization while industry had developed rapidly and the urban-rural gap had expanded. Collectivization in China, as in the Soviet Union and Yugoslavia, was primarily an extractive mechanism that subordinated the interests of rural producers to those of industry and the state. This theme is taken up from several different angles in subsequent chapters exploring China's strategies of cooperation, collectivization, and accumulation.

In China as in the Soviet Union, forced collectivization and crackdown on rural markets set back the prospects of socialist development by undermining the link between cooperation and mutual prosperity, undermining the democratic and popular sources of cooperation, driving a wedge between city and countryside and increasing state manipulation of village and peasantry, reducing the overall credibility of the party and of cooperative institutions, divorcing policy from economic reality and popular welfare, projecting a distorted vision of class polarization and class struggle in the countryside, undermining rural production incentives, and turning cooperative forms from instruments primarily for the improvement of peasant welfare to those tied increasingly to the accumulation and industrialization goals of the centralized state.

Questions and Conclusions

This brief examination of the implications of imposed collectivization in the Soviet Union, Yugoslavia, and China (in light of the origins of Marxist strategies of agrarian development) has uncovered common threads and problems that have been and remain central to a systemic crisis of socialist agriculture. At one level, one can trace the issues back to the belief in economies of scale in agriculture, the efficacy of cooperative and/or collective agriculture, the conviction that the central economic, social, and political issues of socialist development are those of industry and the cities, and the polarizing and exploitative consequences of the market, beliefs shared in essence by Marx, Engels, Kautsky, Lenin, and most Soviet, Yugloslav, and Chinese leaders. In each instance advocates of imposed collectivization overrode proponents of strategies of gradual, voluntary cooperation that emphasized linkages among technology, scale, and popular consciousness. In each instance, peasant interests, including those of the poor and middle peasants, were thrust aside in practice, sacrificed to the prior claims of state accumulation and national plan targets.

At another level, other possible outcomes for socialist agriculture within an evolving Marxist tradition have been discerned. That alternative vision of a socialist agrarian policy has yet to be seriously tested, although China's experience prior to the autumn of 1955 constitutes perhaps its fullest implementation thus far. Since the 1950s each of the countries studied here and many others have sought solutions to the problems generated by imposed collectivization with experimentation centered on redefining the relationship between plan and market and among state, collective, and private sectors, and between large-scale and family-centered farming. In each case, one observes the search for greater latitude for the market, the household, and private sectors. But a variety of other, perhaps more basic, issues remain open. These include the appropriate mix of cooperative, collective, and state ownership, and organizational forms for stimulating accumulation and development, contributing to peasant welfare, and building democratic institutions. A fresh consideration of the premises and promise of socialist agriculture is long overdue.

3

COOPERATION AND CONFLICT: COOPERATIVE AND COLLECTIVE FORMATION IN CHINA'S COUNTRYSIDE

In the 1960s, China's Great Proletarian Cultural Revolution resurrected international debate on problems of the transition to socialism. Stalin and his Soviet successors had constricted understanding of the transition to matters of formal ownership and productivity, relegating to an ever-receding future such issues as the mastery of working people over productive processes, the scope and form of institutions appropriate to the flourishing of socialist democracy, and the elimination of all forms of privilege and inequality.[1]

The critique of Soviet socialism associated with the Cultural Revolution, drawing on Maoist theory and practice of uninterrupted revolution which had developed since the 1940s, suggested to many a variety of fresh perspectives on the transition. The crux of the matter was and is the state-society relationship. The issue is framed by the fact that the extension and penetration of state power is the logical outcome of the creation of new systems of ownership and organization, and of the attempt to promote and guide industrialization and comprehensive development of a new type. Concentration of economic and political power in the hands of the state, whatever its contribution to eliminating inequalities of the prerevolutionary social order and initiating rational planning, has the potential to produce state despotism, a new moloch more powerful and hence more dangerous than the more fragmented social systems it replaced. The Maoist critique of bureaucracy distinctively posed certain of these issues and presented uninterrupted revolution as the optimal approach for resolving them. Yet that critique, and Mao's personal leadership, must be reassessed in light of China's experience in rural transformation.

The present essay reconceptualizes the historical options at a critical juncture in the formation of Chinese socialism, the cooperative and collective transformation of agriculture, and explores their resolution in the creation of collective agriculture. Close analysis of leadership conflict and grass-roots practice centered on the 1955–56 "socialist high tide" suggests new conclusions about both the distinctiveness of the Chinese path and the strength of the legacy of Stalinist approaches to collectivization in particular and socialism in general.

At the center of this analysis is the question of the relationship between transformation of relations of production (embracing both ownership and the organization of productive processes) and the productive forces, that is, between social change and economic development. I will explore conflicts among the state, cooperatives, and individuals over appropriate rates of accumulation, state revenues, individual income and consumption, the scope of the market, and the autonomy of rural producers.

The issues are central to assessment of China's socialist transformation. For it is the countryside that has been most closely associated with the achievements and unique contributions of the Chinese revolution. It was in the countryside that Chinese revolutionaries first developed independent strategies en route to national power. It was over rural policy that Chinese revolutionary praxis diverged most sharply from inherited Soviet wisdom in the 1940s and early 1950s. Collectivization was the decisive event shaping the Chinese economy and society for decades to come. It was over rural policy that Mao eventually broke with many of his closest colleagues in the leadership. Finally, the reform strategy that has advanced farthest in the countryside in the 1980s, in breaking with central premises of the collective order, invites reassessment of China's collective agriculture. This analysis probes the ways in which the peasantry and fractions of it reacted to, participated in, and resisted state-directed sociopolitical and economic change, in particular how it interacted with the party and state in the course of the cooperative and collective transformation of the countryside.[2]

I will consider the constellation of policy choices pertaining to cooperation with respect to production, accumulation, peasant income, and welfare against the background of the Marxist-Leninist tradition and in light of Chinese conditions and conflicting approaches to cooperative formation. At the center of this effort is an attempt to gauge the significance of cooperative and collective transformation in terms of its impact on productivity, accumulation, and income distribution, on the one hand, and peasant control over production, planning, and consumption, on the other.

Marx, Lenin, Mao: Visions of the Transition to Socialism in the Countryside

Marx and Engels provided few specific ideas clarifying their understanding of institutions appropriate to the socialist transition. At numerous points in his analysis of capitalist development, however, Marx offered clues pertinent to understanding the challenge that would arise if and when societies with weakly developed capitalist foundations attempted the transition to socialism. In the *Grundrisse*, he observed that "The greater the extent to which production still rests on mere manual labor, on use of muscle power, etc., in short on physical exertion by individual laborers, the more does the increase of the *productive forces* consist in their collaboration *on a mass scale*" (Marx 1973; italics in original). In rural China, to develop the productive forces and create socialist relations of production would require the formation of cooperative labor both in the sense that Marx used the term here to describe the capitalist transformation of individual labor, and in the sense of creating socialist forms of ownership, management, and distribution. It would require, that is, changes associated with both capitalist and socialist development. Nations such as China, whose agriculture consisted primarily of a mix of subsistence family farming and petty commodity production, could not build on highly developed foundations of cooperative labor (even in the capitalist sense) in erecting a new socialist institutional structure.

The pre-Bolshevik origins of the idea that collectivization was the route to socialist transformation in the countryside remain obscure. What is clear is that the profoundly urban-oriented Bolsheviks, preoccupied with the problems and prospects of the proletariat and industrialization, came to power in 1917 unified in the conviction that collectivization, with land ownership in the hands of the state, was the panacea to the dual problems of increased productivity and the formation of socialist institutions in the countryside. Thus in 1917 in his April Theses, Lenin proclaimed the "Confiscation of all estate land. Nationalization of *all* land in the country under control of local councils of agricultural laborers' and peasants' deputies. Conversion of each large estate . . . into a model farm under control of agricultural laborers' deputies and on public account'' (quoted in Wesson 1963: 38). The Bolsheviks ratified Lenin's agrarian program at their April congress. In September, Lenin went still further in spelling out the implications of his program. After calling for the nationalization of all land he stated that ''the *disposal* of the land, the determination of the *local regulations* governing ownership and tenure of land, must in no case be placed in the hands of the bureaucrats and officials, but exclusively in the hands of the regional and local *Soviets of Peasants Deputies*'' (Lenin 1959d: 1980–81; italics in original).

In the struggle for peasant support which followed in the coming months, this vision was thrust aside. Lenin and the Bolsheviks, with no significant organizational roots in the rural areas, advanced a program with quite different implications for agriculture and for the party-peasant relationship. Land-hungry peasants, with Bolshevik support, seized and subdivided the large estates into individually cultivated microholdings. Nevertheless, as a result of harsh grain requisitioning during the civil war, the immense gulf that had existed between the Bolshevik Party and the peasants gave way to direct conflict between the peasantry and the new state.

In 1919 Lenin observed that ''Socialism means the abolition of classes'' and then proceeded to focus on the sensitive problem of the Russian peasantry as a class of petty commodity producers:

> In order to abolish classes it is necessary, firstly, to overthrow the landlords and capitalists . . . it is necessary, secondly, to abolish the difference between working-man and peasant, to make them all workers. . . . It is not a problem that can be solved by overthrowing a class. It can be solved only by the organizational reconstruction of the whole social economy, by a transition from individual, disunited, petty commodity production to large-scale social production. This transition must of necessity be extremely protracted. It may only be delayed and complicated by hasty and incautious administrative and legislative measures. It can be accelerated only by affording such assistance to the peasant as will enable him immensely to improve his whole agricultural technique, to reform it radically. (Lenin 1959: 318)

Here Lenin sensitively broached the long-term tasks of the rural transformation that would culminate in the transformation of rural producers from peasants to workers. Where Marx had noted the importance both of the communal and subsistence elements of Russian rural society (Shanin 1983), from his 1899 *Development of Capitalism in Russia* forward, Lenin overwhelmingly stressed the character of the peasantry as rural petty commodity producers with its implications for capitalism. This is the basis for Lenin's emphasis in the italicized passage, *"make them all workers,"* and the implicit suggestion in much of Lenin's work that social change is to be directed and carried out from above by the urban-oriented vanguard party with little respect for peasant values or preferences. I will consider the implications of *process* in examining cooperative formation in China.

The same passage, however, emphasizes that political tranformation was only the first step in building socialism. Ultimately, the technical transformation of agriculture was inseparable from questions of ownership, ideology, and organization. It held the key to the transformation of the peasantry in socialist society. Two years later, Lenin amplified on the technical/material components of the transition.

> The only way to solve this problem of the small farmer, to improve, so to speak, his whole mentality, is through the material basis, technical equipment, the use of tractors and machines on a mass scale in agriculture, electrification on a mass scale. This would remake the small farmer fundamentally and with tremendous speed. . . . But you know perfectly well that to obtain tractors and machines and to electrify our vast country is a matter that at any rate may take decades. (Lenin 1959a: 358)

In these and other passages, and above all in the formulation of the New Economic Program (NEP) in the early 1920s, Lenin exhibited sensitivity to the necessity for state financial and technological support to facilitate the gradual, long-term transformation of rural social relations. But just as Lenin and the Bolshevik leadership remained distant from the peasantry and rural politics prior to 1917, in the years prior to 1928 they showed little interest in working out appropriate institutional arrangements or charting the politics of a transitional political process to ensure the development of socialist relations in the rural areas. Stated differently, neither Lenin nor other Bolsheviks perceived in the peasantry the revolutionary or creative impulses they attributed to the proletariat, bases on which to construct the foundations of socialist society in the vast Russian countryside.

In his final years, Lenin did suggest the importance of cooperatives as the centerpiece of state policy during the transition to socialism in the countryside. In 1923 he reiterated "how infinitely important it is now to organize the population of Russia in cooperative societies" (Lenin 1975: 708). Lenin saw the modest cooperative elements of NEP as creating preconditions for socialist development in the countryside. "All we actually need under NEP," he argued, "is to organize the population of Russia in cooperative societies on a sufficiently large scale, for we have now found that degree of combination of private interest, of private commercial interest, with state supervision and control of this interest, that degree of its subordination to the common interests which was formerly the stumbling-block for very many socialists." Lenin urged state "aid to cooperative trade in which *really large masses of the population actually take part*" (original emphasis).

"On Cooperation" is Lenin's clearest, albeit brief, exposition on the nature of the transition in the countryside. Private ownership and cultivation of the land would continue throughout the NEP. Simultaneously, on this foundation of capitalist proprietorship, the formation of state-supported cooperatives *centering on trade* would create the basis for peasant support for and participation in protosocialist institutions and eventually for basic cultural or value changes that would facilitate more advanced socialist forms. Collectivization of agricultural production would become feasible, Lenin held, only when the technological revolution could provide the material basis for rural petty commodity producers willingly to create more socialized forms. Trading cooperatives, however, would create important preconditions for change.

Soviet policy favored this restricted approach to cooperative formation throughout the 1920s. By 1929, however, only one-third of rural households had joined trading cooperatives. The countryside was a sea of subsistence and petty commodity production organized at the household level. Trading cooperatives had developed essentially as appendages of the state. The system was inefficient and costly. It did not significantly increase the supply of marketable grain. Its primary beneficiaries were the more prosperous peasants.[3] Agricultural production remained almost exclusively in private hands. Petty commodity production and family-based subsistence agriculture reigned supreme. The gulf between city and countryside widened, and tension mounted over the serious shortfall of marketed grain. There is little evidence that Lenin's hope for deepening socialist consciousness among the peasantry was realized during the first decade of Bolshevik rule. Against this background, and driven by the desire to create the preconditions for rapid accumulation and industrialization spelled out in the Five-Year Plan, Stalin in 1929 moved from the forced extraction of grain and liquidation of the kulaks to universal forced collectivization. Violent clashes between peasant and state and the subsequent destruction of half the nation's livestock dealt a blow to the long-term prospects for agricultural development and for a collective transition based on popular support for socialist construction.

Ignoring Lenin's strictures, beginning in 1929 Soviet collectivization *preceded* agricultural mechanization, and indeed all technical, administrative, and social preparation for such changes as collectivization. Rather than building on peasant consciousness of the benefits of collective agriculture, it rested on naked state coercion. Soviet collectivization, based on no significant experience with production cooperatives and no rural popular base, produced social and economic disasters of great proportions (Lewin 1975; 1985; Bettelheim 1978; Cohen 1985).

Soviet collectivization shaped in complex ways the perspective of the Chinese leadership as it sought to frame an agrarian policy for the transition. China faced material constraints on the socialist transformation of agriculture far more formidable than those encountered by the Bolsheviks, including highly unfavorable population-land ratios, lower per capita grain yields, and levels of mechanization just a fraction of those in the Soviet Union. For example, at the time that each launched its first five-year plan, with ambitious industrialization targets, China's per capita grain output was approximately 269 kilograms while that in the Soviet Union was 480 kilograms; and the percentage of marketable grain achieved in the Soviet Union was far higher (Nolan 1976: 24).

In analyzing cooperation and collectivization in China I will consider under what conditions revolutionary change stimulates—or aborts—accumulation and the development of the productive forces in industry and agriculture. A look at Chinese cooperative and collective formation also permits us to assess their effects on stratification and inequality, the nature and degree of participation and support for social change by specific classes, the impact of the changes on the livelihood of the people, and their contribution to strengthening cooperative foundations of rural life.

Land Revolution and the Origins of Cooperation

How was "semicolonial, semifeudal China" to initiate the ascent to socialism? In December 1947, Mao Zedong drafted a Central Committee resolution that etched a theory of stages for the new democratic revolution (including land revolution) and the socialist transition that lay ahead.[4]

> A new democratic revolution aims at wiping out only feudalism and monopoly capitalism, only the landlord class and the bureaucratic-capitalist class (the big bourgeoisie) and not at wiping out capitalism in general, the upper petty bourgeoisie, or the middle bourgeoisie. In view of China's economic backwardness, even after the countrywide victory of the revolution, it will still be necessary to permit the existence for a long time of a capitalist sector of the economy represented by the extensive petty bourgeoisie and middle bourgeoisie. . . . After the victory of the revolution all over the country, the new democratic state will possess huge state enterprises taken over from the bureaucrat-capitalist class and controlling the economic lifelines of the country, and *there will be an agricultural economy liberated from feudalism which*, though it will remain basically scattered and individual for a fairly long time, *can later be led to develop, step by step, in the direction of cooperatives*. In these circumstances the existence and development of these small and middle capitalist sectors will present no danger. The same is true of the new rich peasant economy which will inevitably emerge in the rural areas after the land reform. It is absolutely impermissible to repeat such wrong ultra-left policies toward the petty bourgeois and middle bourgeois sectors in the economy as our party adopted during 1931–34. (Quoted in Selden 1978: 173–74; my italics)

Mao's scenario invites comparison with Lenin's, set forth in 1923 in "On Cooperation" but thrust aside in Soviet practice in Stalin's forced collectivization. By 1947, the Chinese Communists had struck deep roots in the countryside dating from the successful rural policy and practice in North China bases in the 1930s and 1940s, notably the wartime policies of protecting subsistence and market activities while initiating gradual reforms that reduced rent, interest, and tax burdens on the poor and restricted the power of the landlords. Following the defeat of Japan, the party launched a land revolution that fundamentally altered class relationships and freed for peasant consumption and investment the substantial surplus previously captured by the landlord class and created a population of independent cultivators with roughly equal small holdings.

Land reform drew on two decades of rural experience and a legacy of firm linkages between party and peasantry. It is worth recalling that Mao's long-term concern for protecting middle peasants from appropriation in the land revolution in the Jiangxi Soviet in the 1920s and

1930s had repeatedly drawn fire from party superiors who criticized his conservative "rich peasant line." If Mao was among the first Chinese Communists to perceive the explosive revolutionary potential of the poor peasants, preoccupation with safeguarding the interests of owner cultivators and the importance of protecting the middle peasantry as the key to securing broad-based support and ensuring the vitality of the rural economy are continuous themes in his leadership and writings from the early 1930s to the mid-1950s.[5]

To be sure, the party's relationship with the peasantry was riddled with conflicts over such issues as grain requisition, prices, and markets. Nevertheless, from its leadership of the anti-Japanese resistance to the land reform and early stages of cooperation, party-peasant bonds contrast favorably to the chasm that separated the Bolsheviks from the peasantry, both in the decades before and after 1917. In China in the years 1935–1955, those bonds rested above all on the party's ability to tread a fine line which permitted it to support poor-peasant demands for redistributive justice at the expense of the landlord class while protecting the material welfare of all peasant producers including small owner cultivators and even some more prosperous peasants. In this way the poor in the liberated areas became beneficiaries of wartime rent reduction and taxation policies and of the subsequent land revolution. Many of them changed their status from that of tenants, part tenants, or hired laborers to freeholders. At the same time, the party's guarantee of the interests of small and medium owner cultivators made possible the formation of a broadly unified peasantry and permitted the unfolding of a social revolution without seriously disrupting agricultural production and trade.

In the civil war document quoted above, Mao and the party clearly elaborated for the first time the concept of stages in China's transition to socialism and emphasized the commitment to phased development in which each step proceeded on the foundation of broad-based popular support. "All empty words are useless," Mao had observed in 1942 in his first extended foray into political economy. "We must give the people visible material wealth . . . we can organize, lead and help the people develop production, increase their material wealth, and, on this basis, step by step raise their political consciousness and cultural level" (Selden 1978: 715).

As wartime strife ended, the ability of the social system to provide increasing material rewards for the great majority would become an important basis for popular support, above all the support of the large and growing stratum of owner cultivators. Indeed, following land reform, party spokesmen, including Mao and Liu Shaoqi, vigorously promoted the "rich-peasant economy," that is, growth of the productive forces and private prosperity in the peasant economy, by guaranteeing that the fruits of prosperity achieved by nonexploitative means would not be expropriated.[6] This policy carried within it the seeds of a conflict that erupted in subsequent debates on rural policy. The issue was this: Was the party to represent the interests of the poorest peasants or those of all nonexploiting rural classes? In the short run, the former choice led to the continuing emphasis on redistributive justice and class struggle politics, while the latter emphasized protecting the interests of the entire working peasantry to support and stimulate the rural economy and improve peasant livelihood. During land reform the party sought to reconcile these conflicting definitions of its role by supporting poor and landless peasant demands for expropriation while simultaneously safeguarding the interests of middle (and at times rich) peasants, to ensure that the land revolution would stimulate the growth of the rural economy. This was the basis for party leadership of a united front in the civil war against the Guomindang which coincided with the struggle for the land as well as for subsequent strategies of cooperative formation (Selden 1978: 27–39, 208–53).

Agricultural Cooperation, Technological Change, and Peasant Welfare

Mao's 1947 address spelled out the long-range commitment to move beyond the land revolution goals of eliminating exploitation and creating a society of roughly equal peasant cultivators to implementation of principles of cooperation. As early as 1943, he had explictly charted the future of the Chinese countryside in terms of cooperation as a springboard for the realization of "mutual prosperity" (*gongtong fuyu*) and ultimately as a bridge to collectivization. Mao's first significant discussion of cooperation explicitly invoked the authority of Lenin.

> Among the peasant masses for several thousand years the individual economy has prevailed with one family, one household, as the economic unit. This kind of dispersed individual economy is the basis for feudal control and causes the peasants themselves to succumb to permanent impoverishment. The only method to overcome such a situation is to gradually collectivize [*jitihua*], and the only road to achieve collectivization, as Lenin said, is through cooperatives [*hezuoshe*]. (Mao 1965a: 88–89)

As early as 1943, then, Mao advanced the goal of rural collectivization built on a foundation of effective cooperation. Locating Chinese cooperative practice in the tradition of Lenin, Mao made no mention of the disjuncture between Leninist theory and Soviet collectivization practice engineered by Stalin. Nor did he note the fact that where Lenin had looked to marketing cooperatives, China would undertake the more ambitious task of forming production cooperatives. Beginning in 1943, building on traditional cooperative forms, the party fostered small-scale mutual aid and agricultural cooperation in more secure base areas and guerrilla zones.

Mao distinguished the new Chinese cooperatives from the Soviet Union's collectives:

> The numerous peasant cooperatives which we have already organized in the Border Region, however, are not yet the cooperatives which in the Soviet Union are called collective farms [*jiti nongzhuang*]. Our economy is a new democratic one, and our cooperatives [*hezuoshe*], built using collective labor, rest on the foundation of the individual economy (on the foundation of private property).[7] (Mao 1965a: 89)

Mao called for the preservation of private property as the foundation of the new democratic economy, including a growing cooperative sector.

From this time forward, collectives of the Soviet type were the unquestioned prototype for the future transformation of China's countryside. The Chinese leadership focused on processes of a cooperative transformation that would avoid the social and economic disasters associated with Stalin's collectivization. Mao's wartime speeches and writings scrupulously emphasized voluntary participation ("compulsion must never be used") and the necessity to ensure that cooperatives stimulate labor enthusiasm, raise productivity, and contribute to mutual prosperity.[8] Rural cooperatives were promoted as a means to win peasant support and bolster the economy while strengthening the position of the party in the countryside.

Long before the land revolution or the founding of the People's Republic, Chinese peasants in the liberated areas began with party support to organize small-scale cooperatives that characteristically built on indigenous forms of mutual aid. The roots of these cooperatives were deeply planted in Chinese soil. Between 1949 and 1952, the recovery period coinciding with the conclusion of the land revolution, China's total grain output increased at the respectable rate of 7.4 percent annually, rising from approximately 127 to 157 million metric tons (Wiens 1980: 61–63).[9] In the countryside, the possibility of increasing yields while promoting land reform and cooperative formation rested on scrupulous protection and improvement of the livelihood of the majority. Cooperatives suggested an approach to a socialist agriculture that could circumvent the rigidifying, commandist, and alienating tendencies characteristic of state-managed and collective economies while making use of economies of scale, expanded opportunities for accumulation, and rationalization of agricultural and sideline production. This approach required vesting resources and broad administrative-technical powers in small, face-to-face, local communities functioning within the scope of regional and national planning.

In the early 1950s the state directed a portion of its slender financial and abundant leadership and administrative resources to promoting highly visible model cooperative units and providing incentives to cooperatives. However, the state could not smooth the way by immediately providing most fledgling cooperatives with the means for mechanization or even improved traditional tools, although these goals were closely associated with the long-range success of the cooperative program. Unless the new cooperatives quickly produced visible results, or unless they outperformed the private sector to the satisfaction of most participants, the alternatives were a return to family farming or state coercion. The latter course not only would inevitably represent the defeat of the cooperative principles of voluntary participation and community initiative, but would set back agrarian development, increase tensions between the party and the peasants, and retard the socialist transition.

Throughout the years 1950–55 a continuing tug of war took place within the ranks of the central party leadership and between grass-roots cadres and the peasantry over the appropriate pace of formation, scale of operation, and nature of cooperative institutions, particularly with respect to ensuring voluntary participation.[10] Important tactical differences repeatedly surfaced within an overwhelming leadership consensus that the way forward to socialist development of the countryside was through the following stages:

1. The peasantry, with local leadership provided by the party and the Youth League, would organize mutual-aid teams and subsequently more advanced and larger cooperatives on the basis of voluntary participation and mutual benefit. The principal yardstick of success was the ability of cooperatives not only to outproduce individual peasants, but also to ensure steady increases in member *incomes*, particularly

those of highly productive middle peasants.

2. The state would restrict the scope of the market by extending its control over grain, cotton, oil, and other vital commodities and restricting the scope of individual commercial enterprise.

3. China would *eventually* follow the Soviet Union—Mao in July 1955 estimated it would require three five-year plans—in completing cooperative transformation with ownership of land, draft animals, and other means of production transferred from individuals to large-scale mechanized collectives. This was the method of development by stages, from small to large and from rudimentary to advanced forms of mutual aid, cooperation, and eventually collectivization. Significant progress in mechanization and technological development would pave the way for large-scale cooperation of the advanced type, that is, collectives, with private landownership eliminated and remuneration based exclusively on the return to labor.[11]

In the mid–1950s, with no immediate prospects of mechanized agriculture outside of a small number of state farms and model cooperatives, the Chinese leadership formulated an analysis of advancing cooperative stages in step with improved technology (Kojima 1975: 61):

Temporary mutual-aid teams: traditional agricultural implements.
Permanent mutual-aid teams: improved agricultural implements.
Elementary cooperatives: new-style animal-drawn implements.
Advanced cooperatives: mechanization and electrification of agriculture, particularly tractors.

The progression rested on perfecting and expanding the scope of voluntary, small-scale cooperation to create a basis in trust, community bonds of solidarity, and managerial and accounting expertise in order to place larger and more complex cooperatives on a firm footing. This required continually expanding cooperative accumulation to finance new equipment. The leadership envisioned a reciprocally reinforcing process of improved technology whose dissemination would be facilitated by cooperation which would in turn smooth the advance to higher forms of cooperation. Inevitably tensions arose between accelerated accumulation and the necessity to improve incomes and strengthen support for the coops, and between those who stressed the necessity for rapid cooperative formation and those who stressed voluntary participation and firm cooperative foundations.

Even in the absence of technical transformation, and in very poor regions, cooperatives could contribute to rural accumulation through coordination of such labor-intensive projects as water conservancy, forestry, and soil improvement, and through the promotion of expanded sideline production. As Kojima Reiitsu (1979: 61–100) has documented, peasant labor accumulation rose throughout the 1950s in step with the advance of cooperatives. Where this labor produced good results, including higher peasant incomes, it provided a powerful impetus for the expansion of cooperatives.

In 1954, with pressures mounting for accelerated cooperative formation, Deng Zihui, head of the party's Rural Work Department, insisted that, rather than wait until all the technical preconditions were realized, China would move ahead on cooperativization to pave the way for technological breakthroughs in agriculture (Deng 1954a: 144–50). "The first step is to carry out socialist revolution, to organize the individual peasants, to achieve cooperativization and collectivization," he told a Youth League meeting. "The second step then is to carry out the technological revolution, to carry out large-scale mechanization."

The transition to socialism in China's countryside began with land revolution and was followed immediately by staged development of cooperatives. From the early 1950s this process, designed to stimulate rural development, would parallel and reinforce the drive for industrialization focused on heavy industry. Eventually (Mao explictly targeted 1967), the intersection of these two processes would facilitate the formation of collectives with strong technological support. The prospect of immediate economic benefits made possible by mechanization, electrification, irrigation, chemical fertilizer, and large-scale production all rooted in the proven success of cooperative agriculture would then overcome the aspirations to private landownership rooted in peasant experience and world view. Collectivization would emerge logically out of Chinese development experience and, by providing industry with both large markets and revenues and facilitating the ability of the state to tap the rural surplus through tax and purchase mechanisms, would in turn reinforce the accelerating industrialization drive. These principles, formulated and implemented in the course of experimentation with diverse forms of cooperation in the early 1950s, constitute one of China's distinctive contributions to the transition to socialism.

In summing up these principles in July 1955, Mao spoke, I believe, for virtually the entire party leadership (1977a). His speech, however,

touched off new and controversial directions in the cooperative movement and brought to the surface simmering conflicts within the leadership and between the party-state and rural society.

How did Chinese experience measure up to these guidelines? The
official version of China's cooperative transformation is that it proceeded by stages, each predicated on voluntary participation. A close
reading of the evidence from the late 1940s through the summer of
1955 confirms the general implementation of these guidelines. To be
sure, cadres at all levels periodically forced participation in mutual-aid
teams and cooperatives without ensuring adequate preparation. Fulfill-
ing numerical targets for the number and size of cooperatives at times
overshadowed the painstaking tasks of building solid cooperative foundations. But where careful preparations had not been made, cooperatives frequently collapsed. It appears that many that gradually grew in
size and complexity had found ways to win the support of their members through solid economic and distributive performance. At the same
time, conflicts deepened between the cooperative and the private economy as the state favored the former and gradually restricted the scope of
the latter. In the summer and fall of 1955 central premises of the
strategy of voluntary participation were thrust aside as China plunged
ahead, basically completing collectivization in one year and culminating in the Great Leap Forward two years later. The task here is to assess
this phenomenon and its significance for the subsequent course of
socialist development in China.

Contradictions in the Chinese Development
Strategy: The First Five-Year Plan and the
Countryside

In the early 1950s China's leaders embarked on a dual strategy to
achieve the economic goals of the transition:

1. Cooperative formation to stimulate rural productivity and, in
conjunction with market controls, to facilitate state access to a larger
share of the agricultural surplus for investment in industry, to obtain
foreign exchange, and to feed China's rapidly growing cities.

2. Urban-centered industrialization to create the agricultural producers' goods that would eventually underwrite collectivization and
agricultural modernization.

The investment priority of capital-intensive heavy industry threatened to starve the countryside of the sources of accumulation required

to propel agricultural development and provide the higher peasant incomes that were essential to sustain support for the cooperatives. Lagging agricultural productivity would inevitably impede industrialization by curbing possibilities for rural accumulation needed to finance industrial projects, by depriving industry of a potential market in the countryside, and by reducing a major source of foreign exchange.

During the First Five-Year Plan period (1953–57) China accumulated at the high rate of 24 percent of national income. Much of the surplus was siphoned out of the countryside by the state in the form of agricultural taxes and compulsory sales at low state purchasing prices. These funds primarily financed a heavy industrial base and urban construction (see chapter 5; also Lardy 1980). By contrast, just 15 percent of state investment was directed to agriculture, where more than 80 percent of the Chinese people labored (Yeh 1967: 334; Liao 1955: 1–8). Kojima Reiitsu has shown that the 25-billion-yuan income the state derived from the agriculture-based food and textile industries alone approximately equaled the entire value of state investment in industry during the First Five-Year Plan. The state bought agricultural commodities including grain and cotton cheaply from the countryside at a fraction of their price on the proscribed free market and exchanged high-priced industrial goods. Although the price scissors working to the detriment of the countryside was somewhat reduced after 1949, prices remained stacked against the peasantry (Kojima 1975: 36–37; *Tongji gongzuo* 1959: 5).[12]

Other state measures served to siphon resources out of the countryside. Prior to land reform, myriad handicrafts and sidelines made it possible for tens of millions of land-poor families to supplement meagre agricultural earnings and survive. Throughout the early decades of the century, significant sectors of Chinese handicraft industry, notably cotton spinning but also silk, tobacco, and vegetable oil, were undermined or destroyed by the influx of foreign manufactures. Nevertheless, almost without exception, rural households engaged in one or more sideline activity to attempt to make ends meet. After 1954, however, state procurement and marketing policies systematically destroyed remaining rural handicrafts, particularly handicrafts based on the processing of agricultural commodities, which passed out of the hands of peasants and into urban factories. The number of handicraft workers dropped significantly from 8,910,000 in 1954 to 6,583,000 in 1956 as individual handicraft was largely eliminated in favor of cooperative enterprise (*1954 Quanquo geti shougongye diaocha ziliao* 1957:

52).[13] I hypothesize that the decline in part-time handicraft and sideline activity by peasant producers was still greater. Hidden beneath these aggregate statistics is the demise of important rural handicrafts. The Chinese study cited above records, for example, a 47 percent drop in the number of workers in Henan's cotton yarn industry between 1954 and 1955; a 45 percent reduction in households engaged in cotton spinning in Liaoning between 1949 and 1954; a 90 percent drop in the number of households employed in sugar refining in Heilongjiang between 1950 and 1954; and a reduction of 34 percent in those processing vegetable oils in Henan between 1953 and 1954 (State Statistical Bureau 1960: 36; Kojima 1975: 52–53).[14]

The heart of the problem was the conflict between centralizing resources for efficient modern processing, export, and state-centered accumulation, on the one hand, and promotion of rural handicrafts that would expand rural incomes and disperse accumulation throughout the countryside, on the other. The state won, with devastating effect not only on the eleven million full-time rural handicraft workers but on the entire structure of rural income and employment. The countryside suffered a double blow. Not only did resource centralization deprive rural households of vital direct sources of income and jobs, but secondary effects compounded the damage. Consider native oil pressing, an industry dispersed throughout the countryside, which made use of cotton, sesame, peanuts, and other crops to produce oil for lighting and cooking. When this rural industry was virtually eliminated by state centralization in 1954–55, not only did the countryside lose jobs and income and find itself more dependent on the state for a scarce staple, but the cycle linking agricultural production, processing, and animal husbandry was broken. The shells used as pig fodder were lost to the peanut-producing localities, and this is but one of several important fodder losses that contributed to the decline of animal husbandry in the rural areas. Likewise the bran from rice, whose milling was also centralized. Centralization meant that prosperous suburban communities near oil-pressing facilities gained access to the processed ''waste'' materials lost to the great majority of more distant villages. State centralization policies directed toward accumulation and industrialization shattered the natural cycle of the preindustrial economy in eliminating a multitude of rural handicrafts.

At the same time, beginning in 1953, the state restricted the scope of petty commerce and transport which provided important sources of rural income in many (particularly poorer mountain) areas. The loss of

Table 3.1

Cooperative Development in the Countryside, 1950–1958
(percent of peasant households)

	1950	1951	1952	1953	1954	1955		1956			1958		
						June	Dec.	Feb.	June	Dec.	Apr.	Aug.	Sept.
All mutual-aid teams	11	18	40	39	58	50	n.a.	n.a.	n.a.	n.a.	—	—	—
Permanent MATs	2	n.a.	10	11	26	28	n.a.	n.a.	n.a.	n.a.	—	—	—
Elementary agricultural producers' cooperatives	—	—	0.1	0.2	2	14	59	36	29	9	—	—	—
Advanced APCs (collectives)	—	—	—	—	—	0.03	4	51	63	88	100	70	n.a.
Rural people's communes	—	—	—	—	—	—	—	—	—	—	—	30	98

Sources: Shi Jingtang et al., *Historical Materials on the Chinese Agricultural Cooperation Movement*, pp. 989–1019; Kenneth Walker, "Collectivisation in Retrospect: The 'Socialist High Tide' of Autumn 1955-Spring 1956," *The China Quarterly* 26 (April-June 1966): 14–18; Frederick Crook, "The Commune System in the People's Republic of China, 1963–1974," in Joint Economic Committee of Congress, *China. A Reassessment of the Economy* (Washington, D.C.: USGPO), p. 373; Peter Nolan, "Collectivization in China: Some Comparisons with the USSR," *Journal of Peasant Studies* 3, 2 (January 1976): 193.

these supplemental income-earning activities was felt by *all* rural strata and communities (Solinger 1983; 1984).

By June 1955 China had embarked on voluntary, staged cooperative transformation. Sixty-five percent of the peasantry reportedly joined mutual-aid teams; approximately half of these were seasonal, and the remainder operated on a year-round basis. Beginning experimentally in 1953 and in significant numbers in 1954, particularly in North and Northeast China, elementary producers' cooperatives began to form. The diverse institutional practices of these small but increasingly ambitious cooperatives, the organization and remuneration of labor, and the breadth and scope of their activities emerged out of repeated local experimentation. In this early phase, flexibility and adaptation to local conditions were at a premium. There was no single blueprint to which the experiences of mountain and plain, grain and animal husbandry regions, large and small villages were required to conform (see table 3.1).

By June 1955, 14 percent of all rural households, nearly all in North and Northeast China, reportedly belonged to elementary cooperatives. These year-round cooperatives preserved individual landownership rights and provided remuneration to their members on the basis of both land investments and labor inputs. Progress toward cooperation, however, proceeded by fits and starts, or rather by leaps followed by periods of consolidation and retrenchment. Divisions within both leadership and people surfaced over the speed with which new cooperatives could and should be created so as to function effectively, as well as over the size, management, and methods of remuneration appropriate to the new cooperatives.[15]

The extensive and frank discussion of cooperative experience in the press and in technical agricultural and economic journals in the years 1953–55—illuminating not only diverse achievements and models for emulation, but also numerous problems and conflicts—enables one both to pinpoint areas of contention and to gauge the process of discovery and adaptation of institutions suited to specific local needs and resources. While one notes divisions over speed of cooperative formation, size of unit, form of remuneration, management practices, and concern over rich-peasant domination, perhaps the most formidable problem centered on devising policies to ensure the protection and strengthening of poor-peasant interests while guaranteeing the welfare of middle peasants, whose contributions to the cooperative were essential to its economic success. In this context, devising systems of equitable remuneration was the central issue if cooperation was to be based on voluntary participation and to ensure mutual prosperity of its members.

The example of Wugong Agricultural Producers' Cooperative, a leading Hebei model of early cooperation, illustrates the complexity of the problem. In 1953 Wugong overcame high-level official objections that the experiment was premature and organized one of the nation's largest cooperatives embracing nearly all the more than four hundred families in the village. A contemporary article in the *Chinese Agricultural Bulletin* (1953, no. 4) cited three preconditions for the successful formation of a big coop (*da she*) in Wugong: (1) The original small cooperative is run well; (2) a strong popular basis for expansion exists; (3) the change is being made in an area and at a time when a good harvest can be expected. The article detailed the careful preparatory steps required while pointing out obstacles to creating effective large-scale cooperatives.

By 1953 Wugong had the benefit of a full decade of fruitful cooperation on a small scale, beginning with four households and eventually extending to twenty-five households. It also enjoyed access to preferential technical and administrative support from the state as it gained prominence as a successful model. With the widely publicized formation of the big cooperative in late 1953, Wugong became the site of the first village tractor station in Hebei province. With all these advantages of being first, advantages that tens of thousands of new cooperatives which followed could not enjoy, between 1953 and 1955 Wugong nevertheless revised the remuneration ratio of labor to land almost yearly, as its predecessor, the smaller model Geng Changsuo Cooperative, had done earlier. Searching for methods that combined equity with sufficient inducement to ensure enthusiastic participation while satisfying official definitions of socialist equity, the village experimented with ratios that shifted the apportionment of income based on land and labor from 60:40 to 50:50 to 40:60.[16]

Mao Zedong explicitly and repeatedly instructed the cooperatives that they must not only raise yields but must increase the incomes of 90 percent of their members *in the very first year of operation*. The translation of such goals into reality necessitated successfully incorporating more prosperous peasants. These farmers had access to superior draft animals and tools as well as better land. To set too low the return on investment of land and other means of production in order to emphasize the socialist principle ''to each according to one's work'' was to issue a death warrant for the cooperative. For it ensured that more successful farmers would seek to withdraw their labor and capital. Yet the opposite extreme, placing too low a value on labor, would impoverish households with abundant labor power. The leadership looked to cooperatives as a means of increasing the size of state revenue and the share of marketed agricultural commodities as well as the rate of rural accumulation. Nevertheless, in these early experimental years, it restricted cooperative accumulation in order to ensure rising personal incomes as a means of demonstrating to skeptical peasants the superiority of cooperatives and guaranteeing the support of their members. The economist Xu Dixin, noting the 5 percent ceiling on cooperative accumulation stipulated in model regulations, observed that "later on, *following the development of production*, it may be raised gradually to 10 percent" (cited in Schram 1969: 33).

The short-run solution proposed by party leaders was to move gradually toward distributive systems that provided a higher return for labor while holding steady the return on land as the cooperative expanded its own base of accumulation and the state circumscribed opportunities for private profit. Eventually it would be possible to make the transition to fully socialist cooperatives modeled on Soviet collectives in which remuneration rested on the principle of equal pay for equal work supplemented by the provision of minimum subsistence guarantees for all. To attempt to advance too rapidly, however, was to jeopardize the fragile consensus essential for stimulating productive enthusiasm of the majority of the peasants.

The Central Committee's decision to strengthen the foundations of cooperatives in the spring and summer of 1955, including a reduction of twenty thousand trouble-plagued units, consolidation of others, and slowing the pace of cooperative formation, emphasized the importance of hewing to the principles of voluntary participation and advancing by stages (*Renmin ribao*, February 28, 1955).

Mao Zedong and the Crisis of Cooperative Transformation

The end of the debate that had been brewing throughout the previous five years came with Mao's decisive intervention of July 31, 1955. The magnitude of the issue is underlined by the fact that Mao went over the head of the Central Committee, where he was outvoted, carrying his message directly to an unprecedented specially convened meeting of provincial and lower party secretaries. Before considering Mao's conclusions and their impact on rural policy, the problem of cooperation must be located in the context of national development policy as expressed in the five-year plan, which assumed final shape in the summer of 1955 and was publicly unveiled one day prior to Mao's pronouncement on rural policy (MacFarquhar 1974: 15–91).

The evidence is overwhelming that, at the very moment when the party finalized its five-year plan, its ambitious targets were already gravely threatened. China's agriculture performed creditably in the years 1949–1957. Nevertheless, where the state projected grain increases of 9 percent in 1953 and 1954, in both years the actual increase was less than 2 percent. Cotton targets were still more demanding—and the shortfall greater in the raw material for China's most important light industry and export commodity. The state projected increases of 16 and 18 percent for these years, but with state procurement prices set low and a ban in effect on private marketing of cotton, the harvest registered *declines* of 11 percent in 1953 and again in 1954 (Walker 1966; Wiens 1980: 63).

From the perspective of the central planners, however, the situation may have looked even grimmer. For in China, as in the Soviet Union in the 1920s, the decisive issue for the state was not output but the quantity of marketable commodities that could be captured for centralized industry and urban consumption. As Ishikawa Shigeru has documented, while commodity sales of grain and cotton increased by substantial margins between 1950 and 1956 (2.7 times in the case of grain), the rate of increase was held back by the increase in peasant consumption, including rising grain and cloth consumption (Kojima 1975: 42–43). In 1954 the state sought to increase agricultural commodification through the imposition of enlarged compulsory grain sales quotas and higher taxes. For the first time the marketed grain ratio (gross) exceeded 30 percent of annual production. The response was angry peasant protest. The state had moved too far too fast in enforcing sales quotas at low state prices. In some areas where excessive procurement had taken place, villagers faced starvation. Mao and Zhou Enlai were among those who issued public self-criticisms. The state increased grain relief and reduced tax quotas. And in 1955 and 1956 the ratio of marketed grain fell sharply to the levels of the early 1950s. The problem of accumulation confronting planners committed to the ambitious industrialization goals of the plan was intensified by the fact that beginning in 1956, and continuing for the next eight years, China had a net foreign exchange deficit with the Soviet Union. Between 1956 and 1964 China repaid Soviet loans in the amount of more than $200 million per year (Kojima 1975: 45, 49–50; Chen Yun 1955: 3–14).

The First Five-Year Plan, from the moment it was finalized in the summer of 1955, confronted severe bottlenecks. The heart of the problem lay in the countryside. In his speech and subsequent pronouncements, Mao, who had pressed for accelerated cooperative formation for the last four years, sought to cut the Gordian knot: Accelerated cooperative formation, he held, would simultaneously solve a range of problems of class exploitation and inequality and pave the way for accelerated economic growth. The implicit burden of Mao's message was that only large-scale, rapid cooperation would enable China to fulfill the ambitious targets of the five-year plan. The economist Tong Dalin turned the logic of gradual cooperation on its head to explain Mao's strategy: "It was precisely because of the lack of tractors that cooperation had to be accelerated. That is to say, we had to create favorable conditions primarily by developing agricultural production, so that the cause of socialist industrialization would be assured of a reliable base, supplying it with enough grain and raw materials" (Tung 1959).

Lashing out at the Central Committee's decision to reduce the number of cooperatives in the spring of 1955, Mao charged that the leadership ("some of our comrades, tottering along like a woman with bound feet") had restrained the mass movement at the very moment when the peasantry, above all its poorest strata, was demanding accelerated cooperation. The party and state, Mao insisted, tailed behind a peasantry that was ready and eager—as no peasantry in the world had ever been—to carry forward large-scale cooperation, that is, collectivization, which would shortly abolish private ownership of land. This was the burden of Mao's message, which he laced with a brilliant mixture of biting sarcasm and detailed attention to concrete issues of cooperation (Selden 1978: 57–62; Friedman 1982).

Mao persuasively defined the Chinese road to socialism in the countryside in terms of voluntary peasant organization based on mutual benefit through successive stages from mutual aid to elementary and eventually to advanced cooperatives. "These steps," he concluded, "make it possible for the peasants gradually to raise their socialist consciousness through personal experience and gradually to change their mode of life, thus lessening the feeling of abrupt change. Generally, these steps can avoid a fall in crop production during, say, the first year or two; indeed they must ensure an increase each year, and this can be done'' (1977a: 195). Ironically, it was precisely this process of voluntary participation and staged advance based on mutual benefit that Mao's collectivization drive swept aside in the fall of 1955.

Let us consider more closely the reasons behind the new strategy. In addition to presenting an eloquent case for rural cooperation, Mao pinpointed a vital reason for stepping up the pace of transformation: growing class polarization.

> What exists in the countryside today is capitalist ownership by the rich peasants and a vast sea of ownership by individual peasants. As is clear to everyone, the spontaneous forces of capitalism have been steadily growing in the countryside in recent years, with new rich peasants springing up everywhere and many well-to-do middle peasants striving to become rich peasants. On the other hand, many poor peasants are still living in poverty for shortage of the means of production, with some getting into debt and others selling or renting out their land. If this tendency goes unchecked, it is inevitable that polarization in the countryside will get worse day by day. (1977a: 201–202)

Was Mao's characterization emphasizing ''capitalist ownership by the rich peasants'' correct in capturing the problem and prospects of the countryside, and what were the consequences of this assessment? Land revolution had eliminated landlord exploitation and extremes of wealth and poverty, indeed all major intravillage property-based inequalities. It had not produced absolute equality; nor could it have without severely undermining growth and dividing the poor and middle peasants. Land revolution, in continuing and extending the party's wartime policies, contributed to the growth of a solid owner cultivator majority and laid the foundations for cooperative unity. In general, effective party leadership in the land revolution made it possible to protect owner cultivator interests, enlarge their ranks, and stimulate economic growth. In reconstituting the system of free purchase and sale of land, and encouraging enterprising households to prosper in the early 1950s, the party opened the possibility of concentration of wealth in private hands.

The most significant evidence available on the question of polarization, apparently the best evidence of national scope available to the party leadership, is a 1954 national survey of sixteen thousand rural families. That survey documented significant inequalities of land, draft animals, and income between poor and more prosperous households.[17]

Table 3.2

Land Cultivation and Ownership by Social Classes After Land Revolution and in 1954[1]

Classification at time of land revolution	After Land Revolution (1947–1952)[2]						1954			
	Share of households as classified during land revolution	Average household size[3]	Average cultivated area per household (acres)	Average cultivated area per person (acres)	Average owned area per household (acres)	Average owned area per person (acres)	Share of households (%)	Average cultivated area per household[4] (acres)	Average cultivated area per person (acres)	Average cultivated area per worker (acres)
Poor peasant	57.1	4.1	2.08	0.50	2.02	0.48	29.0	2.29	0.54	1.09
Middle peasant	35.8	5.0	3.17	0.63	3.09	0.62	62.2	3.26	0.65	1.63
Rich peasant	3.6	6.2	4.18	0.67	4.38	0.71	2.1	4.27	0.69	2.07
Former landlords	2.6	4.2	2.03	0.48	2.00	0.48	2.5	2.18	0.52	1.14
Cooperative members	0.0	5.1	0.00	0.00	0.00	0.00	4.2	2.70	0.53	1.04
All households	99.1	4.8	2.55	0.53	2.49	0.52	100.0	2.63	0.55	1.10

1. Based on a survey of sixteen thousand households in twenty-five provinces.
2. Land revolution took place at different times between 1947 and 1952 in the areas surveyed.
3. Household sizes are given for 1954 only. I assume that these figures remain constant from land revolution to 1954.
4. No 1954 data are available for landownership. With the advance of cooperation and restrictions on hired labor the gap between ownership and cultivation rapidly narrowed. By 1954 it is likely that the difference between the two was slight, particularly in North China where cooperative formation was most advanced.

Source: "Concise and Important Materials on the 1954 Rural Income Survey," *Tongji gongzuo* (Statistical Work) 10 (1957): 31–32.

The national survey data reveal that at the end of 1954 rich peasant households, that is, households classified as rich peasants on the basis of pre-land reform position, enjoyed a 1.9:1 advantage over poor peasants in the area of land cultivated, and an income advantage of 1.9:1. Was the problem acute? Above all, was the situation deteriorating? The available evidence suggests that, Mao to the contrary, the answer to these questions is no. The data are revealing.

Landownership and cultivation data in table 3.2 permit one to compare the immediate aftermath of land revolution (from 1947 to 1952 depending on the area) with the situation at the end of 1954 when the survey was completed. The survey data indicated that while inequality in landholding existed, the issues were not acute. For example, in 1954, this small group of former rich-peasant households enjoyed a 28 percent advantage in per capita cultivated area over those classified as poor peasants. Moreover, state policy contributed to narrowing differences. Whatever income-earning advantages this small group enjoyed, and they were among the smallest in the world, as the scope of cooperative agriculture expanded, the former rich peasants constituted no political threat and their opportunities for enrichment in the market were severely circumscribed. It is difficult to conceive of a group politically more isolated, stigmatized, and vulnerable, unless it is the post–land revolution landlord class, whose condition continued to worsen.

Most significant is the trend in landownership and cultivation. Between the land revolution and 1954 the already diminished rich-peasant advantage over poor peasants in per capita cultivated acreage had dropped from 1.34 to 1.27:1. The reduction in the gap between poor and rich peasants was probably greater as the state restricted tenancy and the use of hired labor and curbed market activity.

We are fortunate to possess some particularly intriguing evidence on the question of class polarization offered by Chen Boda, Mao's secretary and, with Mao, the most forceful advocate of accelerated collectivization. In his February 1956 report on "The Socialist Transformation of China's Agriculture," Chen cited statistical evidence from Baoding prefecture, Hebei province (table 3.3), which he presented as indicative of trends in sales since the land revolution (Chen 1956: 36–44; cf. Friedman 1982). Chen pointed out that "after the launching of the agricultural cooperation movement, the amount of land sold and purchased dropped." Indeed, by 1954, as the cooperative movement shifted into high gear and as strictures against hiring labor took effect, individual land sales dropped to virtually nothing (table 3.4).

Table 3.3

Land Sales in Baoding Prefecture, Hebei Province

Year	Number of acres of land sold
1949	7,315
1950	9,082
1951	19,200
1952	15,237
1953	6,071
1954	1,382

This did not, of course, mean that inequality had been eliminated. Those classified as rich peasants in land reform continued to enjoy advantages over poor peasants in ownership of land and draft animals and higher incomes. Nationally, their per capita advantage in draft animals was on the order of 2.5:1, in plows 2.2:1. Poor peasants as late as 1954 sold an average of 4.5 days of labor power per person per year, while rich-peasant families hired labor an average of 10.8 days per person per year. Finally, rich-peasant per capita incomes were 1.8 times those of poor peasants and 1.4 times those of middle peasants. The point, however, is not only that these differences are extremely small, whether cast in international perspective or compared with the pre–land revolution situation, but that *already by 1954 it was clear that cooperation was eliminating the largest distinctions based on differential ownership of the means of production.* The writing was on the wall. It was several years since the party had trumpeted the slogan of the "rich-peasant economy." Cooperation was the wave of the future, and, together with market controls, it spelled the doom of rich-peasant economic advantage (Deng 1954b: 1–10).

These conclusions are reinforced by the research of Kojima Reiitsu (1975), Peter Nolan (1976), and Vivienne Shue (1980), which documents the effect of national and local policies expanding cooperation, breaking the grip of former landlords and rich peasants over commerce, restricting the scope of such private economic activity as trade, speculation, and transport, and reducing individual and household income inequality.

The most acute rural problems and obstacles to effective cooperative formation and rural development were not those of class polarization or

Table 3.4

Ownership of the Means of Production and 1954 Income of Social Classes and Cooperative Members

Social class[1]	Average house-hold size	Average no. of workers per house-hold	Draft animals			Plows			Net days hired labor		Income	
			(1) per house-hold	(2) per capita	(3) per worker	(1) per house-hold	(2) per capita	(3) per worker	(1) per house-hold	(2) per capita	(1) per house-hold	(2) per capita
Poor & hired	4.2	2.0	0.51	0.12	0.26	0.36	0.09	0.18	-18.7	-4.5	488.7	116.4
Middle	5.0	2.5	1.10	0.22	0.44	0.74	0.15	0.30	-1.5	-0.3	774.4	154.9
Rich	6.2	3.0	1.84	0.30	0.61	1.22	0.20	0.41	66.9	10.8	1,297.0	209.2
Former landlord	4.2	2.2	—	—	—	—	—	—	-8.7	-2.1	497.2	118.4
Coop-erative members[2]	5.1	n.a.	n.a.	n.a.	n.a.	n.a.	n.a.	n.a.	n.a.	n.a.	704.6	138.2
Average	4.8	n.a.	n.a.	n.a.	n.a.	n.a.	n.a.	n.a.	n.a.	n.a.	692.9	144.4

1. Social classes are the designations made during the land revolution.
2. The authors note that cooperative members' income is not comparable to that of private cultivators since it excludes cooperative welfare guarantees. When the value of welfare is included, the per household income rises from 704.6 to more than 850 yuan, and in per capita terms to more than 165 yuan, that is, it exceeds middle-peasant levels.

Source: "Concise and Important Materials on the 1954 Rural Income Survey," *Tongji gongzuo* (Statistical Work) 10 (1957): 31–32.

exploitation but the general poverty of the countryside, the limited availability of improved means of production and skilled technical and administrative personnel, the tension generated by high targets, low state prices, and extractive, centralizing policies of the five-year plan, and the organizational difficulties associated with large-scale coopera- tion. To use Mao's phrase, did not some of these policies amount to draining the pond to catch a fish? The real (though unstated) urgency behind Mao's call for intensified cooperative transformation lay in the crisis of the five-year plan. Acceleration of cooperative formation, Mao now held, could stimulate productive energies, making possible fulfillment of the plan and opening new possibilities for accumulation.

Mao's speech introduced a critical new element into the discussion of cooperative formation. Earlier leadership analysis of cooperation, including Mao's, while warning of rich-peasant domination, had fo- cused on the necessity to create institutions responsive to the interests of both poor and middle peasants, who constituted the great majority. In July, however, Mao offered a new class analysis. Cooperation, he held, was a matter of urgency for the poorest ''60 to 70 percent of the entire rural population'' whom he now designated as ''the poor and lower-middle peasants.'' Mao (1977a: 194–95) rightly perceived that the more prosperous peasants vacillated on the question of cooperation. He held, however, ignoring the doubts of many poorer cultivators, that ''most of the peasants are enthusiastic about the socialist road . . . the only way for the majority of the peasants to shake off poverty, improve their livelihood and fight natural calamities is to unite and go forward along the high road to socialism.''

Here one discovers the origin of a theme whose explosive overtones became clear after 1962 when Mao issued the call ''never forget class struggle.'' The accent in Mao's earlier writings on cooperation and in Chinese practice in periods of united front was on the harmony, unity, and mutual benefit required for and reinforced by a successful coopera- tive strategy to assure mutual prosperity. In introducing the category ''poor and lower-middle peasants,'' Mao offered a startling redefini- tion of rural society: Instead of a countryside perceived as having made substantial progress toward enlarging and strengthening the middle group of owner-cultivators moving toward cooperation, this reclassifi- cation placed the emphasis on a new and greatly expanded category of have-nots.[18] Mao thus prepared the ground for a new wave of class conflict that could be directed principally against middle and ''upper- middle peasants'' who were fearful that cooperative formation and particularly collectivization would represent, in effect, expropriation of their land and a reduction in their income.

The "Socialist High Tide" in the Countryside

Throughout late 1955 and the spring of 1956 Mao pressed for a radically accelerated program of cooperation. The three-volume compilation of exemplary accounts of cooperation, which he edited in the summer and fall of 1955 and published as *Socialist Upsurge in China's Countryside*, carried this message: If these hundreds of communities and individuals, many of them poverty-stricken and confronted with imposing obstacles to development, can successfully organize and creatively solve the numerous concrete problems that arise, why can't the entire countryside move forward to cooperation?[19]

In the October debates at the Central Committee's Sixth Plenum, which formally committed the party to accelerated cooperation targets, Mao subjected to withering attack each of the arguments put forward by those who insisted (as he had throughout the preceding twelve years!) on adhering to policies of gradual and voluntary cooperative expansion. Mao's wrath centered particularly on those who cited material preconditions for the transition, specifically, those who held that the formation of advanced cooperatives required large-scale mechanization if they were to succeed. He concluded (1977a: 216–17) with sweeping declamation that "the masses demand a big expansion . . . in areas which were liberated late, in mountain areas, in backward townships and in areas affected by natural disasters . . . [even] without funds, carts and oxen or without the well-to-do middle peasants . . . and [without] farm machinery." There were, in short, no insurmountable obstacles—material, organizational, or psychological—to rapid, large-scale cooperation. Differences in material conditions, historical experience, leadership, and consciousness were of little consequence. Cooperation could and must advance rapidly, based on the "demand" by peasants, above all by the poorer strata. It must advance everywhere rapidly regardless of concrete conditions. As Mao's irritation grew at Deng Zihui's cautious leadership of the cooperative drive, in July 1955 he installed his personal secretary, Chen Boda, as a deputy (and de facto) director of the party's Rural Work Department to accelerate collectivization. As Chen later observed, Mao had challenged the old concept that without mechanization it would be difficult to realize the large-scale cooperativization of agriculture (cf. Chen 1959; MacFarquhar 1974: 18; Friedman 1982).[20]

Had Mao correctly assessed the mood of the peasantry, particularly of poor peasants, as he had so unerringly done throughout his long revolutionary career? There is scant evidence to support the claim that in the summer of 1955 poor peasants everywhere were demanding rapid, large-scale cooperatives. Yet, in another sense, Mao's forecast was not inaccurate. Once he and a significant portion of the national and local leadership united behind rapid collectivization, poor peasants quickly responded, while many middle and prosperous peasants vainly attempted to resist a collectivization process that they rightly viewed as expropriatory and redistributive at their expense. One need not search far for explanations.

Mao's passionate appeal to take up the cudgels of class struggle imbued poor peasants with the hope that cooperatives would provide a second windfall for them by equalizing incomes between poor and prosperous. Driven forward by a coalition of newly activated poor peasants and local cadres for whom the painstaking requirements of staged, voluntary cooperative transformation were extremely vexing, from the fall of 1955 China telescoped the stages of elementary and advanced cooperative formation. Mao (1956: 8) noted "a fundamental change" in the last half of 1955, as constraints on cooperation, even collectivization, melted away.

Mao's July and October 1955 speeches and the response to his vigorous mobilization from the grass-roots to the party center silenced critics and produced a surge of cooperative formation that swept aside not only his own ambitious targets but the entire logic of voluntary cooperation by stages based on mutual interest. The October 1955 enlarged Sixth Plenum of the Central Committee consolidated Mao's triumph on the issue of cooperation. Like all previous official documents of the cooperative movement, the final resolution is replete with cautioning phrases. Noting "the peasants' predilection for the private ownership of land," for example, it warned that "the amount of dividend which the cooperatives decide to pay on land should remain constant for a certain period, say two or three years," to prevent dissatisfaction or withdrawal by more prosperous peasants (Wilson 1962: 110).

The real message, however, lay elsewhere, and it was twofold: First, the rate of cooperative formation would be dramatically accelerated. For example, in areas where 10–20 percent of peasant households had already joined cooperatives, the formation of elementary cooperatives would be basically completed by the spring of 1958 (Wilson 1962: 115). More important, for the first time in an official document the party unequivocally signaled that the "semisocialist cooperatives" preserving private ownership of land and means of production were but "a transitional form to the fully socialist type," that is, Soviet-style collectives (Wilson 1962: 109). As the cooperative tide swelled from late 1955, the "inconvenience" of the semisocialist form, pressures from above to show "results" in terms of numbers and scale of cooperatives, and the fear of being capped with a "rightist" label encouraged cadres, sometimes with the militant support of the poorest strata, to telescope the stages and to move immediately to collectives. Tens of millions of households moved directly from individual farming or small-scale mutual aid to "fully socialist" large-scale collectives in a matter of weeks. The careful strictures of earlier directives fell before the belief that speed of transformation and expanded size of unit were the real measures of achievement in the socialist transition. Not until January 1956 when the gradualist opposition was thoroughly crushed and the countryside had plunged ahead toward formation of collectives did Mao add qualifications like these: "We should not try to advance anything before the overwhelming majority of the people are satisfied with the advance. . . . What I mean is that we should always make over 90 percent of the people delighted" (Starr 1979: 195). Delighted or terrified, in less than a year the entire countryside passed from a mixed system of private ownership of land and the means of production with varying degrees of small-scale mutual aid and elementary forms of cooperation, to large-scale collectivization; from production organized in most cases on a scale ranging from single households to a few dozen households, to one embracing an entire village or even a township and typically involving several hundred families. For most villages and for the overwhelming majority of households, this was instant collectivization, administratively imposed in the absence of the organic development of cooperative institutions rooted within the community.

The "socialist high tide" overturned central premises of China's innovative strategy of cooperation. As of June 1955 the 14 percent of rural households that participated in cooperatives were concentrated in older liberated areas in the North and Northeast. Virtually all of these had less than one year's experience in small elementary cooperatives, which retained private landownership and paid dividends on the dual basis of contributions of means of production and of labor. In South

China land revolution and cooperation had come later. In Guangdong province, which was among the last to complete land revolution, in the spring of 1955, just 5 percent of rural households belonged to cooperatives, more than 90 percent of them established within the last year. They had time neither to consolidate effective working relationships nor to demonstrate model effects for others to emulate prior to the race to universalize collectives (Vogel 1968: 46–56). Less than half the rural population, including the vast majority of households in South and Central China, had *any* experience with cooperation even at the level of year-round mutual-aid teams (see table 3.1).

By January 1956, six months after Mao's speech, 59 percent of Guangdong's households reportedly belonged to elementary cooperatives and 4 percent to collectives. One month later, official figures listed 93 percent of rural households in cooperatives, and of these 44 percent had joined collectives (Vogel 1968: 155). By the end of 1956, fully 88 percent of China's rural households had joined collectives with another 8 percent in elementary cooperatives. In a word, with the exception of areas with predominantly minority populations, China essentially completed collectivization in just one year. This pace makes the speed of Soviet collectivization look almost glacial by comparison.

Mao's 1955 speeches and the *Socialist Upsurge* documentary collection issued no call for striking a blow at the more prosperous peasants. Nor did they even hint that the formation of Soviet-style collectives with their leveling effect on more prosperous families was anything but a distant goal. But the *practice* of the centrally directed movement, pressing for instant formation of large-scale collectives, the preoccupation with size and speed overriding considerations of voluntary participation, mutual benefit, and advance by stages, introduced features reminiscent of the expropriatory and class struggle methods employed during commandist phases of the land revolution. This time it was not primarily old or new exploiting classes but the middle peasants and labor-short households regardless of class who bore the brunt of these cataclysmic changes.

Elementary cooperatives differed from collectives in two important ways, one quantitative, one qualitative. First, the elementary cooperatives were much smaller, with recommended size in 1955 of twenty-five to forty households. By contrast, the collectives typically embraced an entire village: in 1956 most had one hundred to four hundred families (Walker 1965: 16–17). Second, elementary cooperatives preserved private ownership of land and major means of production. Both elementary and advanced cooperatives based remuneration on work-point systems. But in elementary cooperatives, remuneration was based on the combination of investment of land and labor while advanced cooperatives abolished private ownership of the major means of production and operated on the principle "to each according to one's work."

The model cooperative regulations promulgated on March 17, 1956, stipulated that "the only way to ensure that the peasants take the road of cooperation voluntarily is by adherence to the principle of mutual benefit." They declared that "The cooperative must not violate the interests of any poor peasant, or of any middle peasant" (Tung 1959: 96, 99). The state guaranteed middle-peasant interests against expropriation in the course of a gradual transition to the collective form:

> As production develops and *the socialist understanding of members grows*, the dividend paid on land pooled by members will be gradually abolished. Other means of production brought by members for use under centralized management will, *as need arises and with the approval of the owners*, be gradually converted into common property, that is, property collectively owned by all the members, *after paying the owners for them or taking other mutually beneficial measures*. (Model Regulations 1956: 7)

The clauses I have italicized underscore the recognition by party reformers of peasant sensitivities. The formation of the collective, like earlier stages, was to rest on voluntary participation. There would be no payment for land converted into collective property, but land dividends would be gradually reduced and those who "voluntarily" contributed other means of production would receive equitable payment, or "other mutually beneficial measures" would be implemented. Article 26 points out that collectives that had been established for some time and had sufficient resources would "buy animals belonging to members at normal local prices" (Model Regulations 1956: 7).

These were fine phrases sensitive to peasant concerns. But when collectives were suddenly organized in 1956, most had no such capital fund and those which did preferred to invest it rather than compensate individual cooperative members. The numerous collectives formed directly from individual farms, of course, lacked accumulation funds. They were instructed to pay for draft animals and equipment over three to five years. As Peter Schran has observed, however, in the high tide the great majority of peasants became members of advanced cooperatives [collectives] suddenly. They thus lost title to most of their land and other farm assets abruptly, and they faced distribution according to labor in combination with two to three times as high a rate of accumulation right away. They were organized at once into units which extended in size well beyond the village. (1969: 34)

Deng Zihui put it this way:

There have been deviations in the application of policy: some coopera- tives fixed rather low prices for livestock, farm tools, trees and woods, fruit trees and water conservancy facilities placed under common owner- ship. Others even put certain means of production under common owner- ship without compensating the owners. In certain places, small holdings of trees and fruit trees, poultry, domestic animals privately owned by members were erroneously made the common property of cooperatives. What is more, in inducing members to invest in the cooperatives, not a few cooperatives wrongly adopted the method of coercion. They some- times even froze members' deposits in the bank or credit cooperative or money sent them from other places. (1956: 125–26)

The reality of the transition virtually everywhere was profoundly at odds with that outlined in the model regulations. Poorer peasants join- ing the collective traded their small plots of land and meager means of production with the expectation of immediate income gains as a result of sharing in the higher productivity of middle and more prosperous peasants, and perhaps with the anticipation of longer-term stability and insurance against natural disaster.

The situation looked quite different from the perspective of middle and more prosperous peasants, not exploiters but hard-working peas- ants who were marginally better off than some of their poorer neigh- bors. Perhaps no one has better captured the fears and ambivalence of these and other groups to the pressures of cooperativization than the documentary novelist Zhou Libo (1957) in his *Great Changes in a Mountain Village*. Many of these middle peasants were but recently impoverished peasants, and virtually all, while enjoying a livelihood superior to that of the poorest strata, lived in extremely modest, even precarious, circumstances. The advanced cooperative in most cases meant the transfer without remuneration not only of their land but, despite promises of payment, of their draft animals, groves, wells, and implements. As a result, most middle peasants entered the collective with the expectation of lower incomes, having lost the option of choosing individual or collective farming. There was, to be sure, the hope that the advanced collective would provide the rational basis for development which would eventually bring mutual prosperity at higher levels of production. But this prospect could not have looked bright to most middle peasants facing immediate losses. Indeed, by the early 1980s, China had yet to surpass significantly the rural per capita incomes and grain consumption of the mid-fifties (State Statistical Bureau 1986: 582). *The majority of those who might have been classified as middle peasants at the time of collectivization still had not surpassed income levels achieved twenty-five years earlier.* It is difficult to escape the conclusion that a significant portion of middle peasants experienced collectivization as a form of expropriation, and that this feeling of deprivation and constraint continued throughout the entire collective era.

The problems were not confined to that considerable group of middle and more prosperous peasants. Consider, for example, the case of elderly people relying on modest income from their land to survive when too old to work. For those without family support, transfer of their land to the collective without compensation deprived them of their basic hope for minimal security and threw them on the mercy of the collective. With multiple pressures on fragile new cooperatives to increase both accumulation and the distribution shares of their members, to purchase draft animals and equipment, and to surpass their quotas for grain sales to the state, welfare systems were precarious at best, and with the exception of state disaster relief, welfare payments were entirely dependent on local resources and local priorities. Again looking forward, it appears that despite more than twenty years of discussion of cooperative provision of the "five guarantees," in the 1980s rural support systems for the elderly and infirm continue to rest primarily on their families. In particular, most poorer and less advanced units have yet to implement minimally effective welfare systems. The generous state welfare benefits provided for workers in the state sector do not apply to the more than 800 million rural inhabitants.

Universal collectivization at a stroke "solved" a series of complex problems of the transition period. It completed the egalitarian redistributive logic set in motion in the land revolution (remaining individual differences rested for the most part on differential labor availability and household dependency ratios). It eliminated the fragmented land tenure system based on private ownership which the land revolution had actually strengthened and opened new possibilities for agricultural modernization, including effective capital construction in the fields, rationally planned water conservancy, forestry, tool renovation, and (eventually) mechanization.

A number of astute analysts of Chinese development, including Thomas Bernstein, Jack Gray, John Gurley, Kojima Reiitsu, Peter Nolan, Vivienne Shue, and William Parish and Martin Whyte, have seen in the high tide the successful implantation of cooperative institutions in the Chinese countryside. The present study suggests the necessity to reassess the gains and losses inherent in discarding the tested policy of cooperation by stages so brilliantly articulated—only to be immediately discarded—in Mao's 1955 speech. There the chairman presented cooperative transformation as a fifteen-year process that would grow naturally out of two events bringing together maturing relations and forces of production: the consolidation of cooperatives and the availability of modern inputs for agriculture.

The events of the collectivization drive require assessment of the implications of telescoping stages for the *socialist* transition in the countryside. In a matter of months nearly four hundred million small commodity producers had traded their right to ownership of land, draft animals, and tools and control over labor power for a share in the product of unfamiliar and untested large-scale collectives.

In contrast with earlier laborious advance, consolidation, and sometimes retreat—the painstaking efforts to devise cooperative forms suitable to the contours and needs of each community—collectivization proceeded in an atmosphere of drums and gongs backed by the power of the state. China's collectivization was achieved in the absence of both the violence and the economic collapse that characterized Soviet collectivization. The system, moreover, perpetuated itself in essentials and even achieved production gains over the subsequent two decades. Some have seen this as sufficient proof of the wisdom of a strategy that, building on the solid foundations of earlier cooperative experience, seized the appropriate moment to achieve nationwide collectivization, thereby accomplishing the transition to socialist organizational forms and accelerating the development of the productive forces.

During the Cultural Revolution the history of the early fifties was interpreted to highlight ''two roads'' with respect to rural policy: one a capitalist road associated with Liu Shaoqi, Deng Zihui, and many of the top party personnel then responsible for rural policy; the other a socialist road blazed by Mao Zedong with the support of the poor peasants. This analysis can now be seen to contain fatal flaws:

• It conceals the fundamental shift in 1955 in Mao's own analysis and strategy of cooperative transformation.

• It distorts the leadership consensus around the cooperative path while exaggerating the significance of tactical differences over speed and method. It thus fabricates the existence of a leadership faction opposed to coooperation.

• It considers only the question of relations of production, including ownership and management systems and issues of equality, but ignores questions of their relationship to the productive forces, that is, the impact of policy on production.

• It downplays the importance of the party's previous promise that cooperation would bring mutual prosperity in the form of higher peasant incomes.

• It ignores the question of alliance with the middle peasantry and the importance of achieving unity as a basis for effective cooperation.

• It slights the issues of socialist democracy and coercion which Lenin, Mao, and others had posed clearly since the 1920s.

Bigger, faster, more egalitarian may express aspirations and goals for the formation of socialist communities (though not necessarily the only or the best aspirations). But goals are one thing and implementation quite another. The Chinese leadership, including Mao, had rightly emphasized the importance of proceeding by stages, gradually, in order to construct firm foundations of organizational experience, cooperative values, appropriate technology, capital accumulation, economic growth, and popular consensus and support in the course of the transition. Faced with the multiple crises of 1955, however, Mao jettisoned these proven principles and carried the party with him on a dangerous new course.

The central issues debated within the party in the mid-fifties were not socialism versus capitalism, or whether to restore the individual economy or continue to build agricultural cooperatives. The question of the appropriateness of cooperative and collective agriculture *was* being fought out in a number of East European parties, but not in the Chinese party. China's intraleadership differences centered not on whether to collectivize but rather on the process and speed of the transition, on how to devise appropriate cooperative institutions under diverse conditions in China's rural society, and on the appropriate relationship between cooperative and household and between plan and market.

There were, to be sure, powerful social pressures toward enlarging the private sector in rural production and commerce. The evidence is overwhelming, however, that by 1955 the state had circumscribed many of the most lucrative opportunities for private profit through restriction of commercial endeavor and elimination of channels for speculation. The initiative clearly lay with the expanding cooperative sector.

Policy failures in this period cannot be attributed to "capitalist-roaders within the party." Many of those who were so branded were precisely the most deeply committed to the development of mutual prosperity and rural development through popularly based cooperation. In the medium to long run, the most effective means to replace the private sector was to strengthen the economic, political, and organizational foundations of developing cooperatives. In stressing the importance of combining increased cooperative accumulation with higher incomes for the vast majority of members during the early fifties, state policy astutely addressed these requirements. On the other hand, in eliminating a large share of rural sideline and commercial activity, in transferring those activities from individuals to the state *rather than to newly formed cooperatives*, and in maintaining a price structure detrimental to rural interests, the state undermined the prospects for successful cooperation and set back rural development.

The economic and leadership crises of the summer of 1955 arose out of the conflicting imperatives of fulfillment of the norms of the five-year plan and of the strategy of voluntary cooperation based on mutual benefit, but above all out of the mounting awareness that, barring a major policy initiative, the targets of the plan could not be fulfilled. The Chinese leadership could have recognized that the planned heavy industrial targets were unrealistic and scaled them down or shifted investment priorities to light industry and agriculture. Such choices could have reduced accumulation pressures, increased incentives for rural production, left greater resources in the rural areas for cooperative accumulation and the diversification of agricultural and sideline production, and stimulated cooperative formation. This route, however, implied lower industrial growth targets than the plan stipulated. It was rejected. It is widely held that Mao was preoccupied with politics and prepared to sacrifice economic goals to achieve political and ideological ends. We note, however, that high growth targets for heavy industry remained as sacrosanct in Mao's China as they had been in Stalin's Russia in the initial five-year plans.

To fulfill these economic targets new stimuli would have to be applied. Mao concluded that numerous developmental obstacles could be simultaneously overcome by moving directly to collectivization. By mobilizing the poor, eliminating private ownership of land and some of the remaining intravillage income differentials that divided individuals, and taking advantage of economies of scale and expanded opportunities for labor mobilization, Mao held, collectivization would accelerate accumulation and growth. Collectivization, in this view, would stimulate rural productivity, raise the share of marketed agricultural commodities, stimulate rural accumulation, and increase purchasing power, making possible industrial construction. In the period from the autumn of 1955 to the spring of 1956, Mao threw his authority behind a rural strategy that combined accelerated collectivization with greatly increased agricultural production targets which he advanced in the twelve-year plan for agricultural development (Selden 1979: 358–63).

Putting aside for the moment the question of the feasibility of increasing production on this basis, such a strategy implied a price. This approach to collectivization took place at the direct expense of large segments of the middle peasantry. It is well to recall the warning of one foreign authority on the critical importance of the middle-peasant problem:

> In relation to the landlords and the capitalists our aim is complete expropriation. But we shall not tolerate any violence towards the middle peasantry . . . *coercion would ruin the whole cause*. What is required here is prolonged educational work. We have to give the peasant, who not only in our country but all over the world is a practical man and a realist, concrete examples to prove that the cooperative is the best possible thing. . . . Cooperatives must be so organized *as to gain the confidence* of the peasants. And until then we are pupils of the peasants and not their teachers. . . . *Nothing is more stupid than the very idea of applying coercion in economic relations with the middle peasant.*[21] (Lenin 1959b: 276, 282–83; italics in original)

The comment seems as apt applied to the Chinese countryside in 1955–56 as it was in the context of the Soviet Union's New Economic Policy more than thirty years earlier. China's collective reorganization of rural economic life in a period of less than one year meant, could only have meant, that a significant portion of the peasantry, particularly the more prosperous, but also many poorer people with little or no successful cooperative experience, accepted membership on the basis of various degrees of coercion and with little opportunity to shape cooperative institutions to their needs. Tens of millions of peasants experienced collectivization as expropriation of their land and draft animals or forced participation in a system that lacked legitimacy.[22]

One can approach the problem from another angle. Until 1955, cooperative formation went hand in hand with the gradual development of the productive forces and technological improvement. Early cooperation facilitated tool improvement and semimechanization and above all expanded opportunities for irrigation and rural capital construction, which in turn strengthened the cooperatives. It proved compatible with rising crop yields, expanding rural accumulation, and higher rural incomes. This mutually reinforcing cycle would contribute in the long run to mechanization and electrification, to the material prerequisites for the smooth transfer of landownership to collectives, and ultimately to substantial further gains in production, accumulation, and personal income. In the 1956 rush to collectivization, since imported tractors and electrification were unavailable for all but a few model units (China manufactured its first tractor in 1959), the leadership groped for a will-o'-the-wisp interim technological solution to cushion the slack of rapid social change: In 1956, the double-wheel, double-blade plow, imported from the Soviet Union where it had proven successful in the broad flat wheatlands, was manufactured on a vast scale. Ironically, in light of his subsequent bitter critique of the Soviet Union, it was Mao who threw his prestige behind this Soviet intermediate technology. The moment had come for a production leap to confirm the wisdom of rapid collectivization. Overriding proponents of preliminary testing and evaluation, Mao personally intervened to force through immediate large-scale production to meet the surging demand for plows which would inevitably follow from the high tide of collectivization. The double-wheeler, fully equipped, Mao held, would make possible improvement in the spectrum of agricultural processes from plowing to harvesting and threshing. Where individuals could not afford to purchase full sets of equipment, collectives could. They would be the beneficiaries of the new intermediate technology.

At the height of fervor for the new technology in January 1956, Mao was pictured with the double-wheeler on the front page of the *People's Daily*. As he pressed the ambitious production targets of his twelve-year National Program for Agricultural Development (Selden 1978: 358–63), planners allocated fully 29 percent of the nation's steel to produce 3.6 million sets of the plows and the accompanying equipment. In fact 1.8 million double-wheelers were produced in 1956, plows which the peasants immediately derided as "hanging plows" (they remained hung in the barn) or "sleeping plows" when they proved useless under Chinese soil and crop conditions, sinking, for example, deep into the mud of the rice paddies while water buffaloes strained to drag them forward (Kojima 1975: 62–64; Kuo 1972: 192–93).

The new political priorities of the high tide had triumphed over earlier conceptions of economic-technological imperatives and the politics of voluntary cooperation. Short-circuiting the intermediate process of regional testing precisely mirrored the elimination of local experimentation with advanced cooperatives in the heat of the "socialist high tide." Instant results and giantism (in scale of organization) were the order of the day. China did indeed "complete" collectivization in 1956, but only by inflicting losses on agriculture, undermining the voluntary and participatory features of cooperation, strengthening commandist and adventurist elements within the Chinese leadership, and creating an increasing distance between the complex economic, technical, and political problems of the rural areas and slogans promising instant solutions. Finally, we note that the politics of the high tide reversed earlier strategies of uniting poor and middle peasants and, consonant with increased emphasis on class struggle, tended to drive a wedge between them.

Lessons of Collectivization for the Transition to Socialism

Robert Tucker (1973: 406) has identified "breakneck industrialization with priority for heavy industry, and forcible mass collectivization of the peasantry" as the hallmarks of Stalin's revolution from above. In more than a decade of cooperative formation beginning in 1943 and running through the summer of 1955, China adopted a very different approach to cooperation and to the countryside. However, in the burst of frenetic activity that produced nationwide collectivization in 1956 and then communization two years later, one notes certain striking similarities to Stalin's state-imposed collectivization. Before these are discussed, however, some important differences must be distinguished. In China, little state violence took place during collectivization. The army did not play a significant role in the process, and there is no evidence of killing or violence. Despite significant killing of draft animals and pigs, in comparison with the Soviet Union, no major production sabotage took place. The 1956 harvest was poor, but the rural economy did not collapse.

When the pace accelerated in response to Mao's call, rational arguments for voluntary cooperative formation by stages, using the test of mutual prosperity and deferring collectivization until fulfillment of preconditions of mechanization and semimechanization, were swept away. With the revolution in the relations of production swiftly accomplished, the preconditions for the technical revolution would then be in place. The Chinese economy could then achieve rapid advances. Or so it appeared to many. Yet China paid a heavy price for this and subsequent shortcuts and leaps that imposed universal blueprints with scant regard to local conditions and permitted the state to ride roughshod over the interests of large numbers of people.

I would like to look more closely at that price from two perspectives central to the realization of the socialist promise. One is the problem of socialist democracy, the process by which the *forms* of state or cooperative ownership become invested with the substance of mastery by the immediate producers, in this case by the peasantry. This goal, which ultimately requires mastery by the producers of the highest technological processes as well as institutions of popular expression, cannot be achieved rapidly, much less instantly, with the change from private to public ownership systems. At best, public ownership changes create the preconditions for the full realization of socialism's democratic and egalitarian promise. The process of transition is critical in determining whether the outcome strengthens tendencies toward state despotism or reinforces cooperative forms resting on the support of their members and responsive to their needs. Collectivization reinforced those arbitrary and manipulative tendencies in the party and state and undermined the democratic possibilities inherent in the cooperative form. The long-term viability of cooperatives must hinge on the active support of their members. From this perspective, the instant collectivization and coercive (though not violent) environment of the high tide created endemic problems.

The second and related issue concerns the viability of the collectives as social and economic institutions. Cooperatives or collectives must prove their worth in terms of both social justice and equity criteria *and* superior economic performance measured in productivity, personal income, and security. In the decades since 1955, as subsequent essays in this volume make plain, Chinese collectives failed this critical test.

The collectivization drive and subsequent mobilizations which abandoned the close analysis of socioeconomic and technical conditions, juxtaposed rapid egalitarian social change to tangible material benefits for the majority, and undermined the basis for the alliance of poor and middle peasants, bear heavy responsibility for outcomes that undermined the economic fabric and strained to the breaking point the credibility of cooperative institutions. The view that Mao Zedong alone among Chinese leaders supported the best interests of the peasantry, particularly its poorer strata, is patently false. In the years after 1955 the reverse is often close to the truth.

China's cooperative experience prior to 1955 illustrates the awesome complexity of creating a social system that reduces inequality, satisfies peasant subsistence and equity norms, and outstrips the private sector in increasing productivity and accumulation while raising peasant incomes. The overall performance of this period nevertheless provides encouragement for proponents of cooperative solutions. Whatever the individualistic proclivities of China's hundreds of millions of petty commodity producers, substantial progress was recorded in forming cooperatives whose performance in the realm of production, accumulation, and income distribution offered grounds for continued experimentation. The forced draft mobilization strategies of the collectivization and Great Leap periods, characterized by the projection of impossible economic targets and strengthening of the arbitrary power of the state center over local communities and households, severely undermined both the economic performance and credibility of the cooperative enterprise.

The objections may be raised that this critique of the Maoist collectivization strategy loses sight of the urgent needs and interests of poorer strata of the peasantry, ignores the dangers of deepening class polarization, and slights the difficult developmental choices open in the face of the imminent collapse of the national economic plan. These objections cannot be sustained. In the years 1949–1955, as I have shown, voluntary cooperation by stages, backed by the financial, technical, and organizational support of the state, began to address the needs of the poorest strata within the limits of scarce resources and competing claims on them. They did so in ways far more effective than those attempted during and after collectivization. The long-range solution to the economic problems of the countryside could rest on strengthened cooperative power and expanded local accumulation. The result of forcing the issue of antimarket collectivization, carried to disastrous extremes during the Leap, however, was to undermine both possibilities, an outcome evident by the early sixties.

The initial cooperative strategy lay in gradually raising levels of production, income, commodification, and accumulation, then, within the framework of higher stages of cooperation, expanding step by step levels of productivity and the share of members' income based on labor. The shift from elementary cooperatives to collectives, under the best of circumstances, poses an immense challenge. The experiences of China and Eastern Europe, moreover, raise serious questions concerning the superiority of large collective agriculture to the family farm or to a mixed system involving smaller cooperatives and private households. In any event, the preconditions existed in China for a cooperative transformation that preserved the interests of the middle peasants. The great majority might then have experienced cooperation as a bridge to mutual prosperity, as the slogan of the time proposed. This was also a route that would encourage the expansion of cooperative accumulation, capital construction, and other diversified economic processes by continuously demonstrating their contributions to peasant income, employment, and welfare. As capital and confidence gradually accumulated in the cooperatives, and as an industrializing state became capable of providing tractors, chemical fertilizer, and electricity, perhaps the conditions for formation of more advanced cooperatives or even collectives would ripen. But certainly not before. Mao's 1955 speech on cooperation stands as a monument to the wisdom of this approach, even as it signaled the onslaught against it. Collectivization, and above all the economic and political reverses of the Great Leap Forward of 1958 which extended many of its premises, provide eloquent testimony by negative example to the wisdom of development by stages.[23] The new agricultural policies that unfolded in the early sixties, and particularly those since 1978, addressed many of the problems left in the wake of collectivization, the Leap, and the Cultural Revolution. In each case, policy makers subsequently confronted the necessity to restore the reciprocal relationship between peasant material welfare and strengthened cooperation, and between poorer and more prosperous strata, through relaxing state controls and encouraging policies to raise peasant incomes within both cooperative and private frameworks better attuned to peasant demands.

In advancing this critique I do not wish to minimize the constraints confronting the leadership. The entire Chinese leadership, not just the Mao group, shared with their counterparts in newly independent nations a consensus on the urgency for rapid industrialization, a view reinforced by China's armed confrontation with the United States in the Korean War, by the U.S.-imposed economic blockade, and by the bitter lessons of more than a century in which the imperialist powers rode roughshod over China. Moreover, as cooperation advanced, pressures built toward a comprehensive solution that would overcome conflicts inherent in the mixed system. The fact remains, however, that on numerous previous occasions the party leadership had channeled revolutionary impulses in the service of national interests, including broad unity and protection of the economy. The land revolution did not follow certain policies to their logical conclusion—annihilation of all landlords and rich peasants, absolute equality of land and all means of production, for example—in part because of a broader leadership vision of national development. During the high tide and Great Leap Forward, that modicum of restraint was obliterated. In important instances reason was silenced and the primacy of a manipulated politics of class struggle overrode both economic calculation and the democratic premises that constituted the finest traditions of the revolutionary movement. In each case, immediate goals were achieved—full-scale collectivization and commune formation—only at the expense of long-term economic and political setbacks.

Conclusion

The mobilization logic of the collectivization drive of 1955–56 carried to swift completion the formation of collectives throughout the Chinese countryside. The very fact that collectivization was achieved within a year in the absence of the violence and economic reverses characteristic of Soviet collectivization surely reinforced the conviction among Mao and his closest associates of the efficacy of such approaches to the dual problems of social transformation and economic growth. Mao extended this mobilization strategy in 1958 in the Great Leap Forward and the formation of the communes and again, for a time, won the support of a large section of the party leadership and the peasantry. This time, however, the system was pressed to the point of rupture. The fragility of the collective fabric created in 1956 became exposed, and the economy, particularly the agrarian sector, hurtled toward collapse, sped to be sure by the abrupt withdrawal of Soviet technical support and adverse weather. The attempt to expand rapidly the scale and scope of cooperation to the communes undermined such important bases for cooperation as the reliance on familiar face-to-face relationships and the palpable links between labor and remuneration. Inevitably the boldest innovations of the communes had to be cut back.

The collectivization and Great Leap strategies, for all their boldness, set back the prospects of socialism and development: by undermining the link between cooperation and mutual prosperity throughout the countryside; by undercutting the democratic and popular foundations of cooperation in rural communities; by undercutting the foundations of economic development and accumulation; by increasing state manipulation of village and peasantry; by reducing the overall credibility of the party and of cooperative institutions; by establishing a conspiratorial political milieu conducive to the formation of cliques at the center; by divorcing policy from economic reality and popular welfare; and by projecting a distorted vision of class polarization and class struggle in the countryside.

Under conditions of extreme scarcity in rural China, changing social and institutional relations must raise productivity *and* yield higher incomes for most people or risk undermining the new institutions. Both the successful formation of rural base areas in the face of militarily powerful foes during the thirties and forties and the land revolution rested on this premise which was long shared by Mao, Liu Shaoqi, and the core party leadership. That leadership consensus began to unravel in the summer and fall of 1955. During collectivization, the Great Leap, and the Cultural Revolution, when mobilization strategies juxtaposed the political *versus* the economic, and public interest *versus* individual welfare, many people came to perceive revolutionary change in terms of permanent sacrifice of the individual to party and state. By contrast, the promise of socialism in general and cooperation in particular had earlier seemed to lie in mutual benefit, including improvement in the livelihood of all the people and the creation of new foundations for community solidarity. The Chinese revolutionary experience at its best suggests hopeful possibilities about the prospects for revolutionary change: The periods of anti-Japanese resistance, land revolution, and early cooperative transformation produced far-reaching institutional changes conducive to expanded productivity and personal income for the majority. They rested, moreover, on foundations of broad popular support for major policies and resulted in the expansion of horizons of human freedom and community. These periods of creativity and achievement linking revolutionary change to the promise of cooperation and mutual prosperity offer a standard by which to gauge the course of the transition to socialism in China and elsewhere.

4

ORIGINAL ACCUMULATION, EQUALITY, AND LATE INDUSTRIALIZATION: THE CASES OF SOCIALIST CHINA AND CAPITALIST TAIWAN
With Chih-ming Ka

Are there substantial differences between capitalist and socialist industrialization in late-developing countries? We explore original accumulation in "socialist" China (1953–1957) and in "capitalist" Taiwan (1953–1960) for clues to answers to this question. Our analysis focuses on two dynamic industry-oriented, state-centered accumulation strategies. In each we explore the role of land reform and the use of such extractive and control mechanisms as taxation and compulsory purchase, market controls, and wage, price, and income policies. The comparative analysis provides insight into the possibilities and costs associated with "socialist" and "capitalist" industrialization.

At first glance the China-Taiwan comparison may seem capricious. China, after all, not only is continental in size but, in the early 1950s, pursued a Soviet-inspired strategy of state-centered industrial development, was excluded from major international markets, and had minimal external capital infusions. Insular Taiwan, on the other hand, vigorously pursued capitalist development under U.S. tutelage, was the beneficiary of lavish foreign aid, and moved from import-substitution in the 1950s to export-oriented industrialization in the 1960s and 1970s. At the outset Taiwan enjoyed substantially higher per capita incomes, its agriculture was much more productive, and commodification rates were higher after half a century of Japanese colonial rule. Furthermore, although land reform was an essential part of original accumulation in both China and Taiwan, different social dynamics were involved in the transformation of rural class structures. Land reform in Taiwan involved state buy-out of the landlord class (land reform from above), while mass mobilization and confiscation of land-lord property (land reform from below) characterized the Chinese case.

Nevertheless, in both China and Taiwan, developmentalist states launched agrarian-centered domestic accumulation in the service of urban-based industrialization. The state, not private entrepreneurs working through the market, shaped the contours of the industrial fabric during original accumulation. In both cases, the elimination of the landlords and restructuring of tenure relations was instrumental in the state drive to capture and redirect the rural surplus for industrialization. In both, the state employed a wide array of visible and invisible mechanisms to organize and control the population, to transfer surplus to strategic industries, and to depress income and consumption levels. The analysis of these mechanisms of accumulation constitutes the crux of our study.

Comparison of accumulation strategies pinpoints broad common features helpful in comprehending the nature and limits of original accumulation in two cases that have frequently been cited as divergent models by admirers and critics alike. It also suggests the necessity to rethink analytical categories of the development literature. In highlighting core common elements in the strategies of two late-developing societies in the stage of original accumulation, we reject the conclusions of writers such as Samir Amin (1983) who have erected an unbreachable "Great Wall" between socialist and capitalist patterns of industrialization. At the same time, in contrast with convergency theorists such as Daniel Bell and W. W. Rostow, who have obliterated all essential differences between socialist and capitalist paths, we overlook the significance neither of differential social class outcomes nor of different leadership visions of development.

Original Accumulation

Looking at the dawn of capitalist formation, Marx (1867: 895) concluded that the destruction and transformation of precapitalist property relations was the essence of original accumulation. By means of "ruthless terrorism . . . (t)hey conquered the field for capitalist agriculture, incorporated the soil into capital, and created for the urban industries the necessary supplies of free and rightless proletarians." Marx (pp. 714, 873) held that the prehistory of capitalism required both the accumulation of wealth and the dispossession of rural producers who of necessity become wage laborers in capitalist enterprise. Observing that Marx merged two distinct problems and processes, accumulation of wealth and proletarianization, Gerschenkron (1962: 98) pointed out that historically wealth was created by quite diverse routes of which dispossession and proletarianization of the peasantry was but one. Though he himself noted other sources of accumulation, in a famous passage Marx (p. 714) held that "the so-called original accumulation, therefore, is nothing else than the historical process of divorcing the producer from the means of production."

In the early 1920s Bukharin and then Preobrazhensky addressed the issues of accumulation and expanded reproduction under Soviet conditions of economic backwardness and isolation. In 1920, in the midst of the civil war, Bukharin emphasized the drafting of labor power from the rural, nonsocialist sector into nationalized industry, which constituted the socialized core of the economy. Just as capitalism, by "pillage, class violence, and robbery" mobilized a labor force, so, too, must socialism, arising "from the midst of the debris . . . begin with the mobilization of the living productive forces" (Bukharin 1979: 129).

A few years later, in the midst of the New Economic Policy, Preobrazhenski again addressed expanded reproduction under Soviet conditions of economic backwardness and isolation. He framed the issue of original socialist accumulation in terms of exploitation imposed on the private sector (petty producers in agriculture) by the socialist sector (state-owned industry) primarily through the state's monopoly of the exchange between industrial and agricultural goods, that is, by means of unequal exchange and taxes (Preobrazhensky 1965: 84–85).

Where Marx and Bukharin had emphasized proletarianization of the peasantry, for Preobrazhensky original socialist accumulation pivoted not on the dispossession of agricultural producers but on accumulation processes that extracted their wealth in the service of mechanization and industrialization (p. 80). In exploring analogies between British original capitalist accumulation and original socialist accumulation, he noted a chronological disjuncture. "The original capitalist accumulation on the basis of the commercial capitalism preceded capitalist production" whereas "the original socialist accumulation takes place simultaneously with the beginning of the transition to socialist production and with the accumulation in the socialist complex itself" (p. 83).[1] Preobrazhensky held that industrial development during original capitalist accumulation is spontaneously organized and gradual (guerrilla warfare) compared with the abrupt and consciously planned development of socialist accumulation (pp. 80–83).

By following Marx in taking the first industrialized country (Britain) as the model for original accumulation, Preobrazhensky obscured the fundamentally different character of industrialization in late-developing countries including the Soviet Union. In late-developing countries, whether capitalist or socialist, prior merchant capital formation characteristically plays only a minor role in the creation of the material prerequisites for industrialization (Gerschenkron 1962). Nor do late developers have the opportunity to accumulate capital by plunder or through extraction from colonial territories.

Accumulation of wealth is a necessary but not sufficient condition for sustained industrialization and comprehensive development. In virtually every case of late development, whether capitalist or socialist, original accumulation relies heavily on state power to redirect resources from other sectors, particularly agriculture, to industry. The Chinese and Taiwanese cases shed interesting light on the interconnected processes of social class transformation and accumulation.

The analytical unit for our study of original accumulation is the national economy, albeit a national economy intersecting in various degrees with the world economy. The period of original accumulation ends when self-sustained industrial accumulation no longer relies predominantly on resources derived from other sectors and industry surpasses agriculture in the share of its contribution to the national economy. At that point, the burden imposed on the nonindustrial sectors is not necessarily relaxed. Nevertheless, with the growth of industry, the resources extracted from the nonindustrial sectors in general and agriculture in particular become less important.

Dating the starting point of original accumulation is more complex. Original accumulation frequently begins with vigorous state policies directed to break through existing bottlenecks to mobilize and reallocate resources, including labor power, to achieve self-sustained industrial growth. Despite high growth rates, we distinguish the postwar recovery period (1949–1952 in both Taiwan and China) from the subsequent period of original accumulation. During the recovery phase only minor efforts in accumulation are needed to achieve high growth rates; more important, recovery could be followed by stagnation or even decline (as happened in the Soviet Union in the mid–1920s) in the absence of state-centered original accumulation.

In neither China nor Taiwan did the dispossession and proletarianization of rural producers provide the driving force in, or coincide with, original accumulation, though in each case original accumulation was predicated on transformation of rural social relations and the formation of a small industrial working class. Nor were the market and commercialization central. On the contrary, in both cases the state deliberately (and devastatingly) curbed both domestic and international market activity in early phases of original accumulation. China and Taiwan reveal the decisive role of state-driven processes of accumulation predicated on transformation of ownership and production relations in agriculture and industry. What is particularly striking is the preservation of household-based agriculture in Taiwan under Guomindang rule and the conscious rejection of the dispossession (and proletarianization) of rural producers in favor of a strategy of land reform followed by collectivization and population controls that restrained rural producers from leaving the land in China.

In Taiwan, land reform redirected landlord wealth from consumption to industry and from countryside to city. The state transferred part of confiscated Japanese industrial enterprises to the landlords as partial compensation for the forced transfer of landownership. The conflict over resources between industry and agriculture and between investment and consumption subsequently pitted small family farms against urban industry and a state committed to the priority of industrialization.

China's land reform likewise eliminated the landlord class and created a relatively homogeneous owner-cultivator peasantry. This paved the way for the formation of a collectivized peasantry that, far from being displaced, was bound to the land, facing urban industry and a state bent on extracting a rural surplus to promote rapid industrialization (Selden 1985). Both Bukharin's proletarianization *cum* labor mobilization and Preobrazhensky's concept of original socialist accumulation achieved by manipulation of the terms of trade at the expense of agriculture are thus inadequate to encompass the melange of strategies employed by the socialist state, whether in China (in the 1950s) or in the Soviet Union (under Stalin's First Five-Year Plan).

For Preobrazhensky (1965: 83), original socialist accumulation required state intervention to transfer surplus from the agricultural sector to state-owned industry. Both Preobrazhensky and Bukharin, for quite different reasons, envisaged not the shrinking of rural markets but their expansion. For Preobrazhensky growth of the market would expand (via unequal exchange) the transfer of the surplus to state industry; by contrast, Bukharin favored the growth of the free market and envisaged an agrarian development stimulated by the expansion of equivalent exchange (Preobrazhensky 1965: 144; Cohen 1971; Erlich 1960).[2] Stalin's collectivization, however, short-circuited the protracted process they had envisaged and provided the vehicle for state transfer of the agricultural surplus not by the unequal exchange and expanding market demand proposed by Preobrazhensky but by confiscatory collectivization (Erlich 1950: 75; Lewin 1968: Selden 1983).

It has been widely believed that China under Mao Zedong embarked on a pro-peasant policy that broke unequivocally with Stalin's tribute imposed on the countryside in favor of urban, capital-intensive heavy industry. Samir Amin (1983: 9) provides a pure expression of this view that contrasts China's successful socialist development path, which fully protected the interests of rural producers, with what he terms the statism of the Soviet Union. Similarly, Yu-hsi Chen (1976: 125–49) contrasts China's egalitarian socialist development, characterized by intersectoral cooperation, with Taiwan's "urban-biased" economy resting on intersectoral exploitation. To the contrary, we document the fact that original accumulation in China, no less than in Taiwan, was accomplished at the expense of the countryside. We will focus on the role of the state and the specific mechanisms it employed in both China and Taiwan in transferring resources from agriculture to industry, from the countryside to the city, and from the private and household sectors to the state and the institutions it controlled for purposes of accumulation and industry-centered development.

Perspectives on Original Accumulation in Taiwan and China

In the 1950s in both China and Taiwan the state generated industrial growth through direct and indirect taxation and price manipulation to transfer a significant and growing portion of the rural surplus from consumption to urban industrial investment, including military industry. Both strategies emphasized sectoral inequality between agriculture and industry. In Taiwan, shortly after eliminating the landlord class in land reform, the state introduced a fertilizer/rice barter system as the central mechanism for appropriating a large and growing portion of the agricultural surplus. In China, land reform followed by price controls, compulsory sale quotas, restrictions on private marketing, and collectivization all strengthened state control over the agricultural surplus.

We explore the interrelationships between two types of measures to transfer resources from agriculture to industry: visible transfer mechanisms, such as taxation and compulsory sales, and invisible measures that employ price and exchange mechanisms. Together they restricted the scope of the rural market economy and channeled the surplus to state-directed outlets in both China and Taiwan.

World War II ended the international division of labor that had shaped colonial Taiwan's economy: agricultural Taiwan in the orbit of industrial Japan. Taiwan's agricultural goods lost their protected market and Japan sharply reduced its export of industrial goods to Taiwan. In the 1950s, the Guomindang employed a standard package of import controls, multiple exchange rates, and high tariffs to pursue import substitution. These policies effectively protected Taiwan's domestic consumer goods market against foreign competition and conserved foreign exchange for raw materials and capital goods imports. Only after 1960, with the prerequisites for capitalist accumulation in place, did the state relax its import-substitution policy, encourage private export enterprise, and open Taiwan's economy to the world market (Lin 1973: 83). If Taiwan's rapid growth from the 1960s took place through incorporation in the world market and in the context of foreign investment in Taiwan, during the period of original accumulation foreign trade and investment were restricted.

In the years 1953–57, the Chinese state first controlled international access to the economy and then virtually eliminated the private market as a vehicle for distributing resources and income. With the exception of a brief interlude in the early 1960s, it was not until the 1980s that the state permitted the controlled expansion of private commerce, dramatically expanded imports and exports, and encouraged foreign investment (Solinger 1984; Lardy 1983). Between 1953 and 1956 the Chinese state absorbed and amalgamated private industrial and handicraft enterprise, with collectivization of handicrafts and small industry and nationalization of the modern industrial sector completed in 1956. The market was tightly controlled, with private commercial activity in key commodities such as grain, cotton, and producer goods eliminated and services and consumer activity restricted. The increase in the rate of investment in the 1950s (the period of original accumulation) was due primarily to a net flow of resources from agriculture to state-owned industry (Lardy 1982: 369).

Taiwan's barter system and China's comprehensive collective structure constitute two statist approaches to extraction, accumulation, and market restriction. In both cases original accumulation coincided with a dramatic increase in the economic and political strength of the state and subordination of the countryside.

Institutional Approaches to Original Accumulation

Land Reform and the Barter System in Taiwan

In the colonial period (1895–1945) landlords and the state captured more than one-third of the income originating in Taiwan's agriculture. To fulfill tax and rent obligations, as much as 74 percent of rice took the form of rent and market exchange, one of the highest rates of commodification in Asia (Kawano 1941: 124–25). Agriculture provided the resources for investment in Japanese-owned enterprises and for luxury consumption of imported goods by the landlord class. But with landlords and the state absorbing so much of the surplus, the rural market for industrial goods remained constricted. In the colonial division of labor, Taiwan became a commercialized rural economy while Japan maintained a monopoly on industry.

Prior to land reform, Taiwan agriculture was dominated by landlords but not by large landed estates. In 1939, tenants comprised approximately half of the farming population and cultivated 56 percent of the land (*Statistical Abstracts for the Past 51 Years* 1946: 521). However, there was a long-term tendency toward fragmentation of landownership in the indigenous sector, in contrast to the expansion of large estates dominated by Japanese capitalists. Following the 1945 confiscation of Japanese-owned land (21 percent of the arable land), most remaining landlords owned less than one hectare (Chen 1961; *Statistical Abstracts*).

For Premier Chen Cheng, the initial driving force behind land reform was fear of rural unrest, the basic factor behind the Communist victory on the mainland (Chen 1961: 47). In fact, political stability in Taiwan rested not so much on preempting rural unrest fueled by dissident tenants but on the supply of sufficient food to city dwellers. The February 28, 1947, uprising against the Guomindang was essentially an urban phenomenon (Kerr 1965). This contrasts sharply with China's peasant-based revolution.

With the landlord class weakened by repression following the uprising and by compulsory grain procurement, the Guomindang, with U.S. support, conducted a thoroughgoing land reform (Liu 1975: 76). While the social consequences of land reform were profound, it did not increase agricultural growth rates. Between 1920 and 1939, yields in Taiwan's predominantly tenant agriculture grew at the impressive annual rate of 4.2 percent. In the years 1952–1960, after land reform, annual growth rates averaged 4.0 percent (Hsieh and Lee 1960: 41).

Taiwan's land reform facilitated state surplus extraction with important strategic as well as economic and social implications. Land reform broke the landlords' grip on the rural surplus and strengthened the foundations of a smallholder peasantry owning and cultivating the land. To feed the more than one million mainlanders, most of whom served in the government and army, and to stabilize market prices, the state sought substantial grain procurements. The rice collected by the state, approximately 400,000 tons per year in the early 1950s, rising to 600,000 tons by the end of the decade following land reform, provided rations to meet the needs of the state sector and the cities, facilitated dumping to keep prices low, and provided a source of foreign exchange. The state relied on traditional agricultural exports, particularly rice and sugar, to provide foreign exchange for the import of machinery and raw materials (Guo in Shen 1974: 117).

Land reform proceeded in three stages. In 1949 the Guomindang implemented a rent reduction program initially proposed by American advisers to the Joint Commission on Rural Reconstruction in Sichuan province prior to retreat from the mainland (McCoy 1971: 22). Beginning in 1951, public land previously confiscated from Japanese landowners was gradually sold to tenants (Chen 1961: 63, 307). The landlord system was dismantled in 1953–54 in the "land to the tiller" program, which placed a ceiling on ownership of three hectares of medium grade paddy land for each farm worker. The state then purchased excess land for resale to farmers at the same price, 2.5 times the purchase price of the annual yield. Payment was 70 percent in commodity bonds and 30 percent in shares of stock in four government enterprises. The bonds paid 4 percent annual interest with principal and interest amortized over 10 years. Owner-cultivated land increased from 56 percent in 1948 to 86 percent in 1959 (Chen 1961: 312). Land reform virtually eliminated the big landlords and consolidated the position of the small owner-cultivator as the bulwark of Taiwan agriculture.

Three facts bear note in evaluating the land reform from the perspective of its impact on accumulation. First, the government claimed that compensation conformed with the market value of land, but rent reduction had already brought about a fall in the price of tenant land to one-

Table 4.1

Distribution of Rice in Taiwan (1,000 metric tons of brown rice)

Period	Total production	Distribution (%)		Collected by government	Sale by cultivator (%)	Sale ratio of rice (%)
		Landlords	Cultivators			
1931–35	1,229	34.1	65.9		40.7	74
1936–40	1,304	31.5	68.5		43	74
1950–55	1,571	8.4	62.2	29.5	11.1	50
1956–60	1,858	4.6	67.7	27.8	13.6	46
1950	1,422	16	57	27	6	49.29
1951	1,485	12	62	26	11	49.43
1952	1,570	8	65	27	13	51.11
1953	1,695	5	65	30	14	51.39
1954	1,695	5	61	34	13	50.00
1955	1,615	5	63	32	11	45.98
1956	1,790	5	66	29	12	45.98
1957	1,839	5	66	29	12	46.09
1958	1,894	5	66	29	13	46.56
1959	1,856	5	67	28	13	45.37
1960	1,912	4	71	25	17	45.75

Source: Taiwan Food Grain Bureau (1966).

quarter to one-half its 1948 price (Chen 1961: 310). Moreover, in the period 1914–1943 the average market price of paddy land was about four times the annual yield (Ho 1978: 66). In short, in purchasing at 2.5 times the value of the annual yield, the state grossly undervalued the land. Second, land bonds bore 4 percent interest at a time when three-month bank deposits paid 16 percent a year. The low interest rate constituted disguised forced savings. Third, the remaining 30 percent of compensation was paid with stock in four government enterprises. The market value of all except the Taiwan Cement Corporation fell below the par value of the stocks. In addition, the Taiwan Paper and Pulp Corporation and Taiwan Agricultural and Forestry Development Corporation paid no dividends between 1957 and 1962 (Wu 1971: 150). In essence, land reform constituted punitive forced investment in industry. It marked the involuntary transformation of the landlord class either into peasants or urban workers after bankruptcy (the majority) or, in the case of a minority, into a capitalist class closely tied to the state. Stockholders received shares in such government monopolies as Taiwan Cement and Taiwan Paper and Pulp, as well as in 208 small and medium enterprises (associated under the names of Taiwan Industrial and Mining Corporation and Taiwan Agricultural and Forestry Development Corporation), which were confiscated from the Japanese and gradually returned to the private sector (Liu 1975: 27–29).

Land reform simultaneously broke the power of landlords to control the rural surplus, affected a considerable transfer of value to the state, and created large numbers of small owner-cultivators as the bulwark of Taiwan's agriculture. This shifted the protagonist whom the government faced on the land from the landlords to fragmented smallholders.

The share of the rice output siphoned off by Taiwan landlords fell from one-third in the 1930s (Kawano 1941: 124–25) to 16 percent by 1950, primarily as a result of taxation and the confiscation of Japanese property. Land reform reduced the landlord share to 5 percent by 1953, a level from which it never recovered. Yet in the mid-1950s, following land reform, the share of the harvest going to cultivators was actually slightly lower than it was in the 1930s. Cultivators received 67 percent of the harvest in the 1930s compared with an average of 63 percent in 1953–55. The state secured the lion's share of that portion of the crop formerly appropriately by the landlords (see table 4.1). Likewise, the state's share of marketed rice rose from 55 percent in the early 1950s to 73 percent in the peak years 1954–55 (see table 4.2).

Throughout the 1950s, the state tightly restricted peasant consump-

Table 4.2

The Sale Ratio and Government Collection of Rice in Taiwan (metric tons)

Period	(1) Total sale	(2) Sale by cultivator	(3) Collected by government	2/1 (%)	3/1 (%)
1950	700,650	89,059	387,713	12.71	55.34
1951	733,933	160,675	393,083	21.84	55.34
1952	802,486	196,035	428,788	24.43	53.43
1953	843,596	225,168	496,324	26.69	58.83
1954	847,553	207,268	533,939	24.46	72.22
1955	775,177	173,935	518,739	22.44	73.34
1956	821,352	215,568	519,785	26.25	63.28
1957	847,599	226,923	535,347	26.70	63.16
1958	881,905	251,656	544,847	28.54	61.78
1959	842,211	243,880	513,164	28.96	60.93
1960	874,748	324,392	466,247	37.08	53.30

Source: Taiwan Food Grain Bureau (1966).

tion and directed the surplus to the industrial sector and the cities. In the 1950s, per capita rural consumption (in 1935–37 yen) remained at 1930s' levels, and real agricultural wages declined (Lee 1971: 13). Taking 1953 as the base, in 1960 the index of GNP was 260 but peasant purchasing power was just 106. In the 1950s net real capital outflow from agriculture grew by 17 percent compared with the 1930s (Lee 1972: 10–13). The state monopolized the benefits of land reform.

If the per capita size of the agricultural product determines the sale ratio and the sale ratio in turn determines the size of the outflow of the agricultural surplus, as suggested by economists who insist that the bottleneck for development in the underdeveloped countries is their technological backwardness and insufficient commodification, Taiwan's experience in the 1950s has different implications. There are two facts that do not fit this model. First, the net capital outflow from the agricultural sector increased sharply in the peak years 1953–54 while the sale ratio of agricultural products remained relatively constant (around 60 percent) between 1952 and 1960 (see table 4.3). This means that the increased outflow of agricultural surplus was independent of the sale ratio. The explanation lies in the imposition of state measures to transfer the agricultural surplus from the producers to the state. Second, the sale ratio remained constant despite the substantial

Table 4.3

The Sale Ratio, Net Real Capital Outflow, and Total Production of Taiwan Agriculture from 1952 to 1960

	1952	1953	1954	1955	1956	1957	1958	1959	1960
Sale ratio (%)	59	60	56	55	63	59	58	61	59
Net real capital outflow (million yen)*	102	128	142	97	106	94	92	86	100
Index of total production (1952 = 100)	100	112	112	111	121	128	136	136	137

Source: Lee (1972), Appendices 4 and 6.
*Based on 1935–37 yen.

increase in agricultural output in the course of the decade. Peasants consumed more grain produced by themselves but bought less. Commodification lagged behind the growth of agricultural production. Eventually, the Taiwan economy combined highly capitalized urban industry with a rural economy tied to state-controlled barter arrangements. This division of labor between agriculture and industry, mediated by barter between rural producers and the state, resulted in substantial resource transfers that contributed to industrialization at the expense of rural welfare.

Original accumulation in Taiwan in the years 1953–1960 was principally based on mobilization of the rural surplus through barter arrangements that restricted rural market mechanisms and transferred a substantial portion of the rural surplus to the state and the cities. The stagnation of rural commodification, simultaneous with drastic outflow of the agricultural surplus, resulted in a state-dominated accumulation process and industrial growth at the expense of agriculture and rural people.

Land Reform, Market Control, and Collectivization in China

The Chinese state presided over original accumulation beginning, as in Taiwan, with a land reform that eliminated landlordism and strengthened the position of the state in relationship to a rural population of independent cultivators. Land reform was followed in the early and mid-1950s by state measures that restricted and then effectively eliminated the private marketing of agricultural commodities, imposed heavy compulsory sales quotas on rural producers, and controlled rural consumption. Tenants and smallholders made substantial gains as a result of the land reform carried out in the years 1947–1952. From 1953, however, as state mechanisms replaced market processes built up over centuries, peasants lost crucial sources of income in sideline activities and petty commerce (Fei 1957; Kojima 1982). Finally, in 1955–56, the Chinese state imposed universal collectivization and direct administrative controls over both the rural surplus and the mobility of rural producers. The collectivized peasantry was bound to the land and villages of its birth (or marriage) and effectively barred from urban residence and jobs. We assess state initiatives with respect to their consequences for surplus transfer, industrialization, consumption, and the urban-rural relationship—in a word, for original accumulation.

Land reform eliminated the landlords, tenants, managerial farmers, and hired laborers as classes and created a countryside of basically homogeneous owner-cultivators farming tiny plots of land. Within each village, land reform and economic recovery permitted poorer strata to increase food consumption and raise living standards in the late 1940s and early 1950s. At the same time, the state appropriated a substantial share of that portion of rural surplus formerly appropriated by the landlords. Lippit (1974: 123) has estimated that in 1952 land reform accounted for 5.0 billion yuan in state revenues and 45 percent of the 11.3 billion yuan net investment. Following the recovery period (1949–1952), the Chinese state pursued rapid industrialization while continuing social and economic restructuring through nationalization of industry and commerce and collectivization of agriculture and handicrafts. The "big push" of the First Five-Year Plan (1953–1957) was predicated on acceleration of the transfer of the agricultural surplus to industry and the cities. China's state-centered accumulation rested principally on compulsory sale at low prices of agricultural commodities, which accompanied state control and constriction of rural markets. The state extracted 80 to 90 percent of the rural surplus above subsistence consumption (FGHP 1955: 579; Shue 1980: 235–45; Oi 1983).

With population pressure high and living standards close to subsistence, China could not significantly increase transfers of the agricultural surplus to the state by further lowering consumption. Nor could it long tolerate stagnation of agricultural output while population increased rapidly. Particularly in the face of rapid unchecked population growth, Chinese industrialization required generating a larger agricultural surplus.

A many-faceted debate at the state center came to a head in the spring and summer of 1955 as it became clear that the First Five-Year Plan targets were in jeopardy. The plan's high industrial targets were predicated on substantial increases in grain output of 4.6 percent per year. But with just 1.7 percent growth in 1953–54, it became necessary to attain growth rates of 6.5 percent in grain during the remaining years of the plan (Walker 1966: 25).

In framing ways to accelerate growth and accumulation, the Chinese leadership confronted two thorny issues: first, how to increase agricultural productivity without costly mechanization; second, how to maximize state control of the agricultural surplus to fuel industrial development, particularly the capital-intensive heavy industry that was the focal point of the plan. The institutional choice was accelerated collectivization, which China completed in 1955–56.

From the perspective of original accumulation, the essence of collectivization was mobilization and control of rural resources by the state. By transferring power over the harvest from 100 million peasant households to a much smaller number of collectives subject to state discipline, the state secured control over the rural surplus and positioned itself to control consumption (see chapter 2; also Friedman et al. forthcoming). With collectivization, centralization of processing in state hands, the suppression of rural markets, and the end of free population movement, the subordinating relationship between each individual village *cum* collective and the state was strengthened while the myriad relationships that had linked peasants and villages, on the one hand, and local markets, on the other, were suppressed (Solinger 1984: 179–92; see also chapter 2 this volume). In short, collectivization was part of a process that isolated the village from traditional local and regional networks by eliminating the complex nexus of commercial, social, and cultural ties associated with the marketplace. This was accomplished in 1956 and 1957 by the transfer of rural crafts and commerce from the hands of private artisans, merchants, and peddlers to collective and state enterprises; by outlawing the sale of grain, cotton, and other commodities except through collective and state channels; by providing virtually all industrial products to the countryside through those same collective and state outlets; and by eliminating such economic-cultural features of the market as the temple festivals, which attracted tens of thousands of visitors to the market (Perkins 1966: 14; Solinger 1984: 157–205; Friedman et al. forthcoming). By 1957, private commerce was reduced to 2.7 percent of retail sales (State Statistical Bureau 1960: 40).

Following collectivization, the state accelerated accumulation and curbed consumption. Between 1955 and 1956, China's accumulation rate, defined as the ratio of gross domestic capital formation to gross domestic product, increased from 22.9 percent to 26.1 percent, and at the height of the Great Leap Forward in 1959 it rose to an extraordinary peak of 44 percent (table 4.4). The combination of collectivization, compulsory purchase, and market control enabled the Chinese state to raise accumulation to unprecedented levels in the late 1950s, just as China entered a period of famine brought on primarily by Great Leap policies that took the lives of twenty to thirty million rural people (Ashton et al. 1984).

Peter Schran's (1969) careful study of agricultural accumulation during the First Five-Year Plan period shows net accumulation of 1.3 billion yuan per year in 1953 and 1954; following collectivization this doubled to over three billion yuan followed by further dramatic increases during the Great Leap Forward (p. 145; figures in 1952 prices). Rural net accumulation rose from 2.6 percent in 1953–54 to 5.4 percent in 1956–57 (p. 142). While peasant consumption in 1957 increased only 2 percent over 1954 levels, rural investment increased threefold (Wong 1973: 246). The collectivized peasantry bore the brunt of original accumulation, a pattern that continued into the early 1980s. Agricultural resources were channeled to industry and the cities at the expense both of rural consumption and investment. The priorities of the First Five-Year Plan, with its overriding emphasis on heavy industry, set the tone, moreover, for subsequent decades in which the state slighted agriculture and rural consumption. In the years 1953–57, the state accounted for 90 percent of total investment in capital construction (State Statistical Bureau 1982: 295). Industry received 52.4 percent of total investment, with fully 89 percent of that allocated to heavy industry. A mere 7.8 percent of state investment went to agriculture (Yang and Li 1980: 190; Lardy 1983: 130).

We have pinpointed striking similarities in the processes of original accumulation in Taiwan and China. In both, land reform transformed the principal axis of class conflict in the countryside, the conflict between landlord and tenant, resulting in the elimination of both social

Table 4.4

Accumulation Rates in China (1952–59)

Year	1952	1953	1954	1955	1956	1957	1958	1959
Accumulation rate	18.2	22.4	23.5	22.9	26.1	24.9	33.9	43.8

Source: Yang (1957), p. 51; Yang and Li (1980), p. 24.

classes; in both, the state fostered original accumulation in ways that exacerbated sectoral conflict between rural producers and urban industry and between countryside and city. In both Taiwan and China, the state mobilized the agricultural surplus to promote urban industry through institutional measures that transformed land tenure patterns and curbed or basically eliminated the self-regulating market. Our analysis is also consistent with Gerschenkron's conclusion that the extent of direct state involvement in original accumulation is more deeply affected by levels of economic backwardness than by ideology. Compared with the important role of price manipulation and unequal exchange in original accumulation in Taiwan with its substantially higher yields and commodification, China relied on direct administrative measures, notably sales quotas, market controls, and collectivization, to extract and transfer the rural surplus.

Visible Transfers

According to Bian (1972: 37), from 1952 to 1960 the capital outflow from Taiwan agriculture amounted to NT$28,929 million, of which government transfers constituted the largest part.[3] This outflow accounted for 34 percent of gross domestic investment. The nonagricultural sector, which accounted for 70 percent of GNP, generated less than 30 percent of the capital formation with most of the balance (31 percent) accounted for by U.S. aid (Jacoby 1966: 52). Agriculture, which accounted for only 30 percent of Taiwan GNP in the 1950s, bore a disproportionately heavy burden in support of capital formation.

Recognizing that "peasants are 'notoriously' hard to tax" (Nurkse 1953: 43), the Taiwanese state implemented diverse forced savings measures to secure the surplus. Visible transfer from agriculture to the state consisted of the land tax in kind, compulsory purchase, rent collection in kind from public farm land, and payments for public and private land distributed in land reform (table 4.5). The role of agricul-

Table 4.5

Government Rice Procurement by Sources in Taiwan (metric tons of unhulled rice and %)

	Year								
	1952	1953	1954	1955	1956	1957	1958	1959	1960
Land tax	(16.2) 69,558	(13.5) 67,216	(12) 66,674	(12.7) 64,375	(13.7) 66,012	(13.0) 73,234	(13.0) 70,615	(11.4) 58,564	(16.1) 75,270
Purchased as a part of land tax	(13.8) 58,992	(11.4) 65,722	(14.2) 56,157	(10.4) 54,174	(10.7) 55,469	(11.4) 61,222	(10.8) 59,140	(8.7) 44,518	(12.2) 56,766
Public farm land rents	(3.0) 15,472	(3.5) 17,298	(3.1) 17,198	(−1.8) −9,462	(2.1) 10,938	(1.6) 8,784	(2.8) 15,486	(2.0) 10,120	(0.4) 2,025
Payment for the purchase of farm land	— —	(5.3) 26,148	(2.2) 12,301	(12.6) 65,324	(5.4) 28,283	(4.1) 21,982	(7.6) 41,254	(9.9) 50,780	(3.5) 16,458
In exchange for fertilizer	(60.7) 260,026	(56.2) 278,900	(51.8) 286,991	(59.8) 309,982	(62.1) 322,524	(65.2) 348,944	(62.3) 339,269	(63.5) 325,792	(62.9) 293,102
Repayment of agricultural production loans	(4.6) 19,851	(5.2) 25,602	(5.0) 27,491	(4.3) 22,155	(4.3) 22,502	(3.3) 17,672	(2.4) 13,238	(2.9) 14,961	(2.0) 9,280
Other	(1.1) 4,889	(4.9) 24,438	(15.7) 87,127	(2.3) 12,191	(2.7) 14,037	(10.7) 3,589	(1.1) 5,839	(1.6) 8,429	(2.9) 13,346
Total	(100.0) 428,788	(100.0) 496,324	(100.0) 553,939	(100.0) 518,739	(100.0) 519,785	(100.0) 535,347	(100.0) 544,841	(100.0) 513,164	(100.0) 466,247

Source: Wu (1970), pp. 64–65.

Table 4.6

Agricultural Tax in Taiwan (million NT$)

Year	Agri. tax	Nonagri. tax	Total tax	Agri. tax / Total tax (%)	Nonagri. tax / Total tax (%)
1938				31.3	68.7
1939				25.8	74.2
1940				20.6	79.4
.				.	.
.				.	.
1952	292	407	699	41.8	58.2
1953	466	430	896	52.0	48.0
1954	519	545	1,064	48.7	51.3
1955	578	849	1,427	40.4	59.6
1956	555	862	1,417	39.2	60.8
1957	637	1,001	1,638	38.9	61.1
1958	631	1,047	1,728	39.4	60.6
1959	671	1,281	1,952	34.4	65.6
1960	876	1,427	2,303	38.0	62.0

Sources: *Abstract of Statistics in Taiwan 1895–1945* (1946); *Taiwan Statistics Handbook* (1965), p. 96.

ture in providing tax revenues increased sharply after World War II and throughout the 1950s remained much higher than prewar levels (table 4.6). The agricultural tax played an important role in original accumulation in the early 1950s.

In 1954, about 14 percent of the rice procured by the government, or 4 percent of Taiwan's total rice production, was purchased at compulsory state prices that were slightly less than half the wholesale price (47 percent in the years 1952–58). Compulsory rice procured at low official prices in effect constituted a concealed land tax worth approximately half the tax (table 4.6).

In China, the quantity of grain extracted in the form of agricultural taxes remained roughly constant—19.4 million metric tons in 1952 and 19.7 in 1957. At the same time, the importance of the agricultural tax in total tax revenues declined from 27 percent in 1952 to just 19 percent in 1957 (table 4.7).

The declining importance of agricultural taxes in China's national accumulation was accompanied by an increase in the transfer to the state of the agricultural surplus through compulsory sales of grain,

Table 4.7

Taxes in China (million yuan)

Year	Agricultural tax (1)	Total tax (2)	Agricultural tax as a percent of total tax (%)	Industrial and commercial tax (3)	Industrial tax as a percent of total tax (%)	Grain production (million tons) (4)	Agricultural tax (million tons) (5)	Agricultural tax as a percent of grain production (6)
1952	2,704	9,770	26.6	6,147	63.4	157.3	19.4	12.3
1953	2,711	11,970	22.6	8,250	69.0	159.8	17.1	10.7
1954	3,278	13,220	24.6	8,972	67.8	161.9	18.6	11.5
1955	3,054	12,750	23.2	8,725	68.5	176.3	19.2	10.9
1956	2,965	14,090	21.0	10,098	72.4	176.9	18.3	10.4
1957	2,970	15,490	19.1	11,300	73.1	185.5	19.7	10.6

Source: Chen (1967), p. 441; Wiens in Eckstein (1980), p. 63; Lardy (1983), p. 104.

cotton, and other commodities (table 4.8).[4] The value of agricultural sales to the state increased from 8.2 million yuan in 1953 to 13.3 million yuan in 1956 and 15.6 million yuan in 1957. For the entire period 1952–1957, compulsory sales to the state at low prices were four times as large as agricultural taxes, and in subsequent decades the importance of compulsory sales continued to grow.

In China, land taxes accounted for 18.9 percent of total state grain procurement between 1952 and 1957, compared with 13.4 percent in Taiwan in the years 1952 to 1960. Compulsory purchases accounted for fully 81 percent of Chinese government agricultural procurements in the years 1952–1957, compared with 12 percent in Taiwan for 1952–1960.

China's introduction of compulsory grain sales in late 1953 was spurred by the declining ability of the state to obtain low-price grain through the market at a time when the First Five-Year Plan required substantial increments in state acquisition of grain. In 1952, the state secured 72 percent of the marketable surplus, but the following year, as high demand drove up the market price, sales to the state dropped to just 55 percent (table 4.8). Simultaneously, the income and opportunity disparity between peasants and urban workers generated a rapid flow of migration to the cities, which further exacerbated the grain supply problem. In the mid-1950s the state both increased its control over the agricultural surplus and sought to stem urban migration. Collectivization, combined with a rigorously enforced population registration system, by 1960 halted the flow of population to the cities. Far from easing the urban-rural disparities that gave rise to it, however, this and subsequent policies exacerbated the urban-rural division to the detriment of the countryside (see chapter 5).

The state tightened grain rationing in response to the grain crisis of 1955 (Walker 1966: 26). Serious food shortages, particularly during the spring of 1955, followed the sharp increase in compulsory purchase from 41 percent in 1953 to 57 percent of the agricultural outflow in 1954 (see table 4.8). At the same time the share of agricultural outflow passing through the free market dropped from 45 percent to 28 percent. The volume of grain transactions in the free market dropped from 7–8 million metric tons per year in the early 1950s to just 2–3 million tons by 1954–55 (Lardy 1983: 17). In 1954 the state acquired grain that, according to its own directives, should have been retained by farmers for food, seed, and fodder (Walker 1966: 26). Confronting hungry and angry peasants, the state imposed food ration-

Table 4.8

Outflow of Agricultural Resources in China (billion yuan)

	1952	1953	1954	1955	1956	1957	1952–57
1. Tax in kind	3.1	2.8	3.0	3.0	2.7	2.9	14.5
2. Sale to state	10.3	8.2	12.1	13.0	13.3	15.6	62.2
3. Free market	5.3	8.9	6.0	5.9	6.6	6.3	33.3
4. Total	18.7	19.8	21.1	21.9	22.2	24.8	109.9
(1) + (2)/(4)×100*	71.6	55.4	71.8	72.9	72.0	74.8	69.8
5. (1)/(4)×100	16.4	14.1	14.4	13.7	12.1	11.8	13.2
6. (2)/(4)×100	55.2	41.3	57.4	59.2	59.9	62.9	56.6
7. (3)/(4)×100	28.4	44.6	28.3	27.0	29.6	25.3	30.3
8. (1)/(1 + 2)×100†	29.8	25.5	20.0	18.8	16.8	15.8	18.9
9. (2)/(1 + 2)×100‡	77.1	73.0	80.0	81.2	83.2	84.2	81.2

Source: Ishikawa (1967), Table 1:32–33.
*The rate of government procurement in outflow of agricultural commodities.
†The rate of tax in kind in government procurement.
‡The rate of compulsory purchase in government procurement.

Table 4.9

Grain Procurement in China and Taiwan (percentage)

	Agricultural tax	Compulsory purchase	Barter	Other
China (1952–57)	19	81	—	—
Taiwan (1952–60)	13	12	61	14

Source: Calculated from tables 4.5 and 4.8.

ing in the city as well as restricting migration from the countryside. At no time did it relinquish its ambitious industrial targets. Compulsory purchase and urban rationing were two sides of the coin. The state replaced the market to increase control over the agricultural product and the labor power and movement of the rural population.

Invisible Transfers

Taiwan's Rice-Fertilizer Barter System and Manipulation of Terms of Trade

In Taiwan, government procurement centered on state-directed barter of rice for chemical fertilizer. The rice-fertilizer barter system produced 61 percent of the total rice collected by the state in the 1950s (table 4.5). The state monopolized the production, import, and distribution of chemical fertilizer and required farmers to pay for fixed quantities of fertilizer in rice and other grain. The barter system operated on the basis of unequal exchange by manipulating exchange rates. In 1954–60 the domestic price of fertilizer in terms of rice equivalent fluctuated between 1.7 and 2.9 times above the import price (table 4.10).

To understand the rice-fertilizer barter system, one must understand not only the state's monopoly of imported fertilizer but also its monopoly on rice exports. Throughout the 1950s export prices fluctuated between 2.2 and 3.0 times the compulsory purchase price, which in turn was barely half the market price. Meanwhile, the export price of rice was two to three times the price of the same unit of fertilizer (table 4.10).

In 1959, government profit on the barter arrangement amounted to 170,000 tons of rice, about 35 percent of paddy rice channeled through the barter system (Sasamoto 1968: 34). From 1954 to 1960, the government exported 24 percent of the collected rice to obtain foreign exchange. The government annually reaped U.S. $10.5 million profit from the rice-fertilizer barter system (Rada and Lee 1963: 30).[5] In 1952, the profit from fertilizer imports constituted 92 percent of the profit of rice-fertilizer barter (Lee 1972: table 45). During the colonial period, the outflow of Taiwan's agricultural surplus primarily took the form of rent, while in the years 1950 to 1955 taxation predominated. After 1955, however, invisible transfers, centered on rice-fertilizer barter, accounted for the major part of the outflow (table 4.11).

Growing urban population increased demand for agricultural products—in the first instance, grain. The low price and stable supply of grain are crucial for keeping labor costs low. In Taiwan, rice procured by the state was sold at 20–30 percent below the market price to hold down grain prices for city dwellers. Using 1935–37 as our base,

Table 4.10

Estimates of Unequal Exchange in Taiwan's Barter System Through Compulsory Purchase and Compulsory Rice-Fertilizer Barter, 1954–1960

Year	Domestic barter rate of units of rice to one unit of fertilizer (1)	CIF price per metric ton of ammonium sulfate imported from Japan ($) (2)	Market whole-sale price per ton ($) (3)	(3)/(2)	Official procurement price ($/ton) (4)	FOB price per metric ton of Ponlai rice exported to Japan ($) (5)	(5)/(4)	Ratio of rice export price to fertilizer import price (5)/(2)
1954	1	63	109.8	1.74	58.9	177	3.00	1.86
1955	1	64	118.2	1.85	58.9	171	2.90	2.67
1956	1	66	128.3	1.94	63.0	149	2.37	2.26
1957	1	64	135.6	2.12	65.8	147	2.23	2.30
1958	1	53	95.9	1.80	48.4	147	3.04	2.77
1959	1	47	102.3	2.18	51.4	146	2.84	3.11
1960	1.0–0.9	45	132.2	2.94	56.0	146	2.61	3.24

Sources: Lin (1973), p. 59; "Rice Review" (April 1964).
*The price expressed in NT$ was adjusted according to exchange rate:
  1954–57 US $1.00 = NT $24.78
  1858–59 US $1.00 = NT $36.38
  1960   US $1.00 = NT $40.03

Table 4.11

Net Real Capital Outflow from Agriculture in Taiwan (percentage)

Year	Visible transfer	Invisible transfer
1951–55	57.8	42.2
1956–60	39.7	60.3
1936–40	94.9	5.1

Source: Calculated from Lee (1972), pp. 11–12.

Table 4.12

Indices of Rice Price, Wage, Labor Productivity, and Terms of Trade in Taiwan, 1952–1960

Year	Agricultural terms of trade*	Taipei city rice price†	Industrial labor		Agricultural labor	
			Real wages‡	Produc-tivity‡	Real income§	Produc-tivity‡
1952	—	100	100	100	100	100
1953	100	147	110	125	102	107
1954	84	125	129	125	116	109
1955	79	120	132	136	105	107
1956	73	113	135	142	109	116
1957	76	112	139	149	112	123
1958	78	115	145	150	126	130
1959	77	110	142	162	127	127
1960	102	136	140	177	115	128

The agricultural term of trade is calculated by dividing the average price received by farmers by the average price of nonfood manufactures.
*Lin (1973), Appendix A-12, p. 206.
†Wu (1970).
‡CIECD (1970).
§Hu (1972).

throughout the 1950s, agricultural prices lagged 30 percent behind general price levels, and the price of rice was 40 percent below the general level (Wu 1970: 54, 67).

Beginning in 1953, agricultural prices declined sharply and did not regain their original position until 1959. The comparative disadvantage of agricultural goods inherited from the colonial period did not improve in the decade following the end of Japanese rule (Lin 1973: 61). By providing cheap food and a cheap labor supply, agriculture contributed to labor-intensive industrialization in Taiwan.

Throughout the 1950s industrial wages increased more rapidly than agricultural income. By 1960, industrial real wages had risen 40 percent above the 1952 level while agricultural real income was up by only 15 percent (table 4.12). Nevertheless, between 1952 and 1960, industrial real wage gains lagged 37 percent behind increases in industrial labor productivity. Agricultural real income also failed to keep pace with agricultural productivity.

China's Manipulation of Terms of Trade and the Low-Wage, Cheap-Food Policy

Chinese pricing policy at first glance appears quite different from that employed on Taiwan. The state adjusted the terms of trade to the advantage of agriculture. The agricultural price index for 1957 (1952 = 100) was 122.4 compared to 101.6 for industrial products in the countryside, reflecting a 20.5 percent net increase in agricultural prices over industrial prices (Lardy 1978: 177). Although the purchase price of food grains fell to 95.6 (1952 = 100), overall between 1952 and 1957 agricultural commodities enjoyed a relative advantage over industrial goods (Chou 1966: 652).

But extending our analysis back to the 1930s clarifies the pattern of relative prices. Using 1930–36 as our base, the ratio of agricultural to nonagricultural prices in 1957 was 0.97. By 1952 farm prices relative to industrial prices had fallen 30 percent from prewar levels (Lardy 1983: 102). In the 1950s relative agricultural prices never fully recovered to prewar levels (Jen 1958: 52). In other words, the manipulation of trade terms to the detriment of agriculture was one of the bulwarks of China's socialist original accumulation.

Between 1952 and 1957, Chinese industrial wages rose much more slowly than labor productivity. Nevertheless, the income advantage of industry over agriculture increased. Between 1952 and 1957, agricultural real income increased 18 percent, that is, at an average annual rate of 3 percent. During the same period, workers and employees in the state sector enjoyed a 32 percent increase in real income, or an average rise of 5.3 percent per year, nearly twice as fast as the growth of agricultural real income (table 4.13). The ratio of urban to rural personal incomes widened from about 1.8:1 in 1952 to 2.1:1 in 1957 (Lardy 1978: 179). It would grow substantially

Table 4.13

Indices of Retail Price, Real Wages, Labor Productivity, and Terms of Trade in China, 1952–57

Year	Agricultural terms of trade	Retail price†	Workers and employees		Agricultural labor	
			Real wages‡	Produc- tivity§	Real income‡	Produc- tivity‖
1952	100	100	100	100	100	100
1953	112	103	108	112	104	101
1954	114	106	110	117	105	101
1955	112	106	113	123	114	108
1956	116	106	129	138	117	111
1957	121	109	132	161	118	110

Real wages (income) is calculated from (nominal wage) ÷ (retail price index).
*Lardy (1978), p. 177.
†State Statistical Bureau (1960), p. 173.
‡State Statistical Bureau (1960), p. 216.
§Chen (1967), pp. 488–89.
‖Wong (1973), p. 263; State Statistical Bureau (1960), p. 129; Hou in Eckstein (1968), p. 345.

larger over the next twenty-five years.

In China as well as in Taiwan, the state suppressed agricultural income and industrial wages in order to secure and invest a high proportion of the surplus in industry. The same policies secured cheap food for urban workers, a precondition for a low-wage industrial policy. Agriculture and the countryside bore the primary burden of original accumulation and industrialization in both China and Taiwan in the 1950s.

Conclusion

The perspective of original accumulation provides a coherent framework for comparing Taiwan (1953–1960) and China (1952–1957) so as to cut through official rationalizations that emphasize, respectively, the values and institutions of the free market and of socialism. Our analysis suggests that in both instances of accelerated late industrialization the state restructured a preindustrial social formation that blocked accumulation and development. China's "socialist" industrialization and Taiwan's "capitalist" industrialization reveal important similarities in their initial stage, notably the elimination of landlord and tenant classes and the restructuring of rural social relations in ways conducive to state-led accumulation, laying foundations for state-directed industrialization, the curbing of market activity, and downward pressures on rural consumption. In both cases rapid accumulation directed toward industry was carried out during the period of investigation at the expense of the predominant agricultural population.

There are important differences between original capitalist accumulation and original socialist accumulation in Taiwan and China, of which collectivization and preferences for direct and indirect resource transfers stand out. However, we suggest that these differences are at least as much a product of the different levels of economic backwardness as they are of political-ideological preferences. This is not to deny the significance of social and political choices. It is to pay greater attention to the constraints imposed by economic backwardness that shapes the options employed in the process of economic development, particularly in the initial stage of industrialization.

5

INCOME INEQUALITY AND THE STATE
IN RURAL CHINA

A substantial literature credits the People's Republic of China with impressive gains in the reduction of inequality. Dwight Perkins (1978: 562), for example, observed that China has "clearly reduced intra-village income differentials in a major way; per capita differences of 2:1 from the richest to the poorest family are probably rare."[1] Similarly, Alexander Eckstein (1978: 102) noted evidence of both "a compression of average urban-rural income differentials" and "narrowing of income differentials . . . in the inter-regional distribution of income." Yet, at least until the early eighties, quantitative information about changing local, regional, and national patterns of income and inequality was at best scarce and highly selective. In light of the extensive development literature elucidating the tendency for both interhousehold and spatial inequalities to widen during early phases of development, and the extensive praise for Chinese reduction of inequality, with new data we can now more precisely gauge that performance.[2]

This chapter introduces microlevel data, reexamines interpretive frameworks, and proposes conceptual approaches toward the analysis of Chinese rural income and inequality in the years 1949–1979, prior to the contractual and market-oriented reforms in the 1980s. In focusing on the late 1970s, it provides benchmarks for comparing income distribution in the collective era with the results of subsequent contractual and other reforms. Discussion centers on two important components of rural income inequality and the impact of state policies and institutional change for redressing—or aggravating—them. These are local inequality, or the differentials among households in the same community or income-pooling unit; and spatial or geographic inequality among units, localities, and regions.

Income is an imperfect measure of inequality, and a full treatment of inequality issues would require analysis of many other factors, including differential access to power, nonmonetary sources of prestige and consumption, and the redistributive impact of state and community welfare systems. Nevertheless, even in a society such as China's, in which commodity production remains at a low level, substantial interchange takes place outside the market, and the roles of state and collective are powerful, income distribution provides one vital and measurable gauge of inequality and of the overall performance of the system.

Local Income Inequality

Wugong is a prosperous model village that has had considerable success in collective agriculture. Its per capita income places it among the richest villages in China. This is a position attained in part as a result of its early cooperative achievements, and in part due to the fact that it was selected as a model village in the 1950s and has since made judicious use of state subsidies and a number of other advantages. It is located in southeastern Hebei province in the poor Heilonggang region on the North China plain. In 1977 it had a population of 2,536, farming 243 hectares of land that were mostly in wheat. For administrative purposes, the total village constituted a single production brigade, and this brigade was then divided into three production teams, which were the effective units for collective farming and income sharing.

We have household survey data on income in two of these subunits. The most prosperous team in the village was team 3, consisting in 1977 of 998 people in 232 households. In 1977 team 3's average per capita income from all sources was 245 yuan and from collective sources 214 yuan. Team 2 was the poorest. Its 1977 per capita collective income was 137 yuan. Both did well by national standards, ranking comfortably within the top 10 percent of all teams, yet distinct differences in economic performance and income differentiated the two teams.[3] The per capita collective distributed income of team 3 exceeded that of its neighbors in team 2 by 56 percent despite comparable land endowments and the equalizing effects of income generated by a substantial brigade-level economy.

Sources of Local Inequality

With land reform in 1947 in this area, and then with the collectivization of agriculture in the mid–1950s, major sources of income inequality in the village were removed. Nevertheless, even with the elimination of all significant property-based inequalities as well as the loss of diverse off-farm sideline and commercial activities, some bases of income differentiation remain within the collective sector. Close analysis of the data reveals that the most significant of these was simply the number of able-bodied laborers one had in one's household. In Wugong as elsewhere in China after 1956, the collective farm (usually the team) continued to pay people in cash and in kind on the basis of workpoints according to how much each family member worked. In contrast to many other places, however, in Wugong these workpoints were only minimally differentiated by age, sex, or skill. While most men earned ten workpoints a day, in the late seventies women often earned nearly as much, getting nine to ten workpoints a day. Women earned fewer total workpoints each year primarily because they shouldered the main responsibility for family chores and could not work in the collective fields as much as men. Older men also did well in comparison to younger men, continuing to earn almost as much as younger men long after their strength had declined, so long as they continued to report for work in collective endeavors. All of these features contributed to narrowing income differentials among participants in the collective economy of the village.

Within each team I can nevertheless discern significant interhousehold income differentials. The principal variable is the ratio of income earners to total household population. Households with more children and retired parents to support consistently ranked among the lowest in per capita incomes. The most prosperous households were those with children in the 15–28 age bracket. Typically, these young people had finished school and joined the work force but continued to live at home and contribute their income to the household before getting married. Another group that did surprisingly well was households comprising old people with dependents left to support. There were twenty-one households in team 3 with two people over sixty and no one else to support. These twenty-one households received an average per capita income of 289 yuan per year, well above the team average of only 245 yuan.

Conversely, those village households that fared most poorly had many dependents and few able-bodied laborers. Households with many young, pre-school-age children are doubly hurt when the mother must stay home to tend them, thereby forfeiting her workpoints from the collective farm. (This village had no nursery in 1977.) Old people who cannot work but live alone also obviously have low incomes. The poorest person in team 3 was a woman in her seventies who lived alone and received a total annual income of only 37 yuan.[4] A primary source of income differentials in the village, then, is simply one's place in the family life cycle—what the Russian agronomist Chayanov referred to as demographic differentiation. Those at the beginning have too many young children and sometimes dependent parents or grandparents as well; those near the end may be able to earn no income of their own and must fall back on the support of their children and, in the last resort, on collective welfare payments. Those in the early-middle years of the life cycle with many able-bodied laborers still at home do the best. The cyclical character of this income pattern distinguishes contemporary rural China from many other developing nations in which major intra-village income differentials are the product of highly unequal access to land and other means of production.

The search for sources of income inequality in Wugong produces surprisingly few other important differentiating factors. Service in local village leadership and administrative roles produces no apparent income advantage. In team 3 in 1977, nineteen households had one or more members active as team leader, brigade secretary, commune leader, or external army officer. Among these nineteen households, per capita income averaged only 227 yuan, well below the team average of 245 yuan.

Another group that fared more poorly than expected was households with members working outside the village in state-sector jobs. In team 3, twenty-five households reported remittances of state salaries from parents or children working outside the village. They worked as military and state officials as well as technical and administrative specialists, teachers, and factory workers. These posts are coveted by village youth, and villagers with more education and political connections have a better chance of getting them. State-sector jobs bring secure monthly salaries with important fringe benefits, such as retirement pensions and health insurance, attached. And where a substantial portion of collective income is provided in kind, state jobs offer a coveted infusion of cash income. Nevertheless, assuming that the villagers were forthright in reporting remittances from these kin when we conducted the household survey, in most cases the household back in Wugong village did not reap great financial rewards from having jobholders in the state sector. The twenty-five team 3 households with state jobholders had average per capita incomes of only 238 yuan, slightly below the village average of 245 yuan. And unlike some other villages in which substantial income came from contract and temporary industrial labor or from private commercial activities, such income sources were absent in Wugong.

An example of one person who has been a leader and who has kin in state jobs illustrates the dominance of household life cycle position in incomes. Zhang Duan was the village party secretary for fifteen years before retiring in 1974 as a result of crippling illness. He heads a nine-member household that includes three party members and a PLA officer stationed in Beijing. A daughter-in-law holds the position of commune vice-secretary and a son works in a county textile factory. This household well illustrates how family connections can lead to better jobs. But at the time of our survey the family back in the village reaped few direct benefits in the form of income. With three young dependent children and neither Zhang Duan nor his wife earning income, the reported per capita income was only 82 yuan—one of the lowest in the team.

What do these income differences signify for prosperous and poorer households in a model village? The household survey discloses that as of 1978 the largest differences in consumption patterns centered on the size and quality of housing and possession of five consumer durables: bicycles, sewing machines, watches, clocks, and radios. Comparing the top and bottom deciles of per capita incomes, we find that by these measures households in the top decile were twice as well off as those in the bottom decile. The richest decile had 1.5 rooms and 1.2 items of the five consumer durables per person, whereas households in the poorest decile averaged just .77 rooms and .61 consumer durables per person. Other important differences in consumption patterns centered on the scale and style of weddings, funerals, and other important life cycle moments as well as a more varied diet and superior clothing. Income differences in Wugong at this time did not significantly affect issues of subsistence (due to egalitarian grain distribution and effective collective welfare policies), nor did they substantially affect the life opportunities for the next generation by assuring superior access to education, preferred jobs, or the ability to migrate to the cities.

Two other points should be noted. In poor villages, remittances from kin working outside the village may make a more significant difference in household incomes. But in this prosperous village, remittances from outside workers, including those on state payrolls, have not changed local income distribution that much. From the perspective of the great majority of villages with little land and abundant labor power, however, it is essential to place as many individuals as possible in jobs that produce incomes from the state and from other external sources.

The same point can be made about work in the private sector, including work on private plots and the selling of household handicrafts in peasant free markets. Both private income and salary remittances constituted only a small part of the income of team 3 in the late 1970s—13 percent, divided about equally between private-sector activities and remittances. This was a low figure compared to national figures at that time, and far below national figures in the eighties—in 1981 private-sector earnings constituted 38 percent and remittances and other miscellaneous earnings 10 percent of peasant incomes throughout China.[5] Nevertheless, the same principles probably hold. Households that send their members to work in the private sector or in state-sector jobs outside the village will have fewer members left to work on the collective farm. Thus the increase in alternate earnings will in part be offset by reduced collective farm earnings, notably in units with substantial collective earnings.

Table 5.1 records the distribution of income in team 3 according to a number of measures, including the proportion of village income earned by various income groups, the income ratio of the richest households compared to the poorest, and an overall measure of income inequality called a gini coefficient—a larger gini coefficient implies more inequality. This table shows, not surprisingly, that the distribution of total income per household is less equal than the distribution of per capita incomes. Some large households appear to be rich because they have more members at work. But because they must share this income among more dependents, many such households have relatively low per capita incomes.

Comparing the richest and poorest 10 percent of households shows the importance of the demographic factor in the pattern of per capita incomes in Wugong's team 3. The top 10 percent of households with mean per capita incomes of 427 yuan averaged just 2.8 household members. The bottom decile, which averaged 107 yuan per capita income, had an average of 4.5 members per household. To reiterate,

Table 5.1

Per Capita and Household Income Distribution in Team 3, Wugong Village, 1977 (percentages)

Indicator	Household collective income	Household total income	Per capita collective income	Per capita total income
Poorest 10%	2.6	3.0	3.4	4.3
Richest 10%	19.0	18.7	17.8	17.2
Poorest 20%	7.3	8.1	9.3	10.9
Richest 20%	34.5	33.5	31.8	30.7
Middle 60%	58.2	58.4	58.9	58.4
Poorest 40%	21.1	22.7	25.3	27.3
Decile ratio (richest: poorest 10%)	7.3:1	6.2:1	5.2:1	4.0:1
Gini coefficient	0.27	0.25	0.22	0.19

Source: 1978 household survey of team 3, Wugong Brigade.

the data strongly underline the cyclical pattern of income differentiation within the village in which neither sector (state or collective) nor occupation (agriculture, sideline industry, factory, cadre, or administrator) substantially affects household and per capita household income.

Table 5.1 shows that in this affluent team, extracollective sources of income have tended to moderate rather than exacerbate income inequality. It appears, then, that in Wugong households do trade collective for off-farm and private income, and that the overall effect of these alternate sources of income is either neutral or slightly equalizing in its consequences.

Many of these patterns, with respect to the demographic cycle and the equalizing effects of extracollective incomes, are not restricted to this one rich team in a model village. Data on an average-income team in Guangdong province show a comparable distribution. With an average per capita collective income of 71.6 yuan in 1978, team 12, Xintang brigade, Tangtang commune, was just below the national average of 74 yuan in that year (Griffin and Saith 1982: 175–79; Vermeer 1982: 20). Alternate private and off-farm sources of income constituted only 12 percent of household income, much as in Wugong. Table 5.2 displays the types of incomes just as in the previous table, only this time the overall measure of inequality is not the gini coefficient but the

Table 5.2

Income Distributions in a Rich and Average Team
(coefficients of variation)

Indicator	Household collective income	Household total income	Per capita collective income	Per capita total income
Rich team (Wugong, 1977)	.47	.43	.37	.35
Average team (Guangdong, 1978)	.50	.44	.43	.33

Sources: "Rich," Wugong data for 1977 from our survey. "Average team" data from 1978 report on 27 out of the 28 households in team 12, Xintang brigade, Tangtang commune, Guangdong province, as reported in Keith Griffin and Ashwani Saith, "The Pattern of Income Equality in Rural China," *Oxford Economic Papers* 34 (1982), p. 203.

Note: The coefficient of variation is the standard deviation divided by the mean income for each category of income distribution. It provides a measure of inequality analogous to the gini coefficient. Like the gini coefficient, a larger coefficient indicates greater inequality.

coefficient of variation, which behaves much the same way. By this measure, income inequality again declines steadily as one moves from left to right across the table, from household collective income to per capita total income. In other words, in both Wugong and this Guangdong team, alternate sources of income outside the collective sector moderate rather than exacerbate intrateam income inequality.[6] Indeed, the lion's share of household collective income inequality is the product of the demographic cycle. In this Guangdong village the top decile of households with mean collective incomes of approximately 130 yuan averaged 1.7 persons per household compared with the bottom decile with mean collective incomes of 45 yuan and 5.3 persons per household. More significant still, where the ratio of labor power to household size for the top decile was 1:1.0, for the bottom decile it was 1:4.0. In other words, the households with the lowest collective incomes had the largest number of mouths to feed per labor power (Nolan and White 1981: 4).

The Wugong and Xintang cases illustrate the proposition that the primary determinant of one's income relative to that of neighbors within the team is the stage in the household life cycle, with the ratio between labor power and dependents providing the crucial indicator of per capita household incomes. Stated differently, a substantial portion of the inequality witnessed at any one point in time is a transient inequality that will even out in the course of the life cycle as children become mature laborers earning good incomes and later marry and form their own households. When people become too old to support themselves, they must rely on their sons for support, and in the last resort on village welfare programs. In poorer villages the downswings in a household life cycle have been further cushioned by the collective (team), which would allow households to draw grain for subsistence even when they could not pay for that grain out of current income. The household thus incurred a debt to the team to support current consumption, a debt which in some cases might never be repaid. This leveling out of the effects of the household life cycle suggests that we should consider lifetime inequality rather than income inequality at a single point in time. And by such a standard of intravillage and particularly intrateam lifetime equality rural China appears to be very equal.

Comparisons of Local Inequality

Comparative data on villages in China and elsewhere help place income inequality in Wugong in context. For China itself, data on local inequality within a single collective unit exist not only for the two teams in Wugong and for Xintang but also for six other collective units of different times and in different places. This sample includes prosperous and middle-income communities located in wealthy and poor, mountain, plain, and suburban regions in six provinces in North, Northwest, Southeast, and Southwest China. Like most of the available data on rural China, the sample is nevertheless skewed toward well-to-do communities. In the total of nine units, only Lujiafu in Shandong, Fenghuan in Sichuan, and Xintang in Guangdong (discussed above) were close to the national average for rural incomes. All other units ranked in the top 20 percent of rural household incomes at the time they were surveyed. Several, including Wugong and Liulin, were exceptionally prosperous units in poor regions. In particular, this sample lacks data from hard-core poverty villages and from villages in frontier and minority areas.

Data are most consistently available on collectively distributed income—that is, income paid to each household by the collective (team) and excluding additional income from private endeavors or from work off the farm. The comparative data presented for eight units are not for per capita total earnings but for household earnings distributed by the collective (table 5.3). By our measures of inequality, the two teams in the village of Wugong are quite similar in most respects (columns 7, 8). Although the income ratio between the richest and poorest group differs significantly in teams 2 and 3, the overall degree of inequality captured in the gini coefficient is about the same in both units. The same is also true of Liulin and Xishan in earlier years. Though differing in some specifics, all four units have degrees of local inequality that are in a similar range with gini coefficients ranging from 0.26 to 0.29. A group of villages in our sample exhibits substantially more equal income distributions than those discussed above. They include the middle-income Shandong village Lujiafu and the two relatively prosperous Guangdong villages of Dongguan and Dianbai, with gini coefficients ranging between 0.16 and 0.17. The data now available cannot sustain the hypothesis that higher incomes correlate with greater intracollective income inequality (or the reverse). The sample suggests a plausible range within which estimates for income inequality in most Chinese communities may be expected to fall. Despite the small size of the sample, the internal consistency of the data and its mesh with what we know about rural income structures suggest that it provides a working guide to the range for income distribution in many Chinese rural communities in the era of collectivization from 1955 through the 1970s.

That even the most unequal villages in the sample are quite equal is indicated by comparison with income distribution data on Indian villages. Most available data from other countries aggregate local with regional inequalities into an overall measure of rural inequality. Such aggregate data preclude comparisons with the kinds of intravillage inequality data presented on China to this point. However, one study of eighty-four Indian villages does provide data on inequality structures within villages (Gartell 1981: 776). In that study, the average gini coefficient per village was 0.46, which is well above the 0.16–0.27 range observed in the China sample, indicative of much higher intravillage inequality in the Indian case.

There is reason to believe that most of the Indian differentials, and those in most other developing Third World capitalist nations, far from being overcome in the course of the life cycle, exhibit tendencies to remain or even to become exacerbated. These income inequalities are rooted above all in sharply differentiated access to ownership and control of land, which is frequently the primary source of employment, subsistence, and income (Castro et al. 1981: 402; Griffin 1979).[7] By contrast, China's land reform, followed by the collectivization of land,

Table 5.3

Collective Household Income Distribution in Selected Chinese Villages, 1955–1979 (percent)

Indicator	(1) Xishan Beijing, 1955	(2) Lujiafu Shandong, 1958	(3) Liulin Shaanxi, 1963	(4) Dongguan Guangdong, 1974	(5) Dianbai Guangdong, 1974	(6) Fenghuan Team 2 Sichuan, 1977	(7) Wugong Team 3 Hebei, 1977	(8) Wugong Team 2 1978
Poorest 10%	3	6	3	7	6	2	3	2
Richest 10%	19	16	24	16	16	21	19	21
Poorest 20%	10	13	7	14	14	7	7	7
Richest 20%	35	30	37	29	29	37	35	35
Middle 60%	55	57	56	57	57	56	58	58
Poorest 40%	24	29	22	20	31	18	21	22
Decile ratio	6.3:1	2.7:1	8.0:1	2.3:1	2.7:1	10.5:1	6.3:1	10:1
Gini coefficient	0.26	0.17	0.29	0.17	0.16	0.31	0.27	0.27
Per capita collective income	138	62	126	157	c.150	72	216	130

Sources: Columns 1–5, Marc Blecher, "Income Distribution in Small Chinese Rural Communities," *China Quarterly* 68 (1976):797–816. Column 6, Keith Griffin and Kimberley Griffin, "Institutional Change and Income Distribution in the Chinese Countryside," presented at the Conference on Development and Distribution in China, Hong Kong, March 14–17, 1983. Column 7, author's field research. Column 8, provided by Peter Nolan.

Notes: Xishan—a sample of 26 households in an advanced cooperative; Lujiafu—all 243 households with a per capita collective income of 62 yuan. Liulin—46 out of 50 households in two teams. Dongguan—a sample of 22 out of 98 households in a team. Dianbai—all households in a team. Fenghuan—31 out of 32 households. Wugong—all 232 households in team 3 and all 216 households in team 2.

large animals, and equipment, substantially reduced intravillage income inequality, and that pattern has persisted at least into the early eighties.

Spatial Inequality

To this point I have only examined income inequality within single villages or collective units. But in addition to this type of income inequality, major spatial inequalities exist among Chinese villages and regions. These have persisted and in some cases increased. The major efforts at rural transformation in the 1940s and the 1950s—land reform and collectivization—left essentially untouched large spatial inequalities among villages and regions that were rooted in ecological, demographic, and socioeconomic differences. In spite of this limitation, the changes associated with land reform did have a significant impact on incomes throughout the countryside. In a study comparing household income in the early 1930s and 1952, Charles Roll (1975: 35) found that the poorest peasants, the bottom 20 percent of households, almost doubled their income share from 6.0 to 11.3 percent between the 1930s and early 1950s (table 5.4). The gini coefficient measuring overall inequality decreased significantly. Equalizing resources within each village, then, had a significant impact on overall rural inequality. Roll concluded that 75 percent of the differences in per capita crop income were the product of interregional differences.

The reductions in income inequality were largely restricted to changes within single villages. Spatial inequalities remained. Following Li Chengrui's (1959: 60–63) classification of China into six regions by county per capita agricultural incomes, it is evident that in 1952 following land reform, former rich peasants in the poorest counties still earned less than poor peasants in middle-income counties, despite the fact that in the poor regions per capita rich-peasant income was still twice that of the poor peasants (Roll 1980: 75–76). (The class categories are based on landownership and income *prior* to land reform.) Conversely, poor-peasant per capita incomes in the richest counties (group one) were substantially higher than rich-peasant incomes in the poorest counties (groups four, five, and six). Average per capita incomes in the most prosperous counties were five times higher than those in the poorest. On the basis of Li's data, we can estimate 1952 per capita income of the top 10 percent of counties at 700–750 kilograms of unprocessed grain and the bottom 10 percent at 150–160 kilograms,

Table 5.4

Household Per Capita Rural Income Distribution in China, 1934 and 1952

	Percentage share 1930s	Percentage share 1952	Change in share
Richest 10%	24.4	21.6	−2.8
Richest 20%	42.0	35.0	−7.0
Upper-middle 20%	23.9	21.3	−2.6
Middle 20%	14.9	17.4	+2.5
Lower-middle 20%	13.2	15.0	+1.8
Poorest 20%	6.0	11.3	+5.3
Poorest 10%	2.5	5.1	+2.0
Decile ratio	9.8:1	4.2:1	
Gini coefficient	0.33	0.22	

Source: Charles Roll, *The Distribution of Rural Incomes in China: A Comparison of the 1930s and 1950s* (New York: Garland, 1980), p. 76; derived from Li Chengrui, *Zhonghua renmin gongheguo nongyeshui shigao* (Draft History of the Agricultural Tax in the People's Republic of China) (Beijing: Finance Publishing House, 1959), pp. 60–63.

giving a decile ratio in the range of 4.4–5.0:1. In short, some of the largest rural income inequalities remaining after land reform can be accounted for in spatial or geographical terms, in this case using the county as a unit.

These sorts of spatial differentials are shaped in large measure by ecological factors, including differential terrain, climate, soil quality, precipitation, and access to water, transportation, and urban markets. They are also conditioned by human social factors shaping local and regional developmental processes. Spatial differentiation in contemporary China takes the form of substantial differences in per capita income and opportunity among teams, brigades, communes, counties, and provinces; among mountain, plains, and suburban areas; between coastal and inland, industrialized and nonindustrial, Han and minority regions; and between city and countryside as well as between workers and peasants.[8] How have state policies impinged on these spatial factors?

Nicholas Lardy, who has conducted the most exhaustive analysis of China's regional inequality and redistributive policies, concluded that "the initiation of sustained growth of per capita GNP was accompanied by a simultaneous reduction of regional inequality" (1980: 167).[9]

Lardy documents substantial reductions of interprovincial inequality in domestic product and levels of industrialization. This result, in impressive contrast with the performance of most other nations in early stages of development, he tells us, was achieved by means of a leadership choice "to sacrifice some economic growth in return for achieving improved regional economic balance" (p. 171).[10] Whatever the validity of these conclusions, they rest on two kinds of data: provincial industrial output and interprovincial financial transfers. Lardy presents no significant evidence of reduced urban-rural or intrarural inequality.

Following Mao's 1956 discussion of "The Ten Major Relationships" and his calls during the Great Leap Forward and Cultural Revolution to eliminate "the three great differences," the Chinese leadership has repeatedly called for narrowing the urban-rural gap on behalf of the peasantry. Moreover, in maintaining low industrial wages, in shifting the terms of trade to the advantage of the countryside by raising state purchasing prices of agricultural commodities, and in diverse other ways, the Chinese state has periodically sought to narrow the gap.

Yet our attention is riveted on powerful countertendencies that have preserved or even exacerbated urban-rural and intrarural differentials at the level of both state policies and environmental constraints. Among the most striking features of Chinese rural development has been the official stress on self-reliance, with its favorable implications for units and regions that enjoy natural advantages such as level terrain, good soil, or access to water, sociopolitical advantages such as location in early liberated areas, technological-economic advantages such as a legacy of highly skilled agricultural and handicraft producers, and locational advantages such as proximity to cities or railroads.

A related approach, the emphasis on successful models, has also tended both to channel disproportionate state resources to a very small number of high-flying units and to serve as justification for not providing extensive subsidies to lagging units and poorer areas. Similarly, the transfer of sixteen million educated youth to rural areas from the mid-sixties on balance increased the burden for the already overpopulated countryside. Stated differently, the Chinese state has rejected certain obvious redistributive methods, including progressive taxation and direct subsidies to accelerate development in poor rural regions. Quite the contrary. China's tax policies have been consistently regressive, stimulating rapidly developing units while acting as a brake on the economic performance of those who lag behind. China has not developed social security or national health systems that might work to the advantage of poorer rural areas, nor for the most part has it earmarked special development funds for chronic poverty regions. And in imposing high rates of accumulation on the countryside, in siphoning off much of that accumulation to accelerate industrial growth, and, at least until the 1980s, in curbing such important sources of rural income as those associated with traditional sidelines, handicrafts, and marketing, the state has maintained a series of policies that favored the cities to the detriment of the countryside. Finally, when strategies emphasizing self-reliance and successful models are coupled with the formidable array of population controls that bar migration from poorer to more prosperous regions and from countryside to city, the result is not only to perpetuate but to reinforce spatial inequalities.[11]

Suzanne Paine (1981: 138) has observed that population controls can cut both ways: While the prevention of large-scale migration out of depressed areas tends to perpetuate spatial inequalities, the same policies prevent the drain of skilled labor from poorer regions, to which one may add the energies of youth and those with entrepreneurial and other creative impulses. Paine concludes that on balance the advantages in retaining skilled labor are decisive, and that compared with economies that permit free population movement, spatial inequalities will be relatively small. Population controls undoubtedly help to prevent the formation of the urban slums with their monumental problems of unemployment and marginalization common to most Third World nations. But under Chinese conditions of substantial and, at least until the late seventies, rapidly growing labor surplus in poorer rural regions, the principal effect of population control policies on rural income has been to reinforce intrarural and urban-rural spatial inequalities. Whereas more prosperous regions are in a favorable position to accumulate and absorb surplus labor in a wide range of sideline and industrial enterprises, many poorer regions lag behind and find it increasingly difficult to employ the growing numbers in the labor force. This pattern has been reinforced by such state policies as "taking grain as the key link" (to the detriment of animal husbandry, forestry, and commerce), which hit hill and mountain regions particularly hard.

The most important and least studied structural limits on spatial mobility since the early fifties have been the restriction of peasants to jobs and residence within their teams through a tightly controlled system of work and travel passes and rationing by *hukou* (official residence) of food, cloth, and other necessities. To state the matter starkly, the majority of Chinese people since the mid-fifties have been legally bound by the state for life to residence and collective labor within tiny production units, teams, typically comprising thirty to forty households (Blecher 1984).[12] The weight of this fact, properly understood, shapes much that has been distinctive of Chinese policy and practice at the height of the collective era, including issues of spatial inequality. Rural population control reinforces the fact that each cell— each team, brigade, and commune, which comprise the rural milieu—is a community of destiny that structures the life opportunities and incomes of member households and individuals and, if this argument is correct, works to the disadvantage of poorer and more remote communities.[13]

Chinese national survey data released in 1981 present a clear view of distribution of rural poverty and spatial inequality by county in the late seventies. In 1977, 515 counties had per capita collective distributed incomes below 50 yuan, the officially designated poverty line. And even with the 1979 bumper harvest and increased state purchasing prices, 221 of China's 2,300 counties, altogether 88 million people, had average per capita collective distributed incomes below 50 yuan during all three of the years 1977–79. These poverty-stricken counties, scattered throughout China, cluster heavily in hard-core poverty zones, including 71 in the low-lying saline-alkaline areas of the North China plain, 70 in the Yunnan-Guizhou plateau and mountain regions, and 48 in the dry Northwest loess plateau. Sichuan, which pioneered in expanding the household sector, reportedly led the way in the reduction of poverty counties with per capita collective incomes below 50 yuan from 39 in 1977 to just 3 in 1979. Large gains were also reported by a number of North China plain provinces: Shandong reduced poverty counties from 63 to 26; Hebei from 51 to 13. Others, however, registered little change in the years 1977 to 1979. In Gansu the number of poverty counties barely declined from 35 to 32, and in Guizhou it actually increased from 52 to 53.[14] The evidence underlines the fact that the national development strategy, which combined large-scale collectivized agriculture with heavy accumulation directed to heavy industry, bypassed large areas of the countryside in terms of the capacity to raise incomes.

Combined Rural Inequality

One need not be content with just speculating about the consequences of persistent poverty in some areas combined with growing prosperity in others, such as in rich delta plains and on the outskirts of major cities. In 1979 China's Ministry of Agriculture surveyed over five million rural collective units, or almost all of China's rural production teams. The published survey shows the distribution of average per capita collective incomes in these units at the end of the era of mobilizational collectivism. These data on spatial inequality can be combined with our data on local inequality throughout the nation. The methodological note at the end of this chapter details how these estimates were made.

For the purpose of these estimates, we assume that the distribution of private incomes, including remittances from urban kinsmen, is a more or less constant percentage of collective income. If this assumption produces any error in our estimates, we suspect it is to understate inequality, since teams near cities with higher incomes to begin with may well be more likely to sell to urban consumers and to have close kinsmen at work in town. Nevertheless, this possibility is not out of line with the conclusion that is to be drawn from this exercise anyway—that the Chinese countryside is relatively equal but not all that equal in comparison to some other developing societies.

The first estimate concerns per capita incomes. It uses for an estimate of local inequality the distribution of per capita total income from Wugong's team 3. This distribution was reported in abbreviated form in the last column of table 5.1. As already suggested, Wugong's distributions are not dissimilar to a number of other studies conducted throughout China. If anything, it may be toward the more unequal of the normal range of reported inequalities in a single team. But the distribution of per capita *total* family income is used here, including private-sector income and remittances from urban kin. Because this distribution is somewhat more equal than the distribution of collective incomes alone, the estimate is probably fairly representative of the situation prevailing throughout the Chinese countryside.

In the per capita estimate, deriving from the operations reported in the methodological note to this chapter, the richest 10 percent of all rural households get 25 percent of all income while the poorest 40 percent get 21 percent. The gini coefficient for this distribution is .31. How should these figures be assessed?

The raw figures might suggest greater inequality in 1979 than in 1952, when the data in table 5.4 were collected. But the two sets of figures cannot be directly compared. In preparing the figures in table

5.4, Roll had only very crude data on six regions to index spatial inequality, and local inequality was indexed only by differences among peasants by class origins. These sorts of crude categories tend to underestimate total inequality, giving lower estimates of inequality in 1952 than in 1979 even if actual inequality remained constant. Thus the reaction to the comparison between the 1979 estimate and that of 1952 may be either "Ho-hum, it's all in the methods," or "Aha, we were right. The failure to control spatial inequality has exacerbated overall inequality." A little of both reactions is called for. The change in methods for 1952 and 1979 overstates the worsening situation. But the changing pattern of spatial inequality also caused overall rural inequality conditions either to remain constant or actually to get worse over time.

Comparisons with other countries provide an additional way of assessing China's rural inequality in 1979. For this comparison data on total household income must be used—with the "total" here meaning the combined income from collective, private, and remittance sources. In this estimate, the richest 10 percent of all households get 28 percent of all income, while the poorest 40 percent get 16 percent. The gini coefficient is .37 (table 5.5).

By this standard, the Chinese countryside appears to be only modestly equal in comparison to many other developing societies. It is clearly more equal than the second group of Asian societies in table 5.5, and also more equal than most of the non-Asian developing countries. But it is less equal than most in the first group of Asian societies. In part the first group has less inequality because these countries are geographically smaller and have less geographic variability in climate and terrain.[15] But this only further substantiates the argument that it is spatial inequality in China that inhibits overall equality.[16]

This comparison, it should be noted, is only for current income. It leaves out important relative welfare aspects of these different societies. These welfare aspects include not only health and education, which are far more widely provided in China's countryside than in most other developing societies at comparable income levels, but also the provision of a basic consumption floor below which families are not allowed to fall. The Chinese state had serious problems in providing this floor out of state resources in many rural areas in the early sixties, and again in some places in the seventies. But thus far in the eighties the state has stepped in more frequently to provide grain to grain-deficit areas and even, in the case of severe drought and flood, has turned for the first time to the United Nations and other disaster relief agencies for aid (United Nations 1981; 1982). Another factor affecting rural in-

Table 5.5

Rural Income Inequality in China and Other Countries

	Percent income earned by:			
	Poorest 40%	Richest 20%	Richest 10%	Gini coefficient
China, 1979	16	44	28	0.37
Asian countries:				
Taiwan, 1972	22	39	24	0.29
Pakistan, 1970–71	22	39	24	0.30
S. Korea, 1971	21	39	23	0.31
Bangladesh, 1966–67	20	42	26	0.33
Sri Lanka, 1969–70	19	42	26	0.35
Philippines, 1971	17	47	32	0.39
Indonesia, 1976	16	46	32	0.40
Thailand, 1970	14	51	34	0.45
Malaysia, 1970	13	52	36	0.48
India, 1967	13	53	36	0.48
Non-Asian countries:				
Costa Rica, 1971	18	44	28	0.37
Mexico, 1963	13	55	38	0.48
Honduras, 1967	13	55	38	0.49

Sources: China—see appendix of this chapter. Other countries—Shail Jain, *Size Distribution of Income* (Washington, D.C.: International Bank for Reconstruction and Development, 1975). *Note*: Figures are the distribution of households by total household income.

equality is that for many years poor households have been able to draw subsistence rations even when they lack current income to pay for them. In many instances, debts incurred to the team were never paid back. This system has no counterpart in other poor Third World nations.

By these sorts of subsistence guarantees and other public services measures, then, China has been more equal—or has done better by its rural poor—than the figures in table 5.5 would suggest. Nevertheless, in many ways the figures also attest to a significant reality, as frequent reports in the press indicate. Those in chronic poverty-stricken areas have suffered severely in poor diets, clothing, housing, and other necessities as well as in access to education, culture, and other amenities relative to those in more amply provided regions.

What has happened since 1979? A 1984 report on Chinese survey results gives a first impression that will be surprising to many people but which fits some of the arguments in this chapter. With the increased emphasis on family farming, the gaps in income within any one village may well have increased—the reports of jealousy of rich members and the attempts to confiscate their resources in the initial years of the new agricultural policies support this suspicion. Yet it is certain that many poor households and regions have shared in the rural boom of the eighties. Moreover, allowing poor villages to shift into commercial crops and other products more appropriate to their locale has helped narrow the gap between some rich and poor locales even while the rich were prospering themselves.

Virtually all villages prospered between 1978 and 1983. Including earnings in off-farm activities, remittances from cities, and other miscellaneous sources of income, per capita rural income increased from an annual average of 134 yuan in the first year to 310 yuan in the last (see table 5.6).[17] There was a tremendous jump in the number of prosperous peasants—the percentage of families with a per capita income exceeding 400 yuan rose from less than one-half of a percent in 1978 to over 23 percent in 1984. But the poor profited as well—while one-third of all families had per capita incomes below 100 yuan in 1978, less than 2 percent were this poor in 1984. The net result, as measured by gini coefficients, was that overall income inequality declined steadily since 1978, from a high of .28 to a low of .22 in 1983.[18] With this increased equality China may well have moved toward the egalitarian countryside that many people long thought it to have. And these trends again suggest that in income distribution, things are not always what they seem.

Rapid growth in productivity and income since 1978 has occurred across the income spectrum, in poor as well as prosperous regions, and by poor as well as prosperous households, but as in the former period of high collectivism, the gains have not been shared equally. The appearance of highly visible prospering households has created a new source of tensions in some communities. But with many poorer households rising too, the available evidence does not support the view that intravillage or interregional income differentials have significantly increased in the reform era.

Methodological Note

The estimate of combined rural inequality starts with a 1979 survey of

Table 5.6

Distribution of Rural Households by Per Capita Income

Income groups (yuan)	1978	1979	1980	1981	1982	1983
100	33.3%	19.3%	9.8%	4.7%	2.7%	1.4%
100 –	31.7	24.2	24.7	14.9	8.1	6.2
150 –	17.6	29.0	27.1	23.0	16.0	13.1
200 –	15.0	20.4	25.3	34.8	37.0	32.9
300 –		5.0	8.6	14.4	20.8	22.9
400 –	2.4	1.5	2.9	5.0	8.7	11.6
500 +		0.6	1.6	3.2	6.7	11.9
	100.0%	100.0%	100.0%	100.0%	100.0%	100.0%
Average income	134	160	191	223	270	310
Gini coefficient	.28	.26	.25	.23	.22	.22
Sample size	34,961	58,153	88,090	101,998	142,286	165,131

Source: Gini coefficients estimated from the income figures, which are in *Brilliant 35 Years* (Beijing: China Statistical Publishing House, 1984).

collective income in almost all of China's five-million-plus rural production teams (table 5.7, columns a and b). This distribution is based
on the internal accounting prices of grain distributed in kind to the
members of each production team. In poor teams, which distribute
little cash income, that distribution looms much larger than in rich
teams. Because the internal distribution price is below the state purchase price of grain and other goods, rural income is overstated and
particularly so in poor teams. To correct for this we apply an estimate of
percent of income distributed in kind (column c) and then derive an
adjusted per capita income (column d) by the formula adjusted income
= per capita income + (percent in kind * per capita income * .27),
where .27 is the proportional understatement in price and * is the
multiplication sign. Another needed adjustment is for the size of a
team, which appears to increase in rich areas that can support more
population (column e). A rough estimate of team size (column e)
multiplied by the percent distribution of teams by income group (column b) gives a new estimate of the number of households in each spatial
income group (column f).

The next step in this estimation procedure is to enter columns d and f
from table 5.7 into the first and last columns of table 5.8. The first

Table 5.7

Distribution of Per Capita Collective Income Among Rural Production Teams, 1979

Income groups by average per capita income (yuan)	Percent of all teams	Percent income in kind	Adjusted per capita income	Households per team	Percentage of all households
(a)	(b)	(c)	(d)	(e)	(f)
350	2.3	0.20	369	40	3
200	5.3	0.35	219	40	6
120	17.2	0.50	136	32	17
85	18.2	0.65	100	32	18
60	29.8	0.80	73	32	29
45	19.1	0.95	57	32	19
35	8.2	1.00	44	32	8
84	100.1				100

Sources and derivations by column:
a, b) Ministry of Agriculture survey of almost all of China's 5 million plus rural production
    units as adapted in E. B. Vermeer, "Income Differentials in Rural China," *China Quarterly* 89 (1982):14.
c, e) Estimates.
d) a + (a * c * .27). An adjustment for the market value of income in kind.
f) (b * e)/(sum of b * e for the whole column).

column in table 5.8 provides the spatial dimension of the combined estimate. The last column has been divided by 10 to give the percentage of households in each of the ten interior cells. For example, in the first interior row, 3 percent of all teams earn an average income of 369 yuan. But these teams are divided internally among ten different income groups, each accounting for 0.3 percent of all households, and it is the income earned by each of these household groups that is shown in the interior of this table.

Before the per capita income earned by each of these groups is calculated, "local inequality" must be entered across the top of the table in the first row. The figures in this row are for collective per capita income in Wugong's team 3 as reported in table 5.1—only this time the figures are for decile (10 percent) income groups, arranged from poorest to richest 10 percent of all households and with their income expressed as a ratio relative to average team income. The top "local" row is then multiplied against the left "spatial" column to give the figures in each cell in the body of the table. For example, the adjusted

Table 5.8

Merging of Local and Spatial Inequality to Derive Total Per Capita Collective Income Inequality

Spatial inequality#	Local Inequality* (yuan per capita**)										Percentage households†
	.44	.66	.78	.84	.93	1.00	1.07	1.19	1.36	1.78	
369	162.3	243.5	287.7	309.9	343.1	368.9	394.7	439.0	501.7	641.9	0.3
219	96.3	144.5	170.7	183.9	203.6	218.9	234.2	260.5	297.7	380.9	0.6
136	59.9	89.9	106.2	114.4	126.7	136.2	145.7	162.1	185.2	237.0	1.7
100	44.0	65.9	77.9	83.9	92.9	99.9	106.9	118.9	135.9	173.9	1.8
73	32.1	48.2	56.9	61.3	67.9	73.0	78.1	86.8	99.2	127.0	2.9
57	24.9	37.3	44.1	47.5	52.6	56.5	60.5	67.3	76.9	98.4	1.9
44	19.6	29.3	34.7	37.3	41.3	44.5	47.6	52.9	60.5	77.3	0.8
Household members→‡	4.5	4.6	4.9	5.0	4.8	4.3	4.1	4.0	4.0	2.8	

*Row below is per capita total family income as ratio of the team average as determined in the Wugong survey. Families arranged from the poorest on left to richest on the right.

**Cells below derived by multiplying row above by average team income in far left-hand column.

†Percentage of households in each cell to the left of the given figure. Derived from table 5.1 and from the fact that each column represents 10 percent of all households in a village.

‡Average household membership for each income group in Wugong survey, with some rounding for unevenness in household size.

#The left-hand column is average per capita income per team as reported in table 5.1.

per capita income of 369 yuan at the left multiplied by the ratio .44 at the top gives the upper left cell in the body of the table of 162.3 yuan per year for the poorest peasants within the richest group of production teams. The far right-hand column gives the additional information that this poorest-of-the-richest group of households constitutes 0.3 percent of all peasant households.

Overall, the poorest families tend to be at the bottom left of the interior cells of this table and the richest at the top right part of the table. This ordering by per capita income provides a means of rearranging the families sequentially from poorest to richest. With this ordering, we construct two columns of figures, containing figures for seventy household groups arranged from poorest to richest—these columns are not shown here. The first column gives the total income earned by each household group. It is calculated by multiplying the per capita income of the group by its average household size (as given in the last row of table 5.8) and by the size of the group (as given in the last column). Smaller households have higher *per capita* incomes because they share income with fewer children and retired old people. The percentage of households shown in the right column is for each cell in its row—the percentage is constant among the cells in each row because each column represents precisely 10 percent of all village households.

The second column used in the final calculating step is simply the percentage of households in each group—that is, the figure from the right-hand column of table 5.8. This column, summed from top to bottom, gives the poorest 10 percent of all households, the poorest 20 percent of all households, and so on up to 100 percent of all households. Comparisons of this cumulative column with a similar summing and subsequent percentaging of the left calculating column gives the percentage of total income earned by each successive percentile of households. The gini coefficient is calculated from the same two column.

These are the steps in computing the distribution of per capita incomes in the countryside. The steps in computing the distribution of total family incomes are similar, except that the first row of table 5.8 is for total family income and the last row for family membership has a rather different progression of figures in it. The internal cells are for total family income, and they are calculated by multiplying the left-hand column by the top row of ratios and by family membership.

6

CITY VERSUS COUNTRYSIDE?
THE SOCIAL CONSEQUENCES OF
DEVELOPMENT CHOICES IN CHINA

The antagonism of town and country can only exist as a result of private property. It is the most crass expression of the individual under the division of labor, under a definite activity forced upon him—a subjection which makes one man into a restricted town-animal, the other into a restricted country-animal, and daily creates anew the conflict between their interests.

Marx and Engels, *The German Ideology*

In a socialist society there are still conservative strata and something like "vested interest groups." There still remain differences between mental and manual labor, city and countryside, worker and peasant. Although these are not antagonistic contradictions they cannot be resolved without struggle.

Mao Zedong, Reading Notes on
the Soviet Text *Political Economy*

In the initial stages of socialist transitions the party-state and a coalition of revolutionary classes characteristically eradicate the dominant property-based class divisions between landlord and tenant and between capitalist and industrial worker. In the course of state appropriation of industry and commerce and collectivization of agriculture the largest remaining concentrations of private wealth and power are further reduced. These changes eliminate forms of inequality embedded in the private ownership of property and the ability of property owners to appropriate the labor of producing classes.

However, multiple systems of ownership and attendant production relations (state, cooperative, collective, and private), urban-rural and other sectoral and spatial cleavages, hierarchies of income and power, as well as divisions of labor, survive these changes. Indeed, we observe not only the continued existence of residual sectoral and spatial hierarchies of wealth and power, but the emergence of *new* patterns of inequality, hierarchy, status, and domination that are the direct consequence of specific institutional and developmental priorities of socialist states.

Marx and Engels to the contrary, the town-country antagonism—and that between industry and agriculture—far from inevitably disappearing with the demise of private property, may actually be exacerbated in the initial stages of development of socialist societies. Whereas the market characteristically plays the leading role and the state a secondary role in defining sectoral and class relations in capitalist societies, socialist states have officially sanctioned, reified, and enforced clearcut sectoral divisions in societies in which ownership and control of wealth has passed from individuals to the state and to the collective units it creates and directs. The formalization of divisions between the state and collective sectors, paralleling the historic urban-rural and industrial-agricultural divide, reinforces intersectoral positions. The nature, depth, and hierarchical character of the divide, and its subsequent growth or diminution, however, vary from state to state depending on the specific weight of city and countryside, industry and agriculture, advanced and primitive technology, and the outcome of state-society conflicts.

China offers a particularly fascinating vantage for studying the issues. This chapter reassesses the widely held view, given its purest expression in the work of Samir Amin (1983), that the political economy of the People's Republic of China is distinguished in essence from that of the Soviet Union (and other socialist societies) by a pro-peasant policy that effectively narrowed the city-countryside and worker-peasant gap and made China "undoubtedly the most egalitarian society in the world" (Amin 1983: 59).[1] Recently Amin has suggested that appropriate delinking, making use of "the law of value from a national base and with a popular content," can assure "that the net product of society . . . will be shared equally between rural and urban populations in proportion to their contribution in the quantity of labor" (1987: 437). For Amin, China is the prime example of a nation pursuing such a course of equity for its rural population, a judgment applied particularly, but not exclusively, to the Mao period.

Among twentieth-century leaders, Mao Zedong most persistently drew attention to problems associated with urban-rural and industrial-agricultural inequality. Moreover, he promoted social movements and implemented far-reaching state programs whose explicit goals included reducing and eliminating urban-rural inequalities, both those inherited and some that were the product of the socialist transition. This chapter traces and critically assesses the changing character of city-countryside and state-sector cleavages in China from land reform and collectivization to the post-Mao reforms of the 1980s.

Sectoral Differentiation in the Era of Mobilizational Collectivism (1955–1980)

The events of 1955–56, notably the accelerated nationalization of industry and commerce and the collectivization of agriculture, set in place the main elements of the socioeconomic structure of socialist China including urban-rural and state-collective sectoral divisions (table 6.1). With collectivization and the restriction of private markets, ownership and control of the land, agricultural labor, marketing, and distribution passed from peasant households and small cooperatives to large state-directed collectives. Mirroring Soviet practice in this and other essential respects, the collectivized peasantry was given the right to cultivate small household plots limited to about 5 percent of village land. Subsequent state-society rural conflict during the Mao period, little noted because it took the form of quiet resistance with no manifestoes or organization, and rare violent confrontation, pivoted around state attempts to universalize collective and state spheres and pressures from below to expand the scope of the household and market economy.[2]

The schematic representation of the central sectoral divide in China during the collective era, emphasizing the distinction between urban:state and rural:collective sectors, encompasses more than 90 percent of the population, excluding only the small urban collective sector, a miniscule private sector in both urban and rural areas, and several million state farm workers. Table 6.2 provides an employment profile setting off the small but growing state sector centered in the cities against the mass of the collectivized rural population and a small but growing urban collective sector.

China's extensive industrial growth and the expansion of the state administrative apparatus made possible an increase in state employees from 8 percent of the work force in the early years of the People's Republic to 13 percent in the early 1960s and 19 percent by the early

Table 6.1

Sector and Stratification in the Era of Mobilizational Collectivism (1955–1980)

Sector (ownership)	Managerial principle	Form of labor	Income generation		Income distribution	
			Means	Mode	Source	Benefits
State (urban)	Centralized state administration	State wage labor/Contract and temporary labor	Industry Commerce Administration Other state functions	Mechanical power	State wage in cash	State health insurance, pension, subsidies
Collective/ Household (rural)	Collective administration/ Household management of private plot	Collective/ Household/ Contract/ Temporary	Agriculture Small industry Crafts Trade	Hand and animal power	Share of collective income based on workpoints (mainly in kind)/Income from house- hold production	Collective welfare benefits

Note: Where items are separated by a slash (/) the first item is primary.

Table 6.2

Changing Sectoral Patterns in the Chinese Labor Force (1953–1985)

Year	State-sector employees	Self-employed in urban areas	Collective employees in urban areas	Collective and private producers in rural areas	Total labor force
1953–57	20,980,000 (9.3)	4,800,000 (2.1)	3,220,000 (1.4)	195,630,000 (87.1)	224,630,000
1958–60	47,120,000 (18.0)	1,230,000 (0.5)	7,670,000 (2.9)	206,150,000 (79.6)	262,180,000
1961–65	35,950,000 (13.4)	2,020,000 (0.8)	8,700,000 (3.2)	218,390,000 (81.2)	269,090,000
1966–70	42,470,000 (13.3)	1,260,000 (0.4)	13,400,000 (4.2)	260,930,000 (81.4)	320,380,000
1971–75	58,240,000 (15.9)	520,000 (0.1)	15,980,000 (4.4)	288,460,000 (78.5)	367,330,000
1976–80	74,440,000 (18.6)	320,000 (...)	20,950,000 (5.2)	305,370,000 (76.1)	401,110,000
1981–85	86,800,000 (18.7)	1,560,000 (0.6)	29,006,000 (6.3)	344,392,000 (74.4)	462,920,000

Source: State Statistical Bureau (1986:92).

Notes: Figures in parentheses are percentages.

Totals do not add up to 100 due to rounding.

State-sector employees, while predominantly working in the cities, include workers on state farms and party and government officials stationed at the commune and higher levels in the countryside.

Available statistics on the rural labor force after 1955 do not distinguish individual from collective workers; thereafter virtually all rural labor is collective labor with the exception of state farm workers included under state sector.

1980s. Agriculture, which accounted for 64 percent of the gross output value of agriculture and industry in 1952, accounted for just one-third of the total by the early 1980s. As in the early 1950s, however, more than 80 percent of the population continued to live in the countryside and the collectivized rural work force comprised 75 percent of the total work force; an additional 5 percent worked in urban collectives (State Statistical Bureau 1985: 147, 213, 224).

Three features of this sectoral pattern conflict with widely held interpretations of China's development trajectory. First, contrary to the assumptions of Amin and others, substantial economic, mobility, status, and security advantages of the state (urban) sector over the collective countryside not only were present at the creation of the system in the mid-1950s, when China closely followed Soviet practice, but grew substantially in the subsequent decades of mobilizational collectivism. Second, the state forged elaborate institutional mechanisms to formalize, maintain, and police intersectoral as well as certain intrasectoral positions. These mechanisms of residential control and centralized labor and resource allocation, the source of continuing conflicts in Chinese society, made it possible to stem and even reverse the substantial flow of population from the countryside to the cities in the 1950s. Indeed, in the years 1960–1976 the Chinese state presided over an historically unprecedented urban-to-rural net migration of forty-eight million people (Kirkby 1985: 107, 114; Chan and Xu 1985: 597, 603).[3] Third, the state systematically siphoned resources from the poorer collective sector to the state sector to finance urban heavy industry and to support a growing administrative apparatus. This intersectoral resource transfer, principally executed through compulsory crop sales at low state prices, combined with an investment pattern emphasizing heavy industry, constitutes the heart of China's original accumulation and the crystallization of intersectoral hierarchy (chapter 4).[4]

The Primacy of the State

China's revolution came to power on the basis of rural strength, and few if any twentieth-century leaders have attached greater importance to the peasantry than Mao Zedong. Yet beginning with the attempted construction of socialist institutions and the developmental drive associated with the First Five-Year Plan, and continuing over subsequent decades, China embarked on a course of development and sectoral differentiation that subordinated agriculture and the collective countryside to the state's industrial, military, and urban priorities. Between 1952 and the late 1970s, fixed assets per industrial worker rose from 3,000 yuan for five million workers to nearly 9,000 yuan for fifty million workers. By contrast, in the late 1970s, there were just 30 yuan of fixed assets per rural worker (the value of the land is excluded in Chinese calculations), one-thirtieth of those for industrial workers (Yang and Li 1980: 207; Perkins and Yusuf 1984: 16). Three decades of concentrated state investment in industry enabled industrial growth to far outstrip growth in agriculture. This imbalance in state investment priorities is also mirrored in the relative income and welfare patterns established in the two sectors to the advantage of industry and the detriment of agriculture.

In Republican China, per capita urban income and consumption did not substantially exceed rural levels, a pattern consistent with labor surplus and extensive rural-urban and interregional seasonal and long-term migration. Estimates range from Charles Roll's calculation that in the 1930s rural consumption levels were as high as 81 to 88 percent of urban levels, to calculations of differentials in the range of 1.5–2.0:1. These relatively narrow income differentials were sustained, but not significantly widened, in the early 1950s as income and consumption rose in both urban and rural areas. As late as 1955, Roll (1980: 117, 119) concludes, per capita rural consumption was as high as 87 percent of urban levels. Analyses by Thomas Rawski and the World Bank suggest 1955 differentials no higher than 2:1 (Rawski 1982).[5]

In 1955–56, however, collectivization of agriculture and nationalization of industry, followed by virtual state monopoly over the bulk of marketing activity and the closing of opportunities for urban migration, formalized and deepened the bifurcation between the urban state sector and the rural collective sector.

From the mid-1950s forward the gap in income and benefits grew significantly in favor of the state over the collective sector and the city over the countryside as the fluid conditions of population movement which tended to narrow differentials disappeared and the state curbed important sources of rural labor mobility and income, including household marketing and sideline enterprise. State workers won the eight-hour day, lifetime employment, early retirement (age sixty for men, fifty or fifty-five for women), generous pensions by the standards of poor countries, with retirement pay set at 70–80 percent of salary, free health care, and heavily subsidized housing and food.[6] These extraordinary gains for state-sector workers were made possible by the combination of state direction of the commanding levers of the economy, the reduction of competitive pressures as a result of China's "delinking" from the capitalist world economy, and official priorities systematically favoring the state sector over the collective countryside. Implementing core elements of the Soviet system, China initiated comprehensive and costly wage and benefit packages *in the state sector*. Collectivized rural producers, dependent on self-financed village welfare programs, enjoyed none of these benefits and labored for a fraction of the income of state-sector workers.[7]

This two-tier system extended to education as well. The Chinese state not only financed superior urban schools, with virtually all key-point or high-level schools in cities, but it bore the full cost of urban education while rural communities were enjoined to pay the cost of schools and teachers with only modest state subsidies. Nor did the countryside secure these or comparable benefits in subsequent decades (Eberstadt 1986: 313–16).

The character and size of the subsidies provided uniquely to state-sector workers and their families well illustrate the pattern of sectoral differentiation. By 1978 these subsidies averaged 526 yuan per state worker, 82 percent of the average nominal wage, and accounted for 13 percent of national income. The most important subsidy, which kept urban food prices low while state purchasing prices increased, was for grain and edible oil. In 1978 this subsidy alone averaged 180 yuan per worker. There were also substantial state subsidies for housing, health care, retirement, disability, maternity, and other benefits as well as fuel, transportation, and annual vacation benefits for those working far from home. By contrast, Nicholas Lardy (1983b) has estimated that the total package of price subsidies and fringe benefits for the collective peasantry was less than 10 yuan per person.

To be sure, China's low-wage/low-consumption policy was applied to industry and the state sector as well as to the countryside. Industrial wages stagnated for two decades following the 1956 wage hike. With the entry of new workers at the lower end of the scale after 1957, average real wages actually dropped 17 percent between 1957 and 1977 (Riskin 1987: 263). Nevertheless, real per capita income of state-sector workers, and their advantages over those in the collective sector, continued to grow. One reason has already been suggested: Hidden subsidies continued to multiply throughout these decades (Lardy 1983b).[8]

Another important source of increased differentiation in per capita incomes between state- and collective-sector workers was the steady increase in labor force participation rates, principally the growing numbers of working women. This increased per capita family income and reduced dependency ratios for state employees. In 1957 each urban wage earner supported 3.29 dependents. By 1978 the dependency ratio had dropped to 2.06 and in 1983 each worker supported just 1.71 dependents. Between 1957 and 1980 the urban labor force participation rate rose from 30 to 55 percent of the urban population (Lu Dong 1984; Riskin 1987: 263).[9]

Comparable tendencies were at work in the countryside, but with different outcomes. Tens of millions of additional rural workers were mobilized for collective farm work during the same period, and the number of collective labor days continued to expand with capital construction in the slack agricultural seasons. But with low marginal productivity and high disguised unemployment, rigorous controls on grain distribution and consumption, high rates of accumulation and state extraction of the rural surplus, and with soaring production costs associated with electrification, mechanization, and expanded use of chemical fertilizers and pesticides, rural per capita income and consumption stagnated over the entire collective era.[10]

The issue was not only income. In the countryside, as a result of policies curbing the market and the household sector, *cash* income declined even further. In some poorer rural units from the Great Leap Forward and continuing for two decades thereafter, cash virtually disappeared, forcing people to live almost entirely on income in kind derived from collective production.

Official data on staff wages in different branches of the state sector reveal both the advantages of the state sector over the collective and the ways in which urban-industrial priorities worked to the detriment of those employed in agriculture. In the years 1953–57 the average wage of state workers in agriculture, forestry, water conservancy and meteorology was 470 yuan, while industrial workers had incomes of 627 yuan, one-third higher. By 1971–75, agriculture was the only category in which per capita incomes had actually dropped (to 456 yuan), while industrial wages had increased slightly (to 643 yuan) (State Statistical Bureau 1985: 409).[11] In the early 1950s state-sector income in categories such as commerce, science, culture, education, and public health was roughly comparable to that in agriculture. By the 1970s, all of these were far ahead of agriculture. In short, within the state sector, those employed in agriculture fared poorly in both absolute and relative terms.[12] Within the parameters of a national low-wage policy, China's state-sector workers enjoyed a privileged position as did nonagricultural employees within it.

In sum, the long-term trend was a considerable widening of urban-rural and state-collective income and welfare differentials from the mid-1950s to the late 1970s. The World Bank (1983 Annex A: 175), excluding the considerable value of subsidies to the state sector, estimated the 1979 urban-rural income gap at 2.2 to 1. Thomas Rawski (1982: 12–26) has calculated the gap at 3.4 to 1 excluding subsidies and as high as 5.9 to 1 with subsidies included. Carl Riskin (1987: 240–42) suggests that the differential is no less than 2.5 or 3:1 (with subsidies). Dwight Perkins and Shahid Yusuf (984: 125–27) report an increase in the income gap from 3.9:1 in 1957 to 4.9:1 in 1979. My own estimates, including subsidies to the state sector, are in the range of 4 to 5:1. By virtually every measure, whether that of relative income of 3 to 6:1, status, mobility, educational opportunity, even cultural patterns, the urban-rural and state-collective intersectoral gap widened in the course of two decades of mobilizational collectivism to the detriment of the countryside and rural people.[13]

In addition to this relative decline, following the real gains of the land reform and recovery years of the early 1950s, the countryside experienced a long-term absolute decline in food availability. Per capita grain consumption in the rural areas fell from 197.1 kilograms in the years 1953–57 to 188.7 kilograms in the years 1976–78; at the same time edible oil consumption was reduced from 2.3 to 1.6 kilograms and many traditional goods disappeared from the market (Wang 1985: 416).[14] Many rural communities experienced significant loss of income from handicrafts, sidelines, commercial crops, and the market as a result of state policies proscribing these activities as antisocialist and restricting much of rural economic life to grain production in the name of self-sufficiency. Despite major advances in irrigation and fertilizer production and high rates of accumulation, during two decades of mobilizational collectivism, curbing of the market, and grain-first policies (1955–77), annual growth rates in grain yield were just 1.8 percent. This rate exceeded population growth by just 0.2 percent (World Bank 1983: 169–72; Riskin 1987: 293). Per capita rural income and food consumption, which plummeted sharply in the years 1959–60, did not regain the levels achieved at the start of the collective period in 1955 until the late 1970s. As late as 1978–80 per capita grain output in eleven provinces remained below 1955–57 levels.[15]

These facts may be viewed from two perspectives. First, for a substantial majority of the collectivized peasantry, two decades of high accumulation, labor expenditure, and political turmoil brought few tangible economic gains. Many experienced losses in such areas as the shriveling of markets, the loss of sideline and off-farm income, declining food availability, and restrictions on treasured cultural norms ranging from marriage and burial customs to the enjoyment of traditional festivals. All of this increased the attractiveness of the city, industry, and the state sector and increased the weight of the burden on the peasantry. Second, a substantial minority, which I estimate at roughly one-third of the rural population, experienced net declines in per capita income and consumption following collectivization or lived at income levels comparable to those that existed prior to the founding of the People's Republic. Declining and stagnant areas included many traditional hard-core poverty zones, mountain and hill regions, areas remote from modern transport or cities, as well as localities whose livelihood had traditionally hinged on income from marketing, sideline enterprise, commercial crops, animal husbandry, and so forth, occupations restricted by the state during these decades. Even in those localities that experienced significant income gains, including most suburban areas, villages close to modern transport, and model villages and districts, many former owner cultivators, the substantial group of "middle peasants," experienced few if any income gains.

Any evaluation of inter- and intrasectoral inequalities must be weighed against social and economic achievements which include significant gains in life expectancy, nutrition, and the reduction of illiteracy and communicable diseases in the decades following land reform and substantial growth rates since the mid–1960s. China's life expectancy, according to the World Bank, increased from thirty-two years in 1950 to sixty in 1975 and sixty-nine years in 1982. While this performance must be set against the immense toll of the Great Leap famine (life expectancy dropped by half between 1957 and 1960) and the violent dislocations of the Cultural Revolution, in a single generation China attained life expectancy levels far above those of virtually all low-income countries and comparable to those of many developed countries (World Bank 1984: 3, 113).[16] Comparison with India, Indonesia, and other societies in which substantial landless and land poor rural populations suffer extreme privation and insecurity highlights Chinese achievements in assuring subsistence and basic welfare for the great majority (table 6.3).

In assessing China's gains we note the perpetuation and even intensi-

Table 6.3

GNP and Welfare Indicators in China and Other Large Low-Income Countries

Country	GNP per person (US$) (1985)	Average annual GNP growth (1965–85)	Life expectancy at birth (1984)	Infant mortality rate per thousand (1984)	Calories per person (1983)	Calories as % of requirement (1983)
China	310	4.8	69	36	2,620	111
India	270	1.7	56	90	2,115	96
Pakistan	380	2.6	51	116	2,205	95
Bangladesh	144	0.4	50	124	1,864	81
Indonesia*	530	4.8	55	97	2,380	110
Low-income countries	270	2.9	60	72	2,336	102

*Indonesia, as a significant oil exporter, is included by the World Bank among middle-income countries.
Source: World Bank, World Development Report 1986, World Development Report 1987, pp. 203-204, 258-59.

fication of significant urban-rural differences in health, nutrition, education, life expectancy, and living standards. In 1975 China's urban life expectancy of seventy-two years compared with fifty-seven years in rural China. A national survey revealed that while 3 percent of seven-year-old boys were nutritionally stunted in 1979, the figure was 13 percent for rural areas, and in Sichuan province as many as 37 percent of rural boys were stunted (World Bank 1984). A 1982 Ministry of Public Health survey estimated infant mortality at 13.2 per thousand in cities and 27.2 in the countryside. By the 1980s, the per capita availability of salaried health workers in the cities was 3.5 times that in the countryside; and 1981 urban medical expenditures of 32.5 yuan per person compared with 9.6 yuan in the rural areas (Eberstadt 1986: 271, 193–97). These figures reflect substantial gains for both countryside and city. The data nevertheless show that state health resources too have been (and continue to be) disproportionately allocated to the urban sector long after Mao Zedong's 1965 call for redress of the imbalance.

While income and nutritional levels in China's cities are among the most homogeneous in the world, rural averages conceal quite substantial intrarural inequalities of income and services. In 1976, the year of Mao's death, one-fourth of all teams (24.2 percent) had per capita distributed yearly collective incomes below 40 yuan, the state's official hard-core poverty level, and an additional 18.6 percent were under 50 yuan. In the years 1977–79, 221 counties with a population of 88 million people had per capita collective distributed incomes below 50 yuan in all three years. Virtually all of the households in these localities had no cash income. By 1980 China's rural poor consisted of roughly 100 million people living on per capita annual grain rations of less than 150 kilograms, providing caloric levels of barely 1,500 calories. Many of these people lived in remote hill and mountain areas where their livelihood had barely improved since land reform. [17]

This discussion points to a wide gap between official pronouncements and the reality of intersectoral differentiation in which rural collectives, particularly the poorest, have been virtually bereft of state support. The weakest units and individuals confronted endemic poverty from a position of vulnerability, with the state foreclosing such traditional escape routes as migration.

The divisions between state and collective and between city and countryside, as well as the choice of state investment and welfare priorities, produced or enlarged wide inter- and intrasectoral cleavages. The rural poor, who were primary beneficiaries of the redistributive land reform and whose interests were protected in the initial phases of mutual aid and cooperation, were among the victims of the extreme collectivist, antimarket, grain-first, and class struggle policies proclaimed in their name in the era of mobilizational collectivism and carried to their destructive limits during the Great Leap Forward and Cultural Revolution. To better understand this paradox, I turn to an examination of the institutional fabric of China's sectoral differentiation.

The Institutional Fabric of Sectoral Differentiation

In 1955, coinciding with collectivization, the Chinese state implemented a nationwide system of population registration (*hukou*). Following the frenetic migration to the cities during the Great Leap Forward (the urban population increased from 99 million in 1957 to 131 million in 1960) and the subsequent economic crash, the state effectively barred collective members from migrating to the cities (Kirkby 1985; Chan and Xu 1985). The population registration and control system is the central institutional mechanism defining sectoral differentiation and restricting inter- and intrasectoral mobility. Following the economic crash of the early 1960s, the gap between the state and the collective sector widened as access to state-sector jobs and regular urban work of any kind was virtually closed for rural collective members. In the early 1960s, for the first and only time in the history of the People's Republic, not even state jobs were secure. In the years 1961–64 the state responded to nationwide famine and the budget crisis by laying off twenty million state workers and sending them back to the countryside, including both recent migrants to the city and many who had been employed for a decade or more. These workers lost not only their jobs on the state payroll, but their urban residence permits as well. Most were permanently consigned to the countryside. The burden of assuring their subsistence shifted from the state to the collective and their rural communities.[18] From the early 1960s sectoral position became irrevocable. More precisely, one could change residence or accept a job at a lower point in the locational and sectoral hierarchy in which large nationally administered cities were at the pinnacle, but it was virtually impossible to move to a higher position in that hierarchy.

From the 1960s even the children of urban state-sector personnel faced extreme difficulty in obtaining state jobs and retaining urban residence. The persistent job shortage in the state sector, intensified by the cresting wave of urban youth entering the job market from the late 1960s, was a critical factor that led the state to send seventeen million urban high school and junior high school graduates to settle permanently in the countryside in the decade after 1966.[19] The layoffs of workers in the early 1960s and the "downward" transfer of urban youth to the countryside dramatically reinforced the urban-rural and state-collective divide, a divide, as the peasants described it, between those who ate the state's grain and those who grew their own. Faced with economic, demographic, and employment crises, the state transferred the fiscal burden to the countryside and the collective.[20]

The registration system, in conjunction with elaborate rationing mechanisms that restricted food purchases in the cities to those with urban registrations, and tight restrictions on jobs and housing, froze and formalized sectoral positions. Most individuals were confined to residence and work in the village of their birth or, in the case of women, the residence of their husband. The registration system created a nationwide locational hierarchy with Beijing, Shanghai, and Tianjin at the apex, provincially administered and smaller cities in the middle, and the poorest rural areas at the base. This paralleled and interlocked with the twenty-four or more graded state-sector hierarchies established for different professions including industrial workers (an eight-grade scale), state cadres (twenty-six grades), and college teachers (thirteen grades) (Korzec and White 1983: 251). Collective members, urban as well as rural, virtually alone were ungraded at the bottom of the hierarchy.

The consequences of the registration system were far-reaching and multifaceted. It virtually barred relocation of rural people coveting the benefits associated with urban status and state jobs as well as controlling traditional flows of seasonal job seekers and even beggars fleeing famine. As every foreign visitor notes, China's cities did not experience the familiar Third World syndrome of marginalized, unemployed, and homeless masses of workers and the proliferation of people living by petty peddling, begging, or crime. The other side of the coin, however, is that severe poverty was effectively confined to the rural periphery. The effects of the registration system were not restricted to mediating the urban-rural divide. It also prevented intrarural migration from chronic poverty regions or areas suffering natural or social disasters, thereby eliminating a traditional safety valve in time of famine.[21] The registration system and associated state controls on jobs, housing, rations, and travel made possible the widening urban-rural and intrarural spatial inequalities of income and opportunity.

The household registration system permitted one important exception to the restriction of peasants within their home village: By the 1970s there were more than ten million temporary or contract workers. These rural residents, whose families were required to live, work, and go to school in their native villages, hold industrial and construction jobs in city or countryside, often working side by side with state-sector workers. Temporary and contract workers, including many on the job for years or even decades at a time, receive a fraction of the salaries of state workers for the identical work or for doing the hardest, dirtiest jobs. Contract workers do not enjoy the retirement, health, and other benefits associated with state-sector jobs, and, unlike regular workers with lifetime tenure, they may be layed off at any time. Their official residence remains their home village regardless of the number of years of urban or industrial service. Contract jobs nonetheless attract collective members: They pay cash wages which, even with urban costs of living for contract workers, provide their families in the village substantially higher levels of living than those prevailing in poorer collective units; they provide external earnings comparable to the remittances of urban or overseas workers in other economies; and contract workers cling to hopes of eventually making the transition to urban residence and a state job.[22] Temporary and contract workers constitute an intermediate group that provides limited intersectoral mobility for rural workers, assures the state economy of a flexible source of cheap labor, and preserves intact the formal state-collective divide.

In comparing Chinese patterns of income and opportunity inequality in the collective era with those in large, predominantly agrarian capitalist nations such as India, Indonesia, Mexico, Brazil, and the Philippines, three facts stand out. First, China's elimination of the largest property-based inequalities of private wealth and income and the dominance of the state and collective economy did away with social classes embodying the extremes of wealth and concomitant power. Not only were there no Chinese millionaires, capitalists, or land barons, but the universal distribution of land rights and collective entitlement to land prevented the creation of a class of landless peasants with no entitlement to income. Second, China's urban income distribution is among the most egalitarian in the world (gini coeffect 0.16 by World Bank calculation, compared with 0.42 for India and 0.47 for the Philippines [Riskin 1987: 249]). Indeed, in the 1980s, Chinese reformers targeted this egalitarian income distribution pattern as an obstacle to development requiring transformation in order to raise labor productivity. Third, China has not only preserved but indeed substantially increased both intrarural income and opportunity inequalities and the urban-rural and state-collective income gaps. It has done this through budget, planning, and price priorities and institutional controls, all of which have systematically maintained or increased the primacy of the state sector and the cities and the subordination of the countryside.

How have the post-Mao reforms with their emphasis on commodification, contracts, and the division of labor impinged on sectoral hierarchy and urban-rural inequality?

Reform and Sectoral Differentiation in the 1980s

The Household Contract System and the Reform of Chinese Agriculture

In the 1980s the reform initiatives at the pinnacle of the party-state touched off a powerful reaction among the collective peasantry beginning in poorer and declining regions and spreading throughout the countryside. Emboldened by state efforts to enliven the rural economy, increase production incentives, and raise the rate of commodification, peasants pressed for freedom from collective and state controls.[23] Following market- and contract-oriented changes, collective units continue to retain important residual and contractual landownership rights and frequently direct village sideline and industrial activities, but since 1982 major agricultural production and marketing processes and decisions as well as control of the labor process have passed from the collective to the household. By 1984 fully 95 percent of former production teams had contracted land to households and adopted independent household management (*da bao gan*). The household contract system, in conjunction with sweeping reform measures enacted since the late 1970s, provided a powerful stimulus to agriculture and the rural economy. Table 6.4 compares the performance of essential items of Chinese agriculture in productivity and per capita terms during the collective and reform periods.

While per capita grain increase was negligible and cotton and edible oil actually declined in per capita terms throughout the course of the collective era (1957–1978), in the first six years of the reform per capita grain yields advanced at the solid rate of 3.8 percent per year, and per capita cotton output more than doubled. Other commercial crops registered similarly impressive gains. Moreover, grain output increased substantially in the years 1978–1984 at a time when grain acreage was reduced by 17 million acres and the gross value of grain as a percent of total crop value dropped from 77 to 63 percent (Commentary 1985: 1). The abandonment of grain-first policies in favor of diversification, commodification, and comprehensive development actually stimulated grain production in the context of a general surge in agricultural productivity. A substantial portion of rural labor, an estimated 76 million or 20 percent of the total in 1985, were engaged in village and township enterprises as tens of millions shifted out of grain and crop production to industrial, craft, and commercial activities. In 1986 for the first time the output value of China's rapidly growing village and township enterprises, 330 billion yuan, surpassed the value of agricultural production (Xinhua 1986). Commodification, industrialization, and diversification have begun to transform the character of the agrarian economy and city-countryside relations.

The stimulus of the household contract system, in conjunction with the rejuvenation of the market and rural sideline and industrial production and a substantial boost in state agricultural purchasing prices,

Table 6.4

Agricultural Performance, 1957–1978 and 1978–1984

Per capita output in kilograms*

Year	Grains	Cotton	Edible oils	Meat (pork, beef, mutton)	Aquatic products (fish, seafood)
1957	306	2.5	6.6	6.3	4.9
1978	319	2.3	5.5	9.0	4.9
1984	397	5.9	11.6	14.9	5.9

Average annual growth rates in percent
(per capita annual growth rates in parentheses)

1957–78	2.1 (0.2)	1.3 (−0.6)	1.0 (−0.9)	3.7 (1.7)	1.9 (0)
1978–84	4.9 (3.8)	18.7 (17.5)	14.6 (14.0)	10.1 (9.0)	4.6 (3.3)

*Per capita refers to the national population.
Sources: Riskin (1987: 293); Lardy (1986: 326–27).

generated the first sustained growth spurt in the rural economy since collectivization. Apparently in response to price and market incentives, average annual net grain marketing rose from 40.3 million metric tons in the years 1976–78 to 77.3 million metric tons in 1982–84; the net marketing ratio increased from 13.6 to 20 percent (Riskin 1987: 29–30; Zhao 1986: 12–13). Coupled with sharply rising state purchasing prices, this translated into major income gains for the peasantry.[24]

Rising productivity and expanding market activity translated into substantial income gains for the rural population after twenty-five years of per capita income and consumption stagnation. Chinese government annual surveys highlight changing patterns of rural income distribution in the reform period (table 6.5).[25]

Between 1978 and 1985 rural net per capita income tripled from 134 to 398 yuan (table 6.5). Most important for our purposes are the income gains at the two poles. The 33.3 percent of households with per capita incomes less than 100 yuan in 1978 had dropped to 4.7 percent by 1981, and by 1985 only 11.3 percent of households reported per capita income less than 200 yuan. In 1978, 2.4 percent and by 1982, 36.2 percent of households had per capita incomes exceeding 300 yuan. By 1985, 22.3 percent had passed 500 yuan and more than 60 percent

Table 6.5

Rural Per Capita Net Income, 1978–1985 (percentage distribution)

Income Group	1978	1980	1981	1982	1983	1984	1985
Over 500 yuan	—	1.6	3.2	6.7	11.9	18.2	22.3
400–500	2.4	2.9	5.0	8.7	11.6	14.1	15.8
300–400		8.6	14.4	20.8	22.9	24.5	24.0
200–300	15.0	25.3	34.8	37.0	32.9	29.2	25.6
100–200	49.2	51.8	37.9	24.1	19.3	13.2	11.3
Below 100	33.3	9.8	4.7	2.7	1.4	0.8	1.0
Average income	133.6	191.3	223.4	270.1	309.8	355.3	397.6
Gini coefficient	0.2281	0.2448	0.2505	0.2528	0.2683	0.2666	0.2718

Source: State Statistical Bureau (1986: 582). Data for 1979 are not recorded.
Note: Net income is based on a calculation of the value of income in kind plus cash income.

had per capita incomes exceeding 300 yuan. With many households now active in the market, the cash component of rural incomes also rose significantly.

A 1984 national survey of 37,422 rural households in twenty-three provinces provides more detailed information on the upper end of the rural income spectrum (table 6.6). Per capita net incomes of surveyed households were 399 yuan (compared with 355 in the survey cited above).

With 10 percent of household incomes exceeding 800 yuan, the 1984 survey shows average per capita incomes of the top 10 percent of households as approximately 1,200 yuan and that of the bottom 10 percent as less than 100 yuan, yielding a decile ratio of 12–15:1. Per capita rural income grew rapidly in the years of the reform; indeed, the gains far outstripped those of the entire collective era (1955–1978), with income growing at a real annual rate of 17.9 percent between 1978 and 1984.

The survey and much national data reveal that while poverty remains a problem in the rural periphery, the economic surge of the 1980s has carried many of the poorest rural households and communities well above the official poverty line of the late 1970s, 50 yuan per person. It also underscores continued substantial regional differences. In 1984 rural households surveyed in the six major coastal provinces (including Beijing and Tianjin) averaged 620 yuan per person compared with a national average of 399 and with 314 yuan in eight provinces of the Southwest and Northwest. The gap in productivity, consumption, and

Table 6.6

Distribution of Rural Household Per Capita Net Income, 1984

Household per capita incomes	Percent of households
Over 1000 yuan	5.5
900–1000	1.6
800–900	2.2
700–800	3.4
600–700	5.1
500–600	7.5
400–500	11.2
300–400	16.5
200–300	20.7
100–200	19.0
less than 100	7.2
Gini coefficient	0.2107

Source: *Nongye jingji wenti* (Chinese Agricultural Problems) 6 (1986): 4–13.

income between coastal and inland regions has, moreover, been growing rapidly. Shanghai's *World Economic Herald* reported that the per capita output value of industry and agriculture in the eastern provinces exceeded that of western provinces by 669 yuan in 1981. By 1985 the differential had reached 1,018 yuan (*China Daily*, July 31, 1987).

Since 1978, a significant if relatively small number of highly visible entrepreneurial households (2.3 percent of rural households were officially classified as specialized households in 1984) prospered on a scale inconceivable during the collective era while many of the poorest also improved their lot (Commentary 1985: 17). Yet income and other gains associated with reform policies in the 1980s have by no means been restricted to the entrepreneurial and specialized households whose advance has been most visible: income, savings, and consumption are up for the overwhelming majority of households, including those in poorer regions. As in the preceding collective era, substantial intravillage and regional income differences exist in the countryside, and there is evidence that certain income differentials have increased. Indeed, gini coefficients of intrarural income inequality based on government surveys have risen from 0.22 in 1978 to 0.27 in 1985, indicating a slow but steady increase in income differentiation. These still relatively low income differentials, and accompanying changes in ownership of means of production and labor relations, pinpoint possible sources of future rural frictions, particularly in the event that rural incomes enter a prolonged period of stagnation or decline.[26] The significance of increased income differentiation, including the possible attendant alienation experienced by lagging households, must be weighed against the substantial across-the-board income gains shared—if unequally—by virtually all sectors of the rural population after two decades of income stagnation and policies that favored urban industry over the countryside.

Continuity and Reform in the State Sector

In contrast to the far-reaching reforms in the rural economy and society, until recently, despite China's attempted opening to the world economy, the state sector, industry, and the cities have experienced remarkable institutional continuity. Some widely heralded and far-reaching reforms associated with China's efforts to attract international capital, such as the establishment of the Shenzhen and other Special Economic Zones, have brought economic disappointment and even disasters in the form of massive balance-of-payment deficits, high state budget costs, failure to attract high technology investment, and rampant corruption (Pepper 1986). For the most part, reform attempts to reduce the scope of central and regional planning and control in favor of greater enterprise and managerial authority, to gear income more closely to individual performance through the use of piece rates and bonuses, to foster competition, and to transform the price structure met stiff resistance in state enterprises and ministries. Most were abortive and were quietly abandoned or accommodated to the prereform milieu.

One development, which has been gaining momentum over the last five years, *if sustained*, will significantly redefine the character of labor in the state sector and will transform the city-countryside relationship by undermining the special advantages enjoyed by state-sector employees. On September 30, 1986, China formally ended permanent employment in state enterprises in favor of universal contract labor for new employees.[27]

As noted earlier, contract labor had long existed as an appendage of the state sector, a vehicle for employment of rural workers that maintained the state-collective divide while providing the state with a cheap and flexible labor supply. As reformers pressed state enterprises to raise efficiency, official awareness grew of the large and growing budgetary cost of benefits to state-sector workers. From the 1950s to the 1970s, few among China's young cohort of state workers retired. Between 1978 and 1985, however, many among the first generation of workers retired and the cost of pensions alone increased from 2.8 to 10.6 percent of the state wage bill. At the same time, the cost of food subsidies for state-sector workers spiraled as a result of increases in state purchasing prices. The state responded by increasing the number of contract laborers in state enterprises from 160,000 at the end of 1982 to 5.18 million by December 1986 (Xin Bao 1987, cited in Davis, forthcoming).

In the 1980s the rapid expansion of the urban collective and private sectors, together with the shift toward contract labor in state enterprises, have cast in sharp relief the budgetary cost of underwriting the benefit structure for regular state workers. Between 1981 and 1985 the number of urban collective workers increased from 23 to 26 percent of the urban labor force, and the number of private-sector workers increased fivefold. Most of the proliferating number of contract workers in state enterprises, like rural contracting households, lack benefits associated with regular state-sector employment. The result is deepening division between new and old employees and between workers and managerial/technical personnel in the state sector. The divisions are clearest between contract workers, who are numerous among new industrial and clerical employees and are bereft of the benefits of permanent employment, and technical and managerial personnel, who enjoy the full range of state benefits, ample subsidies, and high guaranteed salaries. Since college graduates and all specialized technical and managerial personnel continue to be hired as regular state workers, and since different cities have interpreted the law in different ways, the evolving system points toward new patterns of differentiation among state-sector employees and between the state sector and the collective economy.

These changes underline not only a tendency toward increased differentiation among technical/managerial personnel and unskilled workers, but also what Davis (forthcoming) has called ''an opportunity structure where cohorts who enter first are systematically favored over those who enter later.'' That is, they suggest the emergence of an important generational rift within the state sector as most new employees are hired on short-term contracts with few benefits while earlier cohorts retain full benefits. I have noted the origin of this trend as early as the 1960s when the combination of demographics and hiring priorities made entry into the state sector difficult even for the children of urban state employees and virtually impossible for rural youth. In the late 1980s young workers face the prospect that few will obtain regular state employment while earlier cohorts of employees as well as technical and managerial personnel enjoy the security and benefits once enjoyed by all state-sector employees. The result may be to redefine urban-rural, state-society, and generation gaps.

Contracts, Commodification, and Changing Patterns of Inequality

In contrast to the income patterns of the collective era, the reforms appear to have worked to the relative advantage of the countryside. For the first time since 1955, with the possible exception of a brief period in the early 1960s, the long-growing gap between state and collective sectors, and between urban and rural areas, may have narrowed. Official data show per capita rural income and consumption gains far outstripping those in the urban areas in the years 1978 to 1984. A 1985 State Statistical Bureau survey of 12,050 households in 82 cities and 31,435 rural households in 600 counties showed average annual income growth rates in comparable prices of 15 percent for rural households compared with 8 percent for urban households; rural consumption on a household basis rose by 13 percent per year compared with 7 percent for urban households (Li Chengrui 1985: 17). While per capita rural income tripled from 120 yuan in 1978 to 397 yuan in 1985, the average annual income of workers in state enterprises increased at barely half that rate. Nevertheless, per capita income of households with state-sector workers rose from 618 yuan in 1978 to 1,148 yuan in 1984, so that the absolute per capita income gap between workers and staff in the state sector and rural producers widened from 488 to 751 yuan a year (Song 1986: 16; State Statistical Bureau 1986: 555).

Many urban people with fixed state salaries view with frustration the fortunes made by highly visible rural (and some urban) entrepreneurs. The sight of two-story homes for prosperous rural households rising on the outskirts of cities is the tangible proof for many urban state workers, who occupy cramped apartments and face mounting inflation with fixed salaries, that the new policies favor the countryside over the city and the private over the state sector. A small and highly visible rural nouveau riche has emerged, and the general level of rural incomes has risen significantly. At the same time poverty zones remain in the rural periphery and, despite impressive gains over a decade, overall rural living standards, with the exception of housing, remain far below urban levels.

In considering changing patterns of rural poverty I begin with State Statistical Bureau estimates that between 1978 and 1984 the proportion of rural households with per capita incomes of less than 200 yuan dropped from 62 percent to just 14 percent (*China Daily* September 28, 1985). By contrast, in 1979, 27 percent of all rural teams, and a somewhat higher percentage of rural households, had per capita distributed collective incomes below the official poverty level of 50 yuan (Vermeer 1982: 14, 28, 29).[28] The reforms have produced a qualitative shift in the position of many of the poorest households and communities. There are also modest indications that the state has begun to accept responsibility to provide minimal welfare for the rural poor—and taken a number of preliminary steps to allocate resources to fulfill those responsibilities.[29] One small example illustrates elements of change from the self-reliant collectivism of the Mao period. Between 1983 and 1985, 132,000 rural residents of three extremely poor arid Gansu and Ningxia counties received assistance in resettling in more hospitable rural areas. In addition to 200 million yuan in state aid for housing, schools, and so forth, a 40-million-yuan grant from the UN World Food Program was allocated to irrigation. The project is to be completed in 1990 when 800,000 people will have been resettled (Xinhua 1985: 21). Nevertheless, with the continued efficacy of the population registration system, one of the most persistent problems remains the poverty of peripheral regions with inhospitable terrain, climate, and soil and primitive transportation.

We suggest the following working conclusions about the urban-rural income gap. First, against the background of long-term relative decline throughout the collective era, measured in per capita income, the countryside with its new collective-household mixed economy has outperformed the cities and the state sector. Second, the state sector and the cities continue to enjoy substantial if declining relative income and benefit advantages over the countryside. Third, a small number of specialized households and entrepreneurs, many of them rural residents, have amassed considerable wealth (by PRC standards). Overall these results produce a small but significant widening in rural income differentials. Finally, the combination of reform policies and modest state assistance has enabled some poor and stagnant areas to move ahead, yet some of the poorest regions, with few resources and primitive transport as well as households with little or no labor power, remain, as they did during the collective era, destitute.

The consequences of the reforms are by no means restricted to changing income patterns. One observes the beginnings of a reshaping of the entire spectrum of social and production relations. Here I note a number of the most important changes in social and class relations in process, emphasizing those that impinge on the urban-rural divide.

The direct relationship between state and collective authorities, on the one hand, and the members of the collective, on the other, has been transformed in essentials. The changes in the countryside are profound. The household contract system, the expanded scope of the market and entrepreneurial opportunities, the reduction of restrictions on extravillage employment, and the end of cadre control over all aspects of work have restored to rural households substantial control over the allocation of their land, labor, and resources.

The redefinition of the collective takes two principal contradictory forms. On the one hand, the contract system is tantamount to collective tenancy in which households lease the land they cultivate to an entity (usually the village) in which they are themselves, in effect, shareholders (cf. Kueh 1985; Crook 1985). On the other hand, the weakening of collective controls results in the dramatic expansion of private economic opportunities for collective members without depriving them of the security inherent in retaining the rights to an equal share of the product of village land.

The changes include the beginnings of class differentiation in both city and countryside: tens of millions of Chinese now earn their living in private or contracted commercial, service, and industrial enterprises. These include merchants engaged in local and long-distance trade; entrepreneurs who hire labor; and tenant farmers including specialized agricultural producers who rent in land in addition to their contracted plots. For the first time since collectivization, the trend toward the homogenization of social classes has been reversed and property-based differentials have reemerged as a factor in defining social and economic relations.

If the consequences of state policies in the first three decades of the People's Republic were to simplify the complex social relations of Chinese society, strengthen the power and penetration of state and collective, restrict the scope of the market and the private sector, and create a deepening urban-rural and state-collective divide, these tendencies have been reversed in the 1980s. Particularly striking are signs of the imminent emergence or reemergence of diverse social classes in a milieu of expanded market relations and reduction in the direct exercise of state power and in the city-countryside polarity.

The changes are clearest in the resurgence of the private sector, whose dominant feature is the predominantly household character of agricultural production—albeit functioning within the scope of collective landownership and collective contracts. Significant rural household activity is at the center of the expanding commercial, sideline, service, and small-scale industrial economy, although the continued strength of the state and collective in these areas should not be overlooked.

The number of private-sector workers has also risen dramatically. A 1986 study (*People's Daily*, January 24, 1986) estimated the number of participants in private enterprises at 17 million and projected an increase to 50 million by 1990. At the same time, in the 1980s the number of urban collective workers is growing more rapidly than that of state workers, virtually doubling from 17.7 million in 1975 to 33.2 million in 1985. Moreover, with the addition of at least 4.5 million urban workers in the private sector and a somewhat larger number of contract workers entering state jobs, regular state workers barely constitute a majority of the urban work force (State Statistical Bureau 1986: 92).

The state has sanctioned significant steps toward the commodification of land and labor. In 1984 households officially won the right to hire labor and, with permission of the collective, to transfer rights to contracted land and enterprises. In the mid-1980s one observes the beginnings of the rental, transfer, and sale of land and the growth of hired labor (see chapter 7). At this writing, very little land has actually changed hands as households, including those most active in commercial and industrial activity, have chosen to maintain cultivation rights to contracted land rather than to rent or sell their land rights.

Large numbers of rural households, while continuing to farm contracted land, have adopted mixed strategies, variations on the diverse survival strategies involving grain production, household sidelines, marketing, and off-farm labor from the arsenal of pre-land reform and precollectivization peasant strategies. At present, those with productive or marketing skills and ambitions, with external contacts and financial resources, become specialized households, many of them contracting the management of small enterprises from the collective, but many others forming independent private enterprises or joint ventures. Some members of the many households lacking these resources or proclivities become hired laborers. In this way we find a resurgence of hired labor in the private, cooperative, and collective sectors, with some employers hiring dozens, and in rare cases even hundreds, of laborers.

Emerging social relations, particularly those in the private sector, generate the sprouts of new classes and actual and potential class antagonisms. At the same time, egalitarian features of the contract system continue to distinguish China from much of the Third World where differential per capita landownership is the single largest factor determining income, entitlements, and life chances (Castro et al. 1981: 402, 418–20). For the present, contractual reform leaves intact subsistence guarantees for rural producers in the form of equal shares of land rights in their villages while contributing to rising productivity and incomes. The result is to redefine the tripartite relationship among the collective, the state, and a growing private sector.

The Crisis of Reform

This discussion has pointed to important achievements of the reform agenda—particularly the income and productivity gains in the countryside and the possible reversal of a thirty-year trend of widening urban-rural gap. At the same time numerous problems have arisen that jeopardize the reform agenda and provide ammunition to its critics. One report (Lu Shaoqing 1985), for example, underscores the rise of child labor in a rapidly industrializing Zhejiang township in which seven hundred peasant children and youth ages ten to fifteen were found working ten- to twelve-hour days (some up to sixteen hours) in aluminum, printing, and plastics workshops. Child wages of one yuan per day compared with the three yuan standard for adult workers in the area. Most of these workers were children of farm families, few of whose adult members earned as much as one yuan per day during the late collective era. At the very moment when the Chinese state is emphasizing the importance of education and technical skills, the reforms have contributed to a rising school dropout rate as families seek the labor of children in farming and household enterprises.

A second consequence is that while their success ultimately hinges in no small part on the ambitious birth planning campaign, the reforms have increased pressures to have more children, particularly males. There are at least three reasons for this. Land is primarily allotted to households on the basis of the number of family members; male children are responsible for the welfare of parents in old age; and the weakening of collective welfare systems has not been accompanied by a national welfare or social security program providing for the elderly.

Third, the reforms have set in motion contradictory processes that make it difficult to sustain the rapid development of agriculture: The state, severely strapped for resources and fearful of a politically explosive urban opposition uniting workers and intellectuals in the manner of Poland's Solidarity, has cut back substantially on investment in support of agriculture. At the same time, there is little inclination by either collectives or households to invest when the potential return on industry and commerce is far higher. The threat to China's elaborate irrigation networks, the lifeline of agriculture, is particularly acute.

China's reforms have contributed to accelerated rural development and a reduction in the sharpest sectoral divisions underlying the social structure, notably those between the city and countryside and between the state and the collective sectors. They have also given rise to new and potentially antagonistic social classes and set in motion contradictory forces that threaten to undermine the reforms themselves. In the 1980s the party-state, with its grip on the industrial-financial core of the economy and deep penetration of the countryside, retains powerful levers to shape sectoral and class outcomes, but the reforms themselves have set in motion processes raising the aspirations and strengthening the power of autonomous classes and groups and redefining the city-countryside conflict.

7

THE REFORM OF LANDOWNERSHIP AND THE POLITICAL ECONOMY OF CONTEMPORARY CHINA
With Aiguo Lu

In the literature of political economy, landownership is a problematic concept. For Marx (1963; 1971), landownership relations embodied not only relations between an owner and the land but the full complement of social relations of production. Others view landownership as the sum total of the rights to own, to possess, to control, to cultivate, and to dispose of or otherwise utilize the land (Jiang 1982; Li Zezhong 1986). This chapter examines landownership rights in China during the era of mobilizational collectivism (1955–1980) and assesses the changes in ownership relations in the 1980s as a result of contractual and market-oriented reforms. Our focus is the multifaceted implications for social and economic relations of changes in landownership.

Land reform (1947–1952) redistributed ownership rights among the peasantry and eliminated the largest intravillage property-based inequalities while affirming the ownership rights of individual cultivators, including the right to buy, sell, or rent their land. With collectivization (1955–1956), private landownership was abolished and formal ownership rights to land and other means of production passed from individuals to collectives organized at the level of the village or a subunit of the village.[1] In practice, however, while collectives secured formal ownership rights, the state assumed tight control over transfer rights including the sale, rent, or exchange of land. Use rights, including the cultivation of the land and its use for industrial, housing, or other purposes, were vested in a collective-state condominium in which the collective exercised immediate authority but crop choice, availability and distribution of inputs, prices both of inputs and crops, and marketing all remained state prerogatives. An important complement to this pattern of collective-state control of land rights was the private plot. Rural households received cultivation rights on approximately 5 percent of the cultivable area. This included crop choice, control of the labor process, consumption rights, and (at times) marketing rights to the fruit of the land.[2] In general, collectives exercised managerial functions on behalf of the state, which monopolized transfer rights and set major guidelines for cultivation and utilization of land and marketing, distribution, and consumption of its product.

Distinctive Chinese concepts of landownership become comprehensible when broken into their component elements. Our discussion of landownership rights in China is organized around five elements that have comprised the essential components of ownership since 1955:[3]

1. Formal landownership rights.

2. Use rights: over the cultivation, investment, industry, mining, and construction on the land.

3. Transfer rights: over the purchase, sale, rent, contracting, or inheritance of the land.

4. Product rights: over the consumption and sale of products of the land.

5. Labor rights: over the labor power of those attached to the land.

The changing character of landownership is at the heart of the continuing debate over rural reforms in the 1980s. Numerous official statements insist that public ownership of land and major means of production, referring principally to formal and transfer rights, is the sine qua non of socialism and will never change. Yet even as that formulation is challenged by the diverse proposals of reformers promoting the commodification of land and labor in order to promote land consolidation, specialization, the division of labor, efficient land use, and agricultural investment, we observe a reality in which essentials of ownership, broadly construed, are in flux.[4] The result at present is a mixed system in which elements of commodification and household ownership are gaining momentum.

Landownership Rights

Formal ownership rights to the land have been vested in the collective from the origins of collectivization to the present. From 1960, following the collapse of the Great Leap Forward, the commune system was based on a three-level system with ownership rights divided among the three primary collective units—the commune, the brigade (usually a natural village), and the team. The team, typically comprising thirty to forty households, was the primary ownership, accounting, and managerial unit from 1960 to the early 1980s. As the Central Committee's Sixty Articles of 1962 emphasized, ''All the land within the production team belongs to the production team.''[5] These ownership rights were, however, essentially restricted to organizing cultivation of the land within the framework of state directives. The team possessed no rights to sell, transfer, or rent the land.

Following the reorganization of China's collective agriculture and formal abolition of the communes in 1984, the National People's Congress issued China's first Land Management Law. The law, which went into effect on January 1, 1987, proclaimed that ''collective land is collectively owned by the peasants of the village and is managed and administered either by rural collective economic organizations such as the village agricultural producers' cooperatives (*cun nongye sheng-chan hezuoshe*) or by villagers' committees (*cunmin weiyuanhui*).''[6] ''Village'' here generally refers to the natural village, although the law permits ownership at the township, the village or a subvillage unit. Published discussion of the household contract system has emphasized the transfer of use rights, that is, the shift of cultivation rights from the collective (principally the team) to the household. This important downward transfer of authority to cultivate the land from collective to household is the centerpiece of the contract system. We note, however, that the Land Management Law also apparently transfers formal ownership and transfer rights to the land from subvillage teams of 3,040 households to village units frequently embracing hundreds of households.[7]

The Land Management Law itself, however, contains contradictory provisions concerning the locus of ownership. The law states that land previously owned by the team is still owned by it, usually under the new name of villagers' small group (*cunmin xiaozu*) (*Selected Documents on Land Management* 1986: 3,22). The Land Management Law not only reiterates the collective's formal ownership rights but adds important transfer rights including the right to contract the land to individuals, to households, and to groups. Ambiguity remains, however, as to whether these rights are exercised by the team (or villagers' small group), by the village (the former brigade), or by a combination of the two. In suburban Shandong and central Hebei, where we conducted investigations in the summer of 1986 and 1987 respectively, the village (brigade) contracted directly with households and the team played no direct role.[8]

Under both the communal and the contractual systems, the formal owner, whether village (brigade) or team, does not possess unfettered transfer rights. In both eras the sale or permanent transfer of possession of land required state approval. The state alone—all levels of state administration and state agencies—enjoys wide rights of eminent domain which permit it to purchase and sell use rights as well as transfer rights. However, in the 1980s a wide range of transfer rights have been formally vested in the collective. The most important of these is the prerogative to contract land to member households.

In 1955–56 collectivization transferred the entire panoply of ownership rights from individual landowners to the collective and the state.[9] The collective exercised major use, product, and labor rights over all land and labor within its purview with the exception of private plots. The state retained exclusive powers to purchase, sell, or transfer land. It controlled a portion of use and product rights by determining crop choice and compulsory sales quotas and taxes, and by establishing guidelines for accumulation and consumption.

The collective directly managed the land and labor of the producers living on that land within the parameters of tight state control. The collective produced what the state specified, purchased quantities of agricultural producer goods at state prices, and sold designated quantities of its produce to the state at (low) official prices. While the state urged collective self-reliance, its antimarket, grain self-sufficiency, and high compulsory sale quota policies left scant room for collective maneuver. Teams and brigades could not sell, transfer, or rent their land, except as directed by the state. Nor could they autonomously decide what to grow, or even *not* to cultivate unproductive land. For their part, collective members had no right to sell, rent, or leave the land and were even heavily restricted in the use of their private plots.

Here we note an extraordinary feature of landownership during the period of mobilizational collectivism. The integration of peasants and land was so tight that one is almost tempted to say that the land owned the people. Collective ownership of the land empowered the collective to control the labor power of all members who lived on it. Indeed, with the 1955 implementation of household registration and control (the *hukou* system), residents were legally and substantively bound to the land.[10] Collective members were bound to the village of their birth not only in the sense that they were barred from migrating elsewhere but also in that they were legally obligated to labor for, and on terms set by, the collective.[11]

State and collective closely restricted the movement of rural residents not only between town and countryside but also among different rural areas. In the rare cases when rural residents secured jobs outside the village as temporary or contract workers, their families were required to remain in the village. The weight of population controls through the household registration system is manifest in the stable proportion of China's rural and urban population in the first three decades of the People's Republic, a pattern which differentiates China from the demographics of accelerated urbanization characteristic of all other industrializing nations. While China experienced rapid industrialization in these decades, the rural population, which accounted for 87.5 percent of total population in 1952, actually increased slightly to 88.0 percent in 1976 as a result of an increase of 332 million residents (Economic Yearbook 1982; Kirkby 1985: 197, 114).[12] China's historically unprecedented rural migration can be understood in part in terms of the landownership issues that are the subject of this paper. How can a net rural migration be absorbed in a society with heavy population pressure on the land? The answer lies in part in yet another dimension of ownership rights exercised by the state. Modest initial subsidies aside, the state required collectives to accept the burden of feeding and housing these migrants, independent of any local calculation of the gain or loss involved.[13]

The Reform of Landownership

The household contract system introduced throughout the countryside in the 1980s has brought far-reaching changes in ownership and production relations, notably in the substantial transfer of the organization and control of agricultural, sideline, and industrial production and marketing from the collective to contracting households. Throughout the countryside rural households have emerged as active contractual partners and semi-autonomous producers operating, to be sure, within a collective framework, but one characterized by sharply reduced collective supervision and control over productive, marketing, investment, and consumption processes. The expanded role of rural households and the reduction in, indeed in many regions the virtual elimination of, collective activity in agricultural production constitute a restructuring of landownership rights involving rural households, the collective, and the state.

In the 1980s the collective exercises transfer rights by contracting the land and other means of production to households or groups of individuals and households. Land is contracted to households on a per capita or labor power basis, or a combination of the two.[14] Contracting households gain the right not only to farm a piece of land but also freely to deploy household labor. This marks a partial shift from the situation in which "the land owns the people." Contracting parties now have wider opportunities for off-farm employment as well as greater autonomy in deploying household labor on their land. Contractual responsibilities include payment to the team or village of specified quantities of crops as well as payment of the land tax, contributions to the public accumulation and welfare fund, and a specified number of days of corvée labor in water conservancy and other public works projects. Y. Y. Kueh (1985: 124) describes this system as one that prescribes a "lump-sum tax (or rental) obligation on the part of peasant tenants" with the collective as de facto landlord collecting income based on ownership of the land.[15] In our terminology, elements of ownership are actually divided among the state, collective, and household.

Throughout China's countryside the relationship between the collective and the agricultural producer has been fundamentally restructured. Instead of the subordination of team members in collective agricultural production, most contracts transfer to the household full or primary responsibility for the major agricultural tasks. In industrially advanced areas, most industry remains collectively administered and some agricultural functions such as plowing and fertilizing may continue to be collectively coordinated. However, the principal collective functions of organizing and managing agricultural production and some sideline and marketing activities have been transferred to contracting households. For example, the utilization of land, including what, how, and how much to produce, is largely decided by contracting households, although with collective supervision and within a framework established by contract. With the elimination of the workpoint system in most units after 1982, the household replaced the collective as the primary agricultural production, income-generating, and distribution unit. With the end of the workpoint system, the essential link between the health of the collective economy and household income has been severed in most villages, particularly with respect to agriculture. This decline of the collective role in agriculture is underlined by the fact that with the end of compulsory sales quotas in 1985, households signed crop sale contracts directly with the state with no collective mediation.

In the mid-1980s several important steps have been taken to clarify and transform land property rights. In 1984 the Central Committee, alarmed by the unwillingness of contracting households to invest in agriculture, extended the contractual term from the original three to "more than fifteen years" and sanctioned inheritance of the land for the duration of the contract. Both steps, designed to boost agricultural productivity by encouraging long-term investment on the part of cultivators, extend the practical ownership rights of contracting households while formal rights remain in collective hands.[16]

The contract system constitutes an agrarian system based on household labor under collective supervision. However, Central Committee Document 1 in January 1983, setting forth the major parameters of the reform for that year, for the first time officially permitted contracting households to exchange and even to hire labor. Document 1 of 1984 empowered contracting parties, with the consent of the collective, to transfer contracts in exchange for payments: "The transferee of a contract should provide the original owner with a certain amount of grain at parity price." The document underlined the fact that contractual terms remained inviolable when the land changed hands, and particularly emphasized that no land could be taken out of production without the permission of the collective. "Private plots and land under contract may not be bought or sold, may not be leased to a third party and may not be transferred as building plots for housing or for any other nonagricultural use" (Circular of the Central Committee 1985). Like so many land policy documents of the 1980s, this one sanctioned, while attempting to control, widespread practices that pressed beyond limits of transfer and use rights stipulated in earlier official directives.

The 1984 directive legalized both vertical transfers between collective and contracting households and horizontal transfers between households. Contracted land may be recovered by the collective if it is abused, wasted, or seriously damaged, and contracting households may also voluntarily return land to the collective in order to pursue other occupations. Potentially most significant are steps to legalize the transfer of contracted land among peasant households, steps which go far toward the commodification of land. Such transfers, with or without compensation, require that existing contractual terms be honored, and they must obtain prior collective approval. Yet contractual terms are frequently violated. A 1984–85 nationwide survey found that 1 percent of land had been subcontracted while 3 percent was left fallow, mainly by households who wish to retain contractual rights even while they neglect farming in order to concentrate on more lucrative activities. Moreover, numerous households have violated contractual terms by building houses on land designated for cultivation (Rural Economic Survey Group 1983).

In response to mounting concern over declining agricultural investment, Document 1 of 1984 provides that households receive compensation for investment in the land. In addition to state compensation in the case of expropriation or return of collective land, compensation for investment is now recognized in contracts between collective and household and in the case of interhousehold transfer of contract. The issue of who pays and who receives compensation, and in what form, implies changes in land property rights to which we return below.

The preceding discussion of the contract system emphasizes the multiple character, increasing complexity, and expanding commodity nature of landownership involving the state, the collective, and contracting as well as noncontracting households. No longer are ownership issues the exclusive prerogative of the state and the collective; individuals and households are also actively involved in redefining relationships involving the collective, the market, and other households. Each of these contracting parties possesses a portion of landownership rights.

The state retains the right of eminent domain: It may take possession of the land in exchange for compensation. Moreover, the state retains extensive prerogatives to determine land use, cultivation patterns, crop choices, and price levels. By 1985, however, the state had abandoned the system of compulsory sales (and guaranteed purchase) of agricultural commodities. Where marketing of agricultural products had once been the domain of collective and state, the state cut back direct administrative controls and expanded the use of administered and market price incentives in a bid to increase the rate of commodification and stimulate the rural economy. Primary responsibility for circulation shifted to the market and the household, cutting out the role of the collective in state purchase of agricultural commodities.

The collective (village) is entitled not only to sell land to the state but also to enter into contracts with other collectives, the state, cooperative and individual enterprises, and peasant households. In addition, the collective retains responsibility for the allocation and utilization of all land within its purview.

Finally, the use, transfer, product, and labor rights of peasant households over contracted land have expanded with the signing of long-term leases of fifteen or more years—up to fifty years for forest and pond land—including the right to organize and exchange household, cooperative, and even hired labor as they see fit (subject to fulfillment of contractual responsibilities); the right to transfer contracted land to other households under certain conditions; and the right to return to the collective land they no longer wish to cultivate, free from contractual obligations. In a word, contracting households actively engage in a wide range of property relations. For contracting households land has taken on essential elements of a commodity, in many ways comparable to those that existed prior to collectivization, yet it is a commodity whose parameters are shaped by the changing collective-state milieu. The landownership relationship may now be seen as a tripartite one monopolized by no single party—state, collective, or household—each of whose powers are in flux.

Land Income

Land income is defined as the return on ownership of land independent of income derived from the labor of the producer. When labor is directly integrated with landownership, that is, when owner and cultivator are one, this portion of income is an inseparable part of total agricultural income. When cultivation is the product of a relationship between landlord and tenant, or between landowner and hired laborer, ownership becomes separated from the cultivation of the land, and, consequently, land income becomes visible, usually in the form of rent or income generated by hired labor. In such cases, land income is an economic form in which landownership can be realized.

The overt forms of land income as rent and as income derived from hired labor disappeared in the land reform that preceded collectivization. We may, however, examine the distribution of the agricultural product during the era of mobilizational collectivism for clues to the existence of land income in China's countryside and for changes taking place under the present contractual system. From this perspective we consider agricultural taxation and compulsory crop sales, collective exactions, and land compensation.

Agricultural Taxation and Compulsory Crop Sales

The agricultural tax and compulsory crop sales constitute the state's claim to a share of the product of the land. Tax levies, established in the early years of the People's Republic on the basis of land size and productivity, remained more or less constant in absolute terms at least until the 1980s. As a result of agricultural development, the proportion of the land tax to total agricultural income has steadily declined from about 12 percent in the early 1950s to 5.6 percent in 1965, 3.1 percent in 1980, and 1.2 percent in 1984 (Zheng and Ye 1985; Ma 1982: 117–18; Li and Tang 1986). There is evidence, however, of subsequent proliferating state tax exactions. A report on a district of Gucheng county, Hubei, for example, notes the doubling of the financial burden on peasant households in the years 1983–85 (Pan 1986: 21). Even before the 1986 implementation of a progressive income tax designed both as a source of government revenue and as a check on income polarization, there were reports of as many as twenty-five different types of levies adding to the burdens of household producers. These included exactions for education, road building, cultural activities, and so forth.[17]

By far the largest source of state extraction of the rural surplus was not agricultural taxes but compulsory sales quotas for all major agricultural products, a system that went hand in hand with the curbing and, by the late 1950s, the virtual elimination of free markets in grain and crops. By keeping prices on agricultural commodities low and those for tractors, fertilizer, electricity, and other modern inputs high, the state effected a major resource transfer at the expense of agriculture and the countryside. This was the primary vehicle for China's rapid accumulation and urban-centered industrialization (see chapter 4 of this volume).

Under mobilizational collectivism, the basic accounting unit, usually the team, was responsible for agricultural taxes and compulsory sales. In the 1980s, however, responsibility for the land tax passed to contracting households, and in 1985, when the state abolished compulsory sales and announced the end of its willingness to buy all available crops, it entered into direct contracts with producing households, bypassing the collective.

While some scholars regard the state agricultural tax as basically equivalent to "absolute ground rent,"[18] the state is not the primary owner of farm land in either formal or actual terms. The land tax does, however, provide a glimpse into both changing ownership relations and the relationship between the state and different social groups. In the 1980s contracting households have replaced production teams as taxpayers (Liang 1986a). This reflects the changing character of ownership and of rural social relations generally. The enlarged position of the contracting household as a participant in landownership and as a relatively independent producer is recognized in the restructured tax system.

Collective Funds

Villages (and in some cases production teams) continue to maintain public funds following implementation of the contract system. In the early 1980s, these funds consisted principally of a public accumulation fund to finance expanded reproduction, accounting for approximately 5–6 percent of total village income; a public welfare fund to support health and welfare programs, accounting for about 2 percent; and a production fund providing circulating resources, accounting for 1–2 percent of gross income.

Under mobilizational collectivism the collection process was straightforward: Following the harvest, the collective deducted production costs, taxes, and collective funds for welfare and accumulation. Only then did the collective distribute the balance, usually about 50–60 percent of gross income, to member households.[19] In the 1980s contracting households still pay collective funds. Such payments are usually fixed in advance and, in theory, are not subject to change during the contract period (Liang 1986a: 61–63). But with the emergence of the household as the primary unit of production as well as of marketing and consumption, the harvest is in the hands of individual households, not the collective. Confronting hundreds of atomized production units (households), and with its own powers diminished, the collective (village) faces growing difficulties in securing resources.

The Shanxi model contract regulations are fascinating with respect to this point: After the harvest, contracting households are instructed first to fulfill their tax and sales obligations to the state in grain and cotton and then "deliver the balance of the commodities to the team." After deducting its share for production, accumulation, and welfare, "if surpluses remain" the team will then return the balance due to each household. These guidelines reflect the effort of the state to insure, first, its own due and, second, that of the collective prior to distribution to the producers as income (Crook 1985: 293, 295).[20]

Collective public funds were originally deducted by production teams from collectively produced products. This merely involved internal bookkeeping. The funds were collectively produced, collectively owned, and collectively used. When the contracting household is the primary agricultural production unit, however, collective funds take on new characteristics: (1) These funds are primarily the product of household production; (2) Their appropriation no longer involves internal distribution within a single economic unit but requires value transfer from contracting households to the collective; (3) The collective elicits these funds from contracting households by virtue of its formal ownership of land and its contractual relationship to the household. Although many collectives provide services and inputs that contribute to agricultural production, and many earn income from collectively managed industries, a considerable part of collective funds are now individually produced but collectively appropriated and collectively used. This is in part the economic realization of collective ownership of the land.

Land Compensation

Another source of income derived from landownership is land compensation. This mainly takes two forms. First, when the state appropriates land it pays compensation to the production team or village. The 1986 Land Management Law stipulates that state compensation for land should be three to six times the average annual output value of that land in the last three years, plus payment of a subsidy for rural people who are displaced. The subsidy ranges from two to three times to a maximum of ten times the average annual output value of the land in the last three years, and the total payment should not exceed twenty times the average annual output value. This constitutes the best indicator available of the state's current official assessment of land value and the entitlement of the formal owner (the collective) in the event of confiscation. It also clarifies the partial ownership claims of contracting households.

Here state policy obliquely acknowledges the partial commodity character of the land, including its differential value based on productivity. That "value," however, is quite independent of the price that purchasers in the market are willing to pay, a value which frequently bears no relationship to the output value of the land: this is above all the case with respect to land in and near the cities, industrial zones, or major transporation lines. In the 1960s in Hebei province, when the state purchased rural land, it normally paid the collective four to six years' cash value of earnings from grain produced on that land; in the chaos of the Cultural Revolution the state sometimes simply confiscated land with no payment to local units.

As the following examples reveal, the state has been unable to enforce the productivity-based guidelines for land prices stipulated in the Land Management Law. In the early 1980s, the Finance and Education College in Shijiazhuang, the Hebei provincial capital, paid 25,000 yuan per mu (one-sixth of an acre) for 100 mu of land needed for campus expansion. Within two to three years, however, the price had risen to 50,000 yuan, exclusive of the costs involved in wining and dining not only collective leaders but representatives of the approximately twenty government units whose chops of approval are required to complete the process, such as the bureaux in charge of education, finance, construction, materials, electricity, utility, and transport. Similarly, the Hebei Normal College bought suburban land for just 4,000 yuan per mu in 1979; in 1987, when it bought additional land, the price had increased tenfold to 40,000 yuan.

We observe diverse peasant strategies coping with the rapidly changing conditions in the suburbs of all medium or large cities. In Huaidi in suburban Shijiazhuang, for example, peasants in one prosperous industrializing village chose not to sell their remaining land to urban institutions. Rather they divided the land among households. Each child in a family who reached age sixteen received a generous plot of land sufficient to build a five-room house on condition that a house be built within one year. Since children in this suburban area were not marrying until well into their twenties, the houses provide a valuable source of income as rental properties convenient to a rapidly growing city, as well as assuring urban residence for all local youth in an expanding metropolitan area.

In the Chongwen district of Beijing in 1987 the purchase price of land reportedly ranged from 10,000 yuan per mu, if jobs, housing, or other benefits were provided to the dispossessed, to 30,000 yuan per mu or higher if no other arrangements were made for the former cultivators. In the same year, however, an institute of the Chinese Academy of Social Sciences purchased a plot of suburban land for a staff apartment building for 50,000 yuan per mu.[21]

A 1986 Jiangxi provincial report states that the price of suburban land ranges from 20,000 to 50,000 yuan per mu with payment shared 20/80 or 30/70 between the collective and contracting households. The breakdown of the payment clearly reveals the strength of residual ownership claims by contracting households (*Jiangxi nongye jingji* 1986).

Villagers and contracting households are increasingly assertive, both individually and corporately, in negotiating land transactions. In the 1970s the Xi'an Foreign Languages Institute purchased land to build a back road. A decade later the neighboring commune presented a bill for 500,000 yuan, claiming that the original payment was too low, that too much land was taken, that water runoff from the institute had lowered their productivity, and that the institute walls cast shadows that further lowered productivity. When the institute refused to pay, the peasants dumped rubbish to block the back entrance. The institute appealed to urban authorities to mediate, but to no effect. Finally, when the peasants blocked the institute's sewers, a negotiated settlement was reached.[22]

Some land sales reveal the intimate relationship between the soil and its resident households. When a factory negotiates the purchase of agricultural land in the 1980s, in addition to cash payment, it frequently guarantees to provide a specified number of jobs on the state payroll for dispossessed villagers. Such contracts are negotiated with the village which in turn compensates households that lose contracted land.

A second type of compensation takes place when contracted land is transferred between the collective and a household or among households. Collectives pay compensation for investment that improves the land when a household returns contracted land, or a fee is paid by the household that assumes the contract.

The shift from mobilizational collectivism to the contract system leaves intact the structure of differential rent in which those born into communities well endowed with fertile land and access to urban markets enjoy lifetime benefits denied those living in infertile terrain or far from lucrative markets.[23] This differential rent was formerly realized by its beneficiaries in the form of higher workpoint earnings for collective labor. In the 1980s it takes the more direct form of higher income on superior contract land or income generated by the transfer or sale of that land.

The household's share of landownership is expressed in its three realization forms. First, as a member of the village (the formal owner), households share land income in the form of public funds. Second, as an independent producer enjoying contractual cultivation and product rights, the household has a claim on the actual and potential income produced on the land. Third, in the event of the sale of land, contracting households are entitled to compensation. This not only underscores the fact that the contracting household is an independent economic unit with a share in landownership rights but confirms its economic interest in the collective.

The emerging pattern of landownership in the 1980s is a complex amalgam of rights shared among the state, the collective, and the contracting household.

Productivity, Social Relations, and the Future of Chinese Agriculture

"There is only one criterion for judging the rationality of the specific form of the ownership system in the elementary stage of socialism," Xue Muqiao has observed in a characteristic formulation of reform economists, "which is to see if it is conducive to the development of the productive forces and the bettering of the people's livelihood" (1986: 31). While our analysis addresses the implications of ownership for the full range of relations of production, including the exploitation and the autonomy of households, as well as issues of income and social inequality, Xue offers a starting point for discussing the performance of the system. In the years since the introduction of household contracts, agricultural yields and per capita rural incomes have increased dramatically. During the period 1978–1985 agricultural output increased at the annual rate of 6.7 percent, twice the 3.3 percent annual increases of the preceding twenty years, 1955–1977.[24] Sideline and rural industrial production advanced at an even faster pace, and rural per capita net income tripled from 134 yuan in 1978 to 398 yuan in 1985 (State Statistical Bureau 1986: 582). Both economic performance and rural income gains since 1978 contrast sharply with two decades of slow growth of agricultural production and virtual stagnation of rural per capita incomes under the system of mobilizational collectivism.

Does this performance constitute the victory of rural institutional reform in general and reform of ownership in particular? The answer cannot be definitive. The contractual reforms have only been in place since 1982, and the reform agenda is far from complete. Moreover, in assessing China's recent agricultural performance, we note that there have been favorable weather conditions; favorable state pricing policies toward agricultural products beginning with a 38.5 percent increase in agricultural purchasing prices in the years 1979 to 1981 and expanded above quota purchases at premium prices 50 percent higher (*Zhongguo nongcun fazhan wenti yanjiuzu* 1984: 38; Zhao Zhanping 1985); greater market autonomy for agricultural producers; increased availability of chemical fertilizer and pesticide; more effective use of technical personnel; and the end of state requirements to grow grain everywhere, thereby permitting more diverse cropping patterns and higher rural incomes. Many of these conditions favorable to agricultural development, such as the sharp rise in agricultural purchasing prices in the early 1980s, are unlikely to be repeated. Above all, the available data do not permit us to disaggregate the effect of each of these elements. We can, however, consider the ways in which changing ownership patterns in combination with all these factors have, on the one hand, contributed to accelerated agricultural development and the first substantial and sustained improvement in the livelihood of rural people since collectivization and, on the other hand, given rise to new conflicts and problems.

By strengthening the relationship between productivity and household income, and permitting rural households to reclaim control over their labor power, the contract system has stimulated individual initiative long stifled under the collective regimen. "To raise the enthusiasm of the masses" is not a hollow slogan here. China's agriculture is still based overwhelmingly on hand labor. The willingness to work long hours with great intensity, care, and intelligence greatly affects yield and income. In addition, the opportunity for rural producers to diversify in agriculture, sidelines, industry, and commerce, and to leave the land to engage in other occupations, has reduced disguised unemployment and placed a premium on more rational use of labor. Between 1978 and 1985, according to one estimate, 67 million people left agriculture to engage in industry, transportation, commerce, construction, and so forth. Most of these people remain in the countryside, contributing to the rapid growth of rural industry, sidelines, and commerce which have stimulated the rural economy. The future of the rural economy hinges on the ability to find nonagricultural employment for an additional 100 million or more rural workers. Complementary changes in ownership, production relations, and price have strengthened labor and entrepreneurial incentives and labor mobility, contributing to higher productivity and higher rural incomes.

While resolving certain problems of the collective system, particularly low incentives to producers and the bondage of rural people to the land, does the new pattern of ownership conflict with such socialist developmental goals as planning, coordination, class harmony, and equality of income? The reforms may be assessed from the perspective of changing patterns of land concentration and dispersion as they affect productivity, income, and social relations. China has dismantled the large fields constructed following collectivization. In 1985 per capita farmland averaged 0.23 acres, including much marginal hill land, and with an average of ten scattered plots per households, fields are indeed of garden scale. The rare specialized households that have been able to gain cultivation rights to three or more acres have been dubbed "big contracting households" (*chengbao da hu*) (Chen Zhong 1985).[25]

While there is no compelling evidence that the sacrifice of economies of scale at Chinese levels of technology has significantly reduced yields, economists have viewed the problem from two aspects. Some have sought to encourage land amalgamation in the hands of specialized farm households to spur agricultural productivity, commodification, and technological advance. Between 1982 and 1985, China's farmland reportedly dropped at an annual rate of 0.5–1.0 percent as housing construction accelerated and much cropland was used for industrial and commercial purposes (*People's Daily*, March 18, 1985). Reports such as one from 1985 listing rural land prices in Jiangsu province as ranging from a low of 120 yuan to 10,000 yuan per mu suggest the existence of an active market in land (Xu and Shi 1985). Sometimes the tone is critical, even sinister. A company "illegally marketing land" in one county of the Guangxi Autonomous Region in the years 1984–86 reportedly removed 2,256 mu from cultivation (*Guangming Daily*, June 27, 1986). In Taicang county, Jiangsu province, in 1984, 1.5 percent of total farm land was taken out of agricultural production for industrial or housing use (Xu and Shi 1985). Nevertheless, with continuing uncertainty about future policy, the overwhelming majority of rural households cling to the land as the bedrock guarantee of subsistence. China's egalitarian land distribution continues to provide basic subsistence guarantees for nearly 200 million rural households, in contrast, for example, with India, where scores of millions of landless households with no such entitlement are forced into the market as hired laborers from an extremely disadvantageous position.

At the same time, critics have posed the issue of exploitation as specialized and entrepreneurial households earn substantial incomes on the basis of hired labor and the return on capital investment. In 1986 vigorous debate focused on whether Communist Party members should be permitted (encouraged?) to hire labor and whether hiring of labor with the promise of boosting incomes of the poorest strata constitutes class exploitation. The scope for hiring labor, the number of hired laborers and tenants involved in agricultural production is extremely small. For the most part, rural hired labor is centered in industrial and laborers and tenants involved in agricultural production are extremely small. For the most part, rural hired labor is centered in industrial and service enterprises. Since 1986 the primary state response to this issue is its vigorous encouragement of the development of new forms of cooperation as an alternative to both household enterprise and hired labor, particularly in industrial and sideline development.[26]

Other critics have noted a contradiction between the predominantly collective ownership of land, on the one hand, and the increasingly private ownership of tools, machinery, and inputs and private cultivation of land, on the other. A 1984 report indicates that nearly half of total fixed rural assets exclusive of land are privately owned (Wu 1986).[27] More immediately pressing is the failure of the contract system thus far to stimulate substantial agricultural investment. The rapid increase of privately owned agricultural means of production is primarily the result of the sale or distribution to households of collective machinery and equipment. With both collective and household investors placing their resources in higher profit industry, sidelines, and commerce, agriculture goes begging. This investment preference mirrors the state's own long-term anti-agricultural investment bias, a phenomenon which continues in the late 1980s, but it also reflects a worldwide phenomenon of slighting agriculture in favor of industry, commerce, services, and other investments.

Changing patterns of landownership and accompanying state policies have boosted labor incentives, productivity, and income and reduced the relative urban-rural income and opportunity gap, which
increased substantially in the course of the era of mobilizational collectivism.[28] At the same time the reforms have given rise to numerous
conflicts as household autonomy increases, the boundaries of the collective and the household producer become more ambiguous, and tenancy and hired labor make their appearance. These include conflicts
between household and collective, between employer and employee,
and among cultivating households competing, for example, for scarce
water rights. The issues of landownership are at the center of the
continuing debate among proponents of further commodification of
land and labor, those who see the future of the countryside in a resurgence of voluntary cooperatives building on the experiences of the late
1940s and early 1950s, and those who look to the resurrection of
collective- and state-directed institutions.

NOTES

Chapter 1

1. The phrase "China's development trajectory" assumes no single trajectory either temporally or spatially. Indeed, the analysis that follows emphasizes contending positions with the framework of the party-state and within social groups and classes, shifting courses and a multiplicity of resource bases and outcomes by region, class, ethnic group, gender, and so forth. This work nevertheless seeks to chart the terrain of some of the larger directions of socioeconomic change within China (particularly the densely populated regions in which the Han predominate) and, to a lesser extent, to observe the consequences of China's involvement in, and at times exclusion from, the world economy. The term "China" in this study at times refers to policies implemented at a given moment by the party-state; principally, however, it refers to the full range of state-society interactions that produce widely variant results among diverse regions, groups, and classes depending on such factors as physical endowment, location, historical evolution, and connections to the world economy.

2. I shared this view in the 1960s. Alexander Eckstein (1978), while presenting a positive view of China's economic achievements, stressed the difficulty of transfer of "the Chinese model."

3. For an insightful alternative approach to the lines of cleavage in Chinese policy making see Solinger (1984), particularly the essays by Edward Friedman and Dorothy Solinger. The rewriting of Communist Party history, and particularly Mao Zedong's pronouncements in the years from 1955 forward, concealed many of these contrapuntal themes to the mobilizational collectivism that prevailed in the years from 1955 until Mao's death in 1976, except during a brief period in the early 1960s. Throughout the final decades of his life Mao retained a monopoly on the ability to make major policy pronouncements, but particularly following economic setbacks associated with the Leap and the Cultural Revolution, his ability to define economic and social policy in practice was restricted. The most important spokesman for alternative rural policies, whose work has been resurrected in China in the 1980s, was Deng Zihui, who headed the party's Rural Work Department in the 1950s and who clashed several times with Mao on the character and pace of cooperative formation and collectivization. See particularly Deng (1984). Nicholas Lardy has elaborated the alternative approaches of

Deng Zihui, Peng Dehuai, and Chen Yun in the 1950s and 1960s (1987: 378–86). See also Su Shaozhi (1983) on reform alternatives.

4. China's national rate of accumulation is defined as the ratio of accumulation to national income where accumulation is basically "that part of national income used to increase fixed capital assets (productive and nonproductive), working capital and material reserves" (Chen 1967: 11).

5. I first addressed these issues in Selden (1971). That study rightly sought to illuminate egalitarian and participatory elements of the revolutionary process; however, it underestimated intraparty conflict and manipulative and repressive features both of the emerging party-state and of rural society in the anti-Japanese base areas. The issues are explored anew in Friedman and Selden (1987) and in Friedman, Pickowicz, and Selden (forthcoming). See also Thaxton (1983).

6. Lenin's NEP policies represented an advance over War Communism in reducing the pressures on the Soviet peasantry. But in contrast to Chinese efforts to promote mutual aid and cooperation, NEP was predicated on the continued Bolshevik focus on the cities and, in effect, extraction of grain. Taxation and military concerns aside, the Soviet countryside during NEP was essentially left to its own devices.

7. The outcomes of the reforms constitute a subject for future research. While many researchers have perceived in the reforms the cutting edge of a "peasant capitalism" or a household economy, others, such as Pat Howard (1987), have stressed a leadership design and emerging institutional focus giving rise to new forms of cooperation. In my view, the dominant leadership consensus recognizes that large-scale collectivization and communization of the 1950s forward were historically premature, so to speak, given the low technical base of Chinese farming. In the 1980s pressures are building, both from above and from below, to "rationalize" agriculture by encouraging farm consolidation and permitting the full commodification of both land and labor to achieve economies of scale. Some reformers also see these changes as the basis for encouraging new forms of small-scale cooperation. Whether these trends toward expanded cooperation will actually materialize remains, of course, an open question. See Victor Nee (1985) on the issues of peasant household individualism in China, and Harry Harding (1987) on "moderate" and "radical" perspectives on reform.

8. In 1957 China's leading sociologist, Fei Xiaotong, called attention to the consequences for the peasantry of the loss of household sidelines as a result of state policies of resource centralization. Fei was deprived of his position and silenced for the next twenty years. See Fei (1983) and McGough (1979).

9. Following Durkheim, Terence Hopkins has defined anomie in ways that seem to me to fit precisely the situation of China's postcollectivization situation, and particularly that following the cataclysmic impact of the Great Leap and the famine it precipitated. The context is one of "such biographically rapid and extreme changes in people's circumstances of existence that the moral connectives they've shared with others, lived by, and made in effect constitutive of their selves (egos) no longer provide guides to ethical conduct." Personal communication, January 25, 1988.

10. It is particularly in this respect that the performance of the East Asian NICs reportedly compares so favorably with that of China. In Korea and Taiwan, according to one study, the productivity of labor rose by 5.2 and 5.4 percent per year respectively between 1965 and 1981, and in Japan in the 1950s and 1960s it increased by approximately 6 percent (Ramon Myers 1987: 134).

11. According to the estimates of Perkins and Yusuf (1984: 38), China's yields were in turn outstripped by the performance of the world's leading agrarian producers, notably the Republic of Korea (4,918 kilograms per hectare in rice) and Japan (5,128 kilograms per hectare).

12. Formidable methodological problems remain for those who wish to undertake

serious comparative study of the development achievements of China versus those of the East Asian ministates, particularly since no state of China's continental proportions has succeeded in making advances comparable to those of, for example, Taiwan and Singapore. The problems of transforming a nation of China's size, diversity, and complexity seem to me far greater than those in the nations compared here. The international political economy can, moreover, encompass the rise of ministates without major overall transformation; the same would be unthinkable with respect to a country the size of China or India.

Chapter 2

1. In subsequent formulations beginning in 1905, Lenin clearly demarcated two stages in rural policy: a first bourgeois-democratic stage in which such remnants of serfdom as landlord and official domination are abolished, and a second socialist stage to abolish the rule of capital (1959b: 122–30). Lenin's ambiguity, and the deep intra-party divisions on the question of nationalization of the land, are well brought out in Lenin (1959a; 1959d). Lenin's shifts on the agrarian question are summed up in Lenin (1985: 291).

2. "The successes of our collective-farm policy are due, among other things, to the fact that it rests on the *voluntary character* of the collective-farm movement and on *taking into account the diversity of conditions* in the various regions of the USSR. Collective farms must not be established by force. That would be foolish and reactionary."

Chapter 3

1. Stalin's mechanical concept of social change in which social relations, institutions, and ideas automatically follow from the level of development of the productive forces took this form in one authoritative pronouncement: "Every base has its own superstructure corresponding to it. The base of the feudal system has its superstructure—its political, legal and other views and the corresponding institutions; the capitalist base has its own superstructure, and so has the socialist base. If the base changes or is eliminated, then following this its superstructure changes or is eliminated; if a new base arises, then following this a superstructure arises corresponding to it" (Stalin 1951).

In a series of important books, the Polish economist Wlodzimierz Brus has focused on the process of achieving socialist forms of ownership *beginning* with nationalization or the formation of cooperative units. The central issue is the political process of investing new ownership forms with the substance of participation in and mastery of the factories and farms by the immediate producers. Brus raises these issues in the context of a critique of centralized socialism. See in particular "Socialisation in the Conception and Practice of East European Socialism," in Brus (1975: 27–102). Mao Zedong's most comprehensive contribution to the debate is *A Critique of Soviet Economics*.

2. Chinese documents delineate elementary and advanced cooperatives (*he-zuoshe*) as the basic socialist units in the countryside in the 1950s, using distinctive Chinese terminology rather than the term used to translate Soviet collectives (*jiti nongzhuang*). Advanced cooperatives are in fact, however, collective units that own and operate the land and the principle means of production, and in which remuneration is based on the principle "to each according to one's work." They are comparable to, and were modeled after, Soviet collectives, the kolkhozes. I will use the term collectives here.

3. See the excellent discussion in Lewin (1975: 93–102). Nicolai Bukharin, leading the opposition to collectivization as premature and unworkable in the years 1925–29, stressed his fidelity to Lenin's emphasis on marketing cooperatives that left intact private landownership and household farming during the transition period. Cf. Cohen (1971: 193–201). Bukharin anticipated many of the failures and problems of Soviet collectivization; he did not, however, successfully frame an alternative policy that would solve issues of the transition.

4. Mao's concept of stages grew organically out of the party's experience. It invites comparison, however, with a seminal statement on the subject by Lenin in his 1918 "Speech Delivered at the First All-Russian Congress of Land Departments, Committees of Poor Peasants and Communes" (Lenin 1959c: 259). "We know very well that in countries where small-peasant economies prevail the transition to socialism cannot be effected except by a series of gradual preliminary stages. . . . We fully realize that such vast upheavals in the lives of tens of millions of people as the transition from small individual peasant farming to the joint cultivation of the land, affecting as they do the most deepgoing roots of life and habits, can be accomplished only by long effort, and can in general be accomplished only when necessity compels people to reshape their lives."

5. I have developed these themes in Selden (1971; 1978).

6. Two articles have analyzed the positions of Mao and Liu on issues related to the rich-peasant economy and subsequent charges directed against Liu during the Cultural Revolution. Both make clear Mao's participation in formulating the position of support for the rich-peasant economy from the late forties. Lieberthal (1971) and Tanaka (1980).

7. The revised text as presented in Mao (1965: 159) reads: "We have already organized many peasant cooperatives in the Border Region, but at present they are only of a rudimentary type and must still pass through certain stages of development before they can become cooperatives of the Soviet type known as collective farms."

8. One can trace Mao's impulses toward mutual aid and cooperation back to a pre-Marxist period. In his 1919 essay, "The Great Union of the Popular Masses," after noting the approach of "one extremely violent party which uses the method 'do unto others as they do unto you' to struggle desperately to the end with the aristocrats and capitalists" (its leader was "a man named Marx"), the young Mao commented on a more promising alternative which "does not expect rapid results but begins by understanding the common people. Men should all have a morality of mutual aid, and work voluntarily. . . . The ideas of this party are broader and more far-reaching. They want to unite the whole globe into a single country, unite the human race into a single family. . . . The leader of this party is a man named Kropotkin." Cited in Schram (1977: xxviii).

9. Comparing the economic results in the Soviet Union, Cuba, Vietnam, and a number of other countries that attempted cooperative solutions to the agrarian problem, China's performance during this period seems exemplary.

10. One of the most serious charges made against Liu Shaoqi and others during the Cultural Revolution was that they had opposed and sabotaged cooperation in the early fifties. The charges, in my view, are unfounded. The intraleadership divisions centered rather on the pace of cooperation and the issue of voluntary participation. Jack Gray (1975: 413) has argued the contrary. Those who urged caution in cooperative formation, he concludes, really opposed cooperation and sought to move the countryside toward individual farming. While there were surely plenty of advocates of such a future among the peasantry, I see no evidence that this view enjoyed significant support in the upper ranks of the party or state leadership. "Had collectivization been slowed up," Gray concludes of the 1955 hiatus, "it would never have taken place at all." This is

precisely the point with which this essay takes issue.

11. The most prominent spokesman for gradual development by stages was Deng Zihui, head of the party's Rural Work Department. See for example Deng (1954; 1955). In his important 1954 address to the Youth League, Deng's projected timetable for collectivization was faster than that which Mao proposed one year later. Deng spoke of the completion of collectivization within two five-year plans, with large-scale mechanization to be achieved in the third.

12. *Tongji gongzuo* (1957: 5) records a 39 percent rise in the price index of agricultural commodities bought by the state between 1950 and 1956, while the price index of industrial goods sent to the countryside increased by only 10.8 percent. This reduced, but did not eliminate, the gap which continued into the 1980s. China's price index, moreover, excluded such costly items as tractors and water pumps.

13. China's leading anthropologist, Fei Xiaotong, offered a brilliant, if low-keyed, description of the destructive impact of national policy on rural handicraft and income in a single village in 1957. It was his last publication before being silenced for the next twenty years. See Fei (1979: 39–74). A recent if muted criticism of 1950s' handicraft policies is Tian Yun (1980: 16–24).

14. The following discussion of handicrafts draws on Kojima's pioneering research in this area.

15. Articles in the theoretical journal *Xuexi* (Study) in the years 1952–55 spell out in rich detail the rationale for and specific measures employed in the attempted gradual, voluntary cooperative transition based on demonstrated ability to contribute to mutual prosperity. See particularly Wu Zhen (1954).

16. The discussion of Wugong is based on field work between 1978 and 1987. See Edward Friedman et al. (forthcoming). The issue of appropriate ratios for remuneration is discussed in numerous articles in *Socialist Upsurge in the Chinese Countryside* (Mao 1956) and by Jack Gray (1970).

17. Substantially wider differentials existed among regions. A 1956 survey of Shaanxi province revealed the following per capita income differentials by region: Compared with a provincial average of 64 yuan, the average in the industrial crop region was 126 yuan; in the main grain-producing area, 75 yuan; in the hill regions, 45 yuan; and in poor mountainous areas, 19 yuan. If regional differences in income were on a scale of greater than five to one, differences between poor and rich villages were many times higher. See Nolan (1979: 450) and Selden (1985). Cooperativization strategies did not directly address these and other regional and intravillage inequalities.

18. In his September 7, 1955, inner-party directive, Mao went so far as to divide the middle peasants into three categories: lower, intermediate, and upper middle. The version of the directive printed in 1977 (pp. 208–209) takes the unusual step of noting that in practice this proved to be a classification "too fine for drawing distinctions."

19. Gray (1975) and Kojima (1975) have used the *Socialist Upsurge* collection to demonstrate the viability of Mao's approach to cooperation. My own research on Wugong, Dazhai, and other model units suggests another interpretation. In the rush to collectivization in 1955–56, the genuine achievements of many of these units could not be *rapidly* duplicated by most others, which lacked such advantages as outstanding leadership, intravillage unity, long cooperative experience, or access to state financial and technical support.

20. It is instructive to compare the tone and implications of Deng Zihui's writings on cooperation between 1953 and 1956 with those of Chen Boda. Deng Zihui attempted to address concretely the specific doubts and hesitations about cooperation of different sectors of the peasantry while emphasizing the importance of voluntary cooperation and mutual benefit. Deng likewise severely criticized commandism and excessive haste in cooperative formation. Two aspects of Chen's approach stand out sharply from much

of the discussion of the period. First, where Deng and others had stressed the dual and complex nature of the peasantry, Chen emphasized the revolutionary qualities of the peasantry, qualities he traced back to the "semiproletarian" character of the majority of semi-tenants and poor peasants which Mao had pointed to in his 1926 analysis of classes in Chinese society. Second, Chen stressed the dominant role of the state in leading the transition: "our socialist transformation of agriculture is a revolution from above to below, led by the state in which the governmental power is in the hands of the working class." What was essential for Chen was "to give active leadership to ensure the consciousness of the masses and mobilize them," not to "Passively wait for the masses or let the masses take whatever action they see fit." Chen's emphasis on mobilizational leadership and immediate collectivization, his lack of sympathy for voluntary cooperation, and the absence of appeal to peasant material interests in striking ways evokes Stalinist approaches to collectivization (Chen 1956: 36–44; cf. Friedman 1982).

21. I have substituted the word cooperative for "kommunia" in the original translation. Cf. Deng Zihui's reiteration of this point in an important article: "Leninism teaches us: In petty commodity agrarian economy, in carrying out the socialist transformation, we absolutely must not use force and methods of expropriation to collectivize (*gongyuhua*) the property of the peasantry. This would be a violation of the party's basic policy toward the peasants" (Deng 1955).

22. Jack Gray's (1970: 55–61) hypothetical example of family budgets, introduced to demonstrate quite different points about the cooperative movement, bears out this hypothesis. In Gray's example, derived from actual cases described in *Socialist Upsurge in China's Countryside*, 60 percent of income is based on inputs to land, 40 percent to labor. Gray's articles on the socialist upsurge period creatively reconstruct the internal logic of the upsurge, the view so to speak from Mao's desk, based on a close reading of the several hundred case studies provided in the *Socialist Upsurge* collection. At one critical moment, however, Gray steps back from this reconstruction to raise serious problems about its results. Commenting on the *Upsurge* collection, he observes that it "represents an experimentalist idea, and contradicts the notion of gradualism. It is enough that the manifold particular problems of cooperativization and cooperative working have all been solved somewhere. They are therefore capable of solution everywhere. This is acceptable on the level of the leadership and the cadres; but it is not a substitute for gradualism at the level of the farmers, who can only be convinced, in the last resort, by their own practical experience over a series of agricultural seasons; and who must get used gradually to a new form of discipline and a new concept of shared profit. This is the nub of the politics of the cooperative movement; it sets an irreducible minimum period for success, and in the event most Chinese farmers were not given this minimum" (1975: 115–16; italics in original). Precisely. Yet Gray's work as a whole is devoted to explaining the logic and success of the transition and of Mao's analysis. The logic that the performance of model units, typically the beneficiary of special financial and leadership support, proves the viability of national policies, is unacceptable.

23. The cooperative transformation of agriculture in general and the high tide and Great Leap in particular became the subject of intensive study in China and Hong Kong in 1980. Among the more significant attempts at reinterpretation are Yang Junshi (1980). The "Resolution on Certain Questions in the History of Our Party since the Founding of the People's Republic of China" (1981: 16) noted (for the first time in an official document) that "from the summer of 1955 onwards, we were over-hasty in pressing on with agricultural cooperation and the transformation of private handicraft and commercial establishments; we were far from meticulous, the changes were too fast, and we did our work in a somewhat summary, stereotyped manner, leaving open a

number of questions for a long time.'' The document does not, however, explicitly hold Mao Zedong responsible for the problems in this area.

Chapter 4

1. Preobrazhensky went further to say "original capitalist accumulation could (even) take place on the basis of feudalism (p. 80),'' because there is a spontaneous transformation of merchant capital into industrial capital, and original capitalist accumulation is characterized by merchant capitalism, which is not incompatible with feudalism.

2. According to Marx, prices would fluctuate around the "prices of production (cost),'' which would assure an equal rate of return on capital; but even equilibrium prices would depart from "values'' defined by the amount of socially necessary labor expended in production, because of differences in the "organic composition of capital (or capital labor ratio)'' in different industries. However, equivalent exchange, in contrast to unequal exchange, is often used as a shorthand way to indicate exchange under market prices (particularly world market prices, to which Preobrazhensky usually referred), as against monopoly or planned prices used for the reallocation of resources.

3. Bian calculated the capital outflow from agriculture as follows: (1) peasant savings invested in the nonagricultural sector, (2) land tax in kind, (3) government purchase as a part of land tax, (4) payment for agricultural production loans, (5) rice-fertilizer barter, (6) government monopoly of agricultural export.

4. Ishikawa (1967a: 321, 323) takes 1952 as the base year in which a real price (equivalent exchange) is assumed that reflects the real cost under conditions of general equilibrium. Taking 1952 as the base year, he discovered a net resource inflow into the agricultural sector. As will be shown in the following section, however, it is debatable whether 1952 is an appropriate base year. Ishikawa's data in value terms nevertheless show the proportion of resources flowing from various mechanisms (market, taxation, and state procurement) each year.

5. Shi Jizeng (1969: 65) had a similar estimate. During 1958–66, the government earned 10.85 million U.S. dollars net profit per year from rice-fertilizer barter. Xu Wen-fu's estimate of $29.03 million is three times as high as Rada and Lee's (Hsu 1969: 53).

Chapter 5

1. Perkins proceeds to note, however, that on a national basis rural income differentials have changed little since land reform.

2. See particularly Kuznets (1963); Adelman and Morris (1973); Hirschman (1958); Myrdal (1957).

3. The team 3 survey was conducted by Edward Friedman, Kay Johnson, Paul Pickowicz, and myself in preparing our study, *Chinese Village, Socialist State* (forthcoming). I am grateful to my collaborators for permission to use a portion of the data here. The team 2 data were graciously supplied by Peter Nolan from the results of a British survey team in 1978. The team 2 data are restricted to household collective income excluding both per capita incomes and incomes from extracollective sources.

4. There are methodological problems here that cannot be resolved utilizing data available at present. Our data take the household as the unit of income but conceal income pooling in larger networks of family, particularly financial support by sons for aging parents. However, the available comparative data likewise use the household unit

in most cases. Our data also do not disclose payments by the team to "five-guarantee households" and other welfare recipients—an important factor in assuring subsistence.

5. *Beijing Review* 25 (1982): 7. Private-sector earnings rose rapidly in the late seventies and early eighties.

6. This finding is in line with the broad conclusions drawn by Griffin and Saith (1981: 16). One should be wary of generalization on this point, however, and not only because of the limited data available. Viewed in spatial terms, income earned in the private sector probably exacerbates certain inequalities among units and among regions.

7. Louis Kriesberg (1979: 99) notes the high correlation between income inequality and land inequality (.59) in the fifteen countries for which data existed for both indicators.

8. Cf. John Logan's (1978) illuminating discussion of "Growth, Politics and Stratification of Places."

9. See also Lardy (1978).

10. Lardy's conclusions have been challenged by Audrey Donnithorne (1976). We now know that a crucial, perhaps *the* crucial, factor in Chinese investment strategy narrowing differentials was military-strategic considerations. The secret Third Front strategy (*da san xian*) implemented from 1965 until Mao's death eleven years later involved the massive redirection of investment and even the physical relocation of major sites near the Soviet border to mountain and inland regions of Sichuan, Guizhou, and the Southwest. Li and Li (1986).

11. Cf. E. B. Vermeer's (1982b) insightful discussion of a number of the issues touched on here.

12. Changes in rural organization and the burgeoning of rural industry and commerce have created important new opportunities for rural labor in the 1980s, yet vital elements of the population registration system continue to restrict rural mobility.

13. This helps to account for the fact that in the early eighties the strongest pressures from below to dismantle collective agriculture in favor of household-based economy came from poorer, frequently mountain, communities.

14. *Xinhua yuebao* (February 1981: 117–20). Cf. the discussion in Vermeer (1982a: 25–29).

15. There may be additional methodological problems in how the data were collected in each country—e.g., I remain suspicious of the Bangladesh and Pakistan figures. Unfortunately, too little detail is given in the Jain source to deal with this suspicion.

16. These comparisons are less favorable to China than those in the World Bank study (1983). However, the World Bank study compares China's *per capita* rural income distribution with the *total household* income distribution of several societies, thereby overstating China's rural equality. And the spatial inequality figures used in the World Bank estimate for China are an earlier, less complete set that also overstate China's rural equality.

17. Data from *Brilliant 35 Years* (Beijing: China Statistical Publishing House, 1984), as cited by Fan Kang, University of Chicago Agricultural Economics Workshop, November 1984. There are two potential concerns about these survey data. The more serious is that there is about one extra person per household in these data compared to the census and other data sources. This could be a legitimate difference, but it could also suggest that the surveys oversampled prosperous, able-bodied, intact households and left aside the elderly and other poor single-family homes. Another potential concern is that the sample expanded rapidly over these years, perhaps maintaining the same sampling frame but also possibly incorporating new locales that were more equal than those in the early surveys.

18. These gini coefficients are estimated from the original Chinese income data.

The high figure of .28 for 1978 or .26 for 1979 is lower than our earlier estimate of .31 for 1979 per capita income, suggesting that we may have overestimated inequality somewhat. However, the discrepancy is so small as not to change our original conclusions.

Chapter 6

1. The most penetrating critical assessment of Amin's perspective is Edward Friedman's (1984) "Maoism and Rural Misery." Analysts of socialist societies have explored in diverse ways the implications for class formation of patterns of inequality of income, power, and opportunity. The ownership relations differentiating state and collective sectors have led Soviet and East European analysts to distinguish the working class and the peasantry as separate (but nonantagonistic) classes which, along with an intellectual stratum, comprise the classes in socialist societies. As Ossowski long ago observed of the official formulations of the Stalinist period, their concept was one of classes without exploitation, class antagonism, or class stratification. Stanislaw Ossowski, *Class Structure in the Social Consciousness*, pp. 110–13. Cf. Murray Yanowitch, *Social and Economic Inequality in the Soviet Union*, pp. 3–22. The reforms of the 1980s in China (discussed below) and those in Eastern Europe have reopened such highly charged issues as unemployment, exploitation, tenancy, and the private accumulation of wealth as well as the full range of issues of class inequality.

2. The fate of private plots well illustrates the playing out of these conflicts. Private plots created in 1955 at the time of collectivization, only to be abolished in many communities during the Great Leap Forward of 1958–1960, revived and expanded almost everywhere following the famine of the early 1960s before being "collectivized," reduced, or abolished in many regions during the Cultural Revolution. The right of individuals to sell in the market followed a similar cycle, with markets curbed or abolished during the Great Leap and Cultural Revolution, revived and expanded in the early 1960s and 1980s.

3. China's 1960s deurbanization pattern stands out sharply against global urbanization trends. The urban component of world population increased by one-sixth in both the 1950s and 1960s as nearly 700 million urban people were added to the world population. The urban population in Asia increased from 15.4 percent in 1950 to 25.4 percent by 1970 (K. Davis 1972: 48–51, 170). Robert Bach called this source to my attention. See also Kojima (1987: 3–34, esp. table 2–2, p. 19).

4. Li Bingkun's (1985) careful study of relative prices concludes that in 1978 the price of industrial goods was 21 percent higher than their value while agricultural goods were 37 percent below their value giving rise to a price scissors of 27 percent. Zhou Qiren (1986:21) has well explained the resource transfer mechanism that underlay the urban-rural divide: "When primary products (including agricultural and mineral products) are subject to state purchase at a low price and their processing is monopolized, land rent is not directly manifested as the realization of land ownership. Rather it takes the form of profits from excessive processing and becomes an important source of accumulation for our country's industrialization."

5. Roll's data do not provide a measure of the important differentials between state employees and other workers already in place by 1955. In 1955 large numbers of urban workers, including industrial workers, still remained outside the state sector. State workers, who have enjoyed substantial income and welfare advantages over rural collective workers, also enjoy advantages over urban collective workers. In 1978 the 74.5 million state employees had average incomes of 644 yuan, 27 percent higher than the 505 yuan of 20 million collective workers—and when the value of retirement and

health benefits and various subsidies is considered, the differential is even larger. Cf. *Zhongguo shehui tongji ziliao* (1984: 39, 67); Riskin (1987: 240–42).

6. The structure of benefits for state-sector employees is elaborated in Whyte and Parish (1984: 57–106). The distinctive character of "proletarianization" in state-socialist societies, as suggested here with respect to China, differs significantly from that under capitalism. The characterization of that phenomenon is the subject of future research.

7. Collective villagers had two kinds of welfare benefits. The state provided disaster relief in cases of extreme natural disaster such as flood, chronic drought, and earthquakes, but no succor for routine poverty—self-reliance being the official injunction. The rural poor, particularly those too old to support themselves and lacking family support networks, basically depended on collective benefits funded at the village level. "Five guarantee" benefits varied enormously depending on the wealth and the priorities of the village. Interviews suggest that recipients frequently experienced collective welfare as personally demeaning. Perhaps the most important form of "welfare" was the widely practiced system of deficit payments in which households whose earnings fell below subsistence received sufficient grain advance (in effect an interest-free loan) to assure survival. Payments of this kind constituted a form of subsistence guarantee that distinguishes minimum entitlements in the collective era from the life-threatening conditions so many confronted in China in the first half of the twentieth century, and from those in, for example, contemporary India where large numbers of landless households receive no significant community or state support. The central point made here, however, is the contrast between the generous provisions made to the minority in the state sector compared with the bare minimum available to destitute collective families. Rural welfare systems proliferated during the Great Leap Forward only to collapse in the subsequent famine. They expanded again during the Cultural Revolution, this time on firmer material foundations, most significantly in the formation of collective health systems and grain distribution emphasizing equal per capita distribution of subsistence rations within each team. But while welfare and pension gains for state sector workers were large, permanent, guaranteed to all who were eligible, popular, and above all paid for by the state, rural health and welfare programs were meagre, often poorly staffed, paid for by hard-pressed local communities and humiliated their recipients.

8. Urban collective workers shared the benefits of increased subsidies for food and housing, but not health care, retirement, maternity, and other benefit packages from which they were excluded.

9. Jeffrey Taylor (1986: 229), defining China's labor force participation rate on the basis of population age fifteen and over, gives a national rate for 1982 of 89.6 percent for men and 74.1 percent for women, the latter being the highest in Asia and one of the highest in the world.

10. Income as a return on labor declined even further. Thomas Rawski (1970: 119–21) has calculated that agricultural labor productivity (gross output value per worker-year) increased by a total of 10 percent between 1957 and 1975 while output per labor-day declined by 15–36 percent. Duan Yingbi (1983: 25–28) has calculated the decline in net income for basic crops between 1957 and 1978 as follows: The procurement price of paddy increased 5.5 yuan per mu but production costs increased 7.78 yuan; for wheat, prices were up 5.8 yuan but costs rose 10.7 yuan; millet prices rose 4.66 yuan but costs rose by 7.3 yuan.

11. The Soviet case offers instructive comparisons. Agriculture ranks extremely low in Soviet popular esteem, as indicated in social surveys and in official priorities. Nevertheless, in recent decades the urban-rural as well as the state-collective gap, as measured by relative incomes as well as by access to education and services, has

narrowed greatly. David Lane (1982: 40–42, 62–74) concludes that the great income gulf that separated collective farmers from workers in 1940 was nearly eliminated by 1978 when real per capita collective farm incomes were 88 percent of the incomes of all manual and nonmanual workers. Moreover, Soviet agriculture has moved steadily toward the expansion of the state farm sector and reduction in size of the collective sector. Despite these gains, the status of the Soviet farmer, as measured by social surveys, is extremely low, ranking close to the bottom.

12. Yu. Arutyunyan's (1966) study of Soviet state-collective and urban-rural differentials found that the per capita payments to collective workers were 30–42 percent below those to state farm workers in the years 1958–1960. However, collective workers earned substantially more than state employees on their larger private plots, thereby narrowing the gap. I am indebted to Martin Whyte for calling this article to my attention. For demographic, developmental, and policy reasons, the Soviet urban-rural and state-collective income gap has narrowed considerably with the advance of agricultural mechanization in recent decades.

13. Martin Whyte (1983) offers an astute discussion of the growing cultural gap between city and countryside.

14. The World Bank (1984: 164) reports that per capita caloric consumption, which averaged 2,049 calories in the years 1956–58, did not recover to that level until the 1970s. Protein consumption levels of 54 grams were likewise not reached until the 1970s. Alan Piazza's figures show an even sharper drop in caloric availability between 1956–58 and the 1970s. Piazza (1986: 77). Cf. Xue Muqiao (1984: III: 21).

15. The most exhaustive study of grain and food production and consumption for the years 1949–1980 is Walker (1984, particularly 167–98). Cf. Alan Piazza's (1983) estimates for 1980 of daily per capita caloric availability ranging from 1,577 calories in Inner Mongolia to 3,084 in Heilongjiang and his 1986 estimates.

16. China's reported life expectancy increased by twenty-seven years in the two decades prior to 1980, reaching sixty-seven in that year; in the same period India's life expectancy increased by nine years to fifty-two, and richer Indonesia's by twelve years to fifty-three. While comparison with other large agrarian nations seems to me primary, it should be noted that on all the indicators of income, health, diet and life expectancy, the performance of Taiwan, Hong Kong, and Singapore is superior.

17. I have discussed spatial inequality and rural poverty in chapter 5. See also Vermeer (1982a: 25–29) and Riskin (1987: 233).

18. The magnitude of the economic crisis is underlined by the fact that these were, to my knowledge, the only significant layoffs of state workers in the history of the People's Republic. See the discussion in Liu Suinian (1984: 27). According to Kirkby (1985: 114), net rural migration, that is, from city to countryside, was 13.9 million in 1962 and 20.3 million in 1964. Kojima (1987: table 1–2, 12) calculates the decline in the "nonagricultural population of cities" (the category closest to international concepts of urban population) from 83 million in 1962 to 67 million in 1970. Interviews suggest that many workers "voluntarily" returned to the countryside in response to the call of the state for specified numbers of workers in each unit temporarily to return home to help in this time of travail. The tight food situation in the city as black market prices skyrocketed, and the fact that more food was available in certain rural areas, led some to return. Bearing certificates such as "Glorious Supporter of Agriculture Answering the Party's Call" and with resettlement payments of 300 yuan, most cherished the promise that they would be restored to urban state-sector jobs as soon as economic recovery permitted rehiring. However, from the mid–1960s, when plants expanded their labor force, most new workers were people with urban registration. Some sent-down factory workers eventually obtained industrial jobs in lower ranking cities in the urban hierarchy.

19. Jonathan Unger (1982) has emphasized the virtual impermeability of the cities and the state sector after the early 1960s. William Parish (1984) details the destratification process affecting youth in the Cultural Revolution generation. Deborah Davis (-Friedmann) (1985) shows the income advantages of older workers who entered the work force in the early 1950s, and the drying up of opportunities for state-sector jobs from the 1960s forward. The demographics of the period are summarized in Judith Bannister (1985: 740–41).

20. A particularly revealing dimension of sectoral inequality is state grain distribution in the famine of the early 1960s. Liu Suinian (1984: 24) notes that between 1957 and 1960 urban grain consumption dropped slightly from 196 to 193 kilograms per person while rural consumption plummeted from 205 to 156 kilograms. For insightful discussion of the position of the peasantry in Chinese society see Sulamith Potter (1983).

21. The system was tight, particularly with respect to entry into major cities. It was not, however, air tight. Interviews reveal that at the time of the Great Leap famine and subsequently, collectives that faced famine conditions and lacked resources to assist the starving sometimes issued certificates to members entitling them to go begging for specified periods of time. Without such a certificate beggars risked arrest as counter-revolutionary or black elements.

22. The fullest discussion of contract workers is Blecher (1984). Cf. Korzec and Whyte (1981).

23. The dynamics of the reform process in the countryside remain controversial. The strongest case for peasant pressures for market-oriented decollectivizing reforms, repeatedly exceeding guidelines issued from the center, is Andrew Watson's "The Family Farm, Land Use and Accumulation in Agriculture" (forthcoming). A view stressing the supremacy of state leaders in conceiving and shaping the reforms is Jonathan Unger's (1986).

24. In 1979 the state increased grain purchasing prices by 20 percent with a 50 percent bonus for above quota sales. Between 1979 and 1981 state purchasing prices of agricultural commodities increased by a total of 46 percent, and in 1981 the state purchased 60 percent of agricultural commodities at above quota or negotiated prices. In the following years increases in state prices of agricultural means of production eroded these gains. The complex changes in state purchasing policies in the 1980s are described in Zhao (1986).

25. For a fascinating discussion of the sampling procedures used from the first national surveys in 1953 to the 1980s see *Zhongguo nongye nianjian* (1983: 227–28).

26. The evidence concerning rural income inequality in the reform era remains fragmentary. Riskin (1987: 306) concludes that "the rural reforms have given rise to growing inequality within the countryside," but he presents little evidence to show significantly greater inequality. Keith Griffin (1984: 306–09), writing early in the reform period, concluded that, by most yardsticks, including urban-rural, state-collective, interprovincial, interregional, and perhaps even intravillage inequality, the evidence did not support the view that the reforms have generated greater income inequality.

27. The legislation is given in "Guoying qiye" (1986: 739–45); see also Xinhua (1986). The far-reaching significance of the change is astutely assessed in Deborah Davis (forthcoming). Andrew Walder (1987: 41) suggests that the impact of the contract system on the state sector, like earlier reform initiatives, may prove limited.

28. The two figures discussed are not strictly comparable. Collective distributed income, which excludes income from private plots, may constitute 75–80 percent of total income.

29. *China Daily*, March 21, 1986, reports that half of the five million rural families

who qualified for government welfare aid in 1985 had achieved sufficient private incomes to get off the dole. The same article announced the first provincial program, in Hubei, to draft provincewide welfare guidelines.

Chapter 7

1. Article 8 of China's 1954 Constitution prior to collectivization stated that "The state protects the right of peasants to own land and other means of production according to law." It also noted that "The policy of the state toward rich peasant economy is to restrict and gradually eliminate it." See Selden (1978: 289). Between October 1955 and 1978, all official documents with which we are familiar restricted formal ownership and transfer rights to rural land to the collective (including team, brigade, and commune) and state. Two transitional documents are particularly interesting in the abolition of individual property rights in land. The Central Committee's October 1955 "Decision on Agricultural Cooperation," the principal document decreeing collectivization, recognized the existence of private ownership rights to land prior to collectivization. It called on newly forming collectives to compensate peasants for their land as investors. Article V directed cooperatives (that is, collectives) to "pay a certain amount of compensation for the use of private land, draught animals and large farm tools . . . when transferred to the cooperatives as common property." Noting "the peasants' predilection for the private ownership of land," the documents called for the payment of dividends on "land pooled in cooperatives," specifying that dividends should "remain constant for a certain period, say two or three years." The available evidence, however, suggests that neither lump sums nor dividends were ever paid to most landowners joining collectives. See Duncan Wilson (1965: 109–10). A rare 1958 mention of private ownership of land is contained in the model regulations of the Weixing (Sputnik) Commune. Article 5 states that "In changing over to the commune, the members of the cooperatives must turn over to the common ownership of the commune all privately owned plots of farmland" (Selden 1978: 398). However, by 1958, members of collectives had at most cultivation rights to private plots. Formal ownership and transfer rights to the land were firmly in the hands of the collective and the state.

2. Household cultivation, marketing, and consumption rights to private plots were under repeated attack from their inception in 1955 to the late 1970s. In many regions household plots were eliminated in the Great Leap Forward of 1958–1960; many were "collectively cultivated" during the Cultural Revolution, and control over the marketing of the produce was largely eliminated.

3. Cf. Marc Blecher's (1985: 104–106) discussion of formal, actual, and practical ownership rights in "The Structure and Contradictions of Productive Relations in Socialist Agrarian 'Reform.'"

4. Outspoken proponents of further commodification of land include Dong Fureng (1985) and Xu Xu (1986). Li Yining's call for ownership reform also extends to the core of state sector enterprises.

5. Seeking to protect the interests of the teams following the disasters associated with the Great Leap, the article continues: "[The commune] is not allowed to rent, buy, or sell the land owned by the production teams, including the private plots, private hills and residential land of commune members." The Sixty Articles was the major Central Committee statement defining the scope and nature of collective agriculture from 1962 to the reforms of the 1980s. *Nongcun renmin gongshe gongzuo tiaoli xiuzheng caoan* (Revised Draft of the Work Rules of the People's Commune), 1962. See excerpts in Selden, *The People's Republic of China*, pp. 521–26. The commune was simultaneously both the highest level of the collective and the lowest level of state power; in

practice the state component was dominant.

6. *Zhonghua renmin gongheguo tudi guanli fa* (Land Management Law of the People's Republic of China). We have used a text and related documents issued in June 1986 by the Agricultural Bureau of Yantai City, Shandong under the title *Tudi guanli wenjian xuanpian* (Selected Documents on Land Management).

7. During the Cultural Revolution repeated attempts were made to raise the unit of accounting from team to brigade, particularly in 1969–70. Such efforts were almost invariably quickly reversed as a result of peasant resistance and economic setbacks. We have seen no official discussion of the rationale for or significance of transfer of ownership rights from the team to the village.

8. It is tempting on the basis of fieldwork to project the disappearance of the team. With the elimination of the team's organizational functions in most villages and the cutback in the number of local cadres, the village level appears to have become decisive. We note, however, official accounts that suggest that the most common pattern is contracts between team and household with administrative supervision provided by the brigade. He Baogui (1985: 83). The Shanxi provincial model contract likewise specifies the team as the contracting party. See Frederick Crook (1985).

9. A partial transition took place in many North China communities in the years 1951–55 as mutual aid and elementary cooperatives initiated small-scale cooperative agriculture. In many, perhaps most, central and southern villages, the transformation took place in a single stroke between the fall of 1955 and the spring of 1956. See chapter 3.

10. William Hinton (1983: 105–107) was among the first to pose issues of bondage to the land and the depth of the urban-rural and cadre-peasant divide. Cf. the discussion of Sulamith Potter (1983).

11. A critical question remains, of course: the relationship between individuals and the collective. The issue cannot be resolved here, and the literature affords wide scope for differences of opinion ranging from the view of the collective as participatory community to that of collective as totalitarian leviathan. Our work emphasizes the structure of collective controls over the economic and political life of members, controls which pinched particularly painfully in the years of the Great Leap Forward and Cultural Revolution, but at all times tended to produce on the part of farmers with no official position a passive dependence on cadres, the collective and the state. For full discussion of the issues see Friedman et al. (forthcoming).

12. This pattern is all the more extraordinary in light of the rapid urbanization of the years 1950–1960 when net urban migration of 49 million accounted for 67 percent of the 73 million net increase in urban population. Between 1960 and 1976 China's urban population actually declined from 130 to 112 million as a result of net rural migration of 48 million people. The migration to the cities in the 1950s reflected a familiar drive for urban residence and the preference for industrial over agricultural employment. The state mandated and enforced migration from city to countryside beginning in 1960 on a scale that has no parallel in world demographics. The impact of the Great Leap famine is manifest in net rural migration of 13.9 million in 1962 and another 20.3 million left the cities in 1964. Net rural migration continued in almost every year to 1976. The largest number of rural migrants in the years 1964 to 1978 were urban high school and junior high school graduates forced to settle permanently in the countryside. Cf. the statistical series on urbanization prepared by Kam Wing Chan and Xueqiang Xu (1985: 603). Using different definitions from those employed by Kirkby, Chan and Xu calculate an increase in urban population from 12.5 percent in 1952 to 19.7 percent in 1960 before declining to 17.4 percent in 1976.

13. This explains the frequent tensions between sent-down urban youth and villagers. While some urban youth were able to contribute literacy and technical skills, the

great majority worked as agricultural laborers and were unable to support themselves. The issues of conflict are well discussed in Anita Chan et al. (1984).

14. The Shanxi province model contract, published in the *Shanxi Daily* on September 3, 1981, specifies the contracting of land to collective members without clarifying whether the contracting "member" refers to an individual or household. Elsewhere, however, the document specifies household obligation (Crook 1985). Land contracts are most often made with households, with the quantity of land based on a calculation of the number of people or laborers in the household. By contrast, most other contracts, for example, contracts to operate workshops, restaurants, stores, or orchards or to provide services such as electricity or irrigation, are auctioned to the highest bidder, and the contracting party is not a household but an individual or group. In the disjuncture between the two systems, one essentially an equal subsistence entitlement for all, the other based on market criteria, we see the continued tension between the revolutionary legacy of subsistence guarantees for all and the reform emphasis on productivity maximization and encouragement of individual households to prosper.

15. Frederick Crook (1985: 302) also explores the analogy between the household contract system and tenancy noting both differences and similarities in the contractual collectivism of the 1980s and the tenancy of the Republican period. It should be observed that if the collective is a putative landlord, the contracting household is also a shareholder in the landowning entity.

16. Interviews in China in 1987 confirm that the problem of investment remains acute even after the lengthening of contracts. Since the route to wealth clearly lies in sideline enterprise, industry, and commerce, neither the rural collectives nor contracting households have invested in agriculture, and state investment has likewise declined since the mid–1980s. One important result is the progressive deterioration of irrigation systems.

17. Andrew Watson reports farmer resistance to rising taxes in Huairong county north of Beijing following 1985 tax changes that raised taxes there to 7 percent of gross agricultural income. Personal communication, July 2, 1987.

18. For the controversy about the land tax as absolute ground rent see *Jingji zhoubao* (Economic Weekly), April 2, 1984; Xu and Shi (1984); *Jingji yanjiu* (Economic Research) 1 (1984); *Nongye jingji cankao ziliao* 6 (1984); *Nongye jingji wenti*, nos. 4, 9 (1985); *Jingji yanjiu cankao ziliao* (Reference Materials on Economic Research) 109 (1985); *Jingji wenti* (Economic Problems), nos. 2, 6 (1985). For Marx's discussion of capitalist agricultural land rent and absolute ground rent see *Capital*, vol. 3, part 6, esp. chap. 45; *The Grundrisse*, pp. 252–53.

19. The distribution of collective income varies from year to year nationally and

Allocation of Rural Income

	Production costs	State tax	Public accumulation fund	Public welfare fund	Distribution to collective members
1957		26.5	9.8	5.0	57.5
1978		34.9	3.3	9.3	52.6
1980		34.6	3.1	8.4	54.5

Note: Some totals in original do not add up to 100.0.

within each collective unit. Ma Hong et al. (1982: 118) provide national data on distribution for the years 1957, 1978, and 1980.

20. Crook questions whether this system is practiced in all areas. Our judgment is that such a cumbersome system, in which each household would turn its crop over to the collective and then receive back its own share, is in operation in few localities. In most, the collective must collect from contracting households with direct control of the harvest; cf. the discussion by Marc Blecher (1985: 121).

21. These figures, drawn from interviews in Beijing and Hebei, illustrate the range of purchasing prices. One might anticipate that land prices in Beijing would be higher than those in Shijiazhuang. However, it should be noted that the population of Shijiazhuang has grown at a more rapid rate than has that of the national capital.

22. Personal communication from Andrew Watson, July 2, 1987.

23. Differentials are also, of course, in part the result of current labor and investment.

24. *Liaowang* 36, September 8, 1986.

25. Recent reports indicate the loss of 55 million mu of agricultural land between 1981 and 1986. Andrew Watson, personal communication, July 2, 1987.

26. Pat Howard (1987) has well summarized the cooperative position and its growing prominence in 1986 and 1987.

27. Under the former collective system only hand tools were owned by households.

28. The issues of urban-rural and intrarural income inequality in the period of mobilizational collectivism and the 1980s reforms are addressed in chapters 5 and 6.

REFERENCES

Abstract of Statistics in Taiwan 1895–1945 (1946). Taipei.

Adelman, Irma, and Cynthia Taft Morris (1973). *Economic Growth and Social Equity in Developing Countries*. Stanford: Stanford University Press.

Agricultural Bureau, Yantai City, Shandong (1986). *Tudi guanli wenjian xuanpian* (Selected Documents on Land Management).

Amin, Samir (1983). *The Future of Maoism*. New York: Monthly Review Press.

————. (1987). "Note on the Concept of Delinking," *Review* 10, 3 (Winter): 435–44.

Andors, Stephen (1977). *China's Industrial Revolution. Politics, Planning and Management*. New York: Pantheon.

Arutyunan, Yu. (1966). "Social Structure of Rural Population of the U.S.S.R.," in *The Current Digest of the Soviet Press* 18, 25:20–25.

Ashton, Basil, Kenneth Hill, Alan Piazza, and Robin Zeitz (1984). "Famines in China, 1958–61," *Population and Development Review* 10, 4:613–45.

Bannister, Judith (1985). "Population Policy and Trends in China, 1973–1983," *The China Quarterly* 100 (December): 717–41.

Barker, Randolph, et al., eds. (1982). *The Chinese Agricultural Economy*. London: Westview Press, 1982.

Bernstein, Thomas (1976). "Leadership and Mass Mobilisation in the Soviet and Chinese Collectivisation Campaigns of 1929–30 and 1955–56: A Comparison," *The China Quarterly* 3.

Bernstein, Thomas (1984). "Stalinism, Famine, and Chinese Peasants: Grain Procurement During the Great Leap Forward," *Theory and Society* 13, 3:339–77.

Bettelheim, Charles (1978). *Class Struggles in the U.S.S.R. Second Period, 1923–1930*. New York: Monthly Review Press.

Bian Yu-yuan (1972). "The Contribution and Role of Taiwan's Agriculture in the Process of Economic Development" (Taiwan nung-yeh tsai ching-chi fa-chan kuo-ch'eng chung chih kung-hsien chi ti-wei), *Taiwan Bank Quarterly* (Taiwan yin-hang chi-k'an) 23, 2:26–40.

Blecher, Marc (1984). "Peasant Labor for Urban Industry: Temporary Contract Labour, Urban-Rural Balance and Class Relations in a Chinese County," in *China's Changed Road to Development*, ed. Neville Maxwell and Bruce McFarlane. Oxford: Oxford University Press, pp. 109–24.

————. (1985). "The Structure and Contradictions of Productive Relations in Socialist Agrarian 'Reform': A Framework for Analysis and the Chinese Case," *The Journal of Development Studies* 22, 1 (October).

Brus, Wlodzimierz (1975). "Socialisation in the Conception and Practice of East European Socialism," in *Socialist Ownership and Political Systems*. London: Routledge and Kegan Paul.

Bukharin, Nikolai (1979). *The Politics and Economics of the Transition Period*. London: Routledge and Kegan Paul.

Business Week (1985). "Capitalism in China: Under Deng Xiaoping It's Okay to Get Rich," January 14, pp. 53–59.

Carr, E. H. (1964). *A History of Soviet Russia: Socialism in One Country*. Vol. 1. London: Macmillan.

Castro, Alfonso, M. Thomas Hakansson, and David Brokensha (1981). "Indicators of Rural Inequality," *World Development* 9, 5.

Chan, Anita, Richard Madsen, and Jonathan Unger (1984). *Chen Village. The Recent History of a Peasant Community in Mao's China*. Berkeley: University of California Press, 1984.

Chan, Kam Wing, and Xueqiang Xu (1985). "Urban Population Growth and Urbanization in China Since 1949: Reconstructing a Baseline," *The China Quarterly* 104 (December): 583—613.

Chayanov, A. V. (1966 [1925]). *The Theory of Peasant Economy*. New York: Irwin.

Chen Boda (1956). "The Socialist Transformation of China's Agriculture," *Current Background* 339.

————. (1959). "Under the Red Flag of Comrade Mao Zedong," *Hongqi* (Red Flag) 4, July 16.

Chen Cheng (1961). *Land Reform in Taiwan*. Taipei.

Chen, Edward (1985). "The Newly Industrialized Countries in Asia: Growth, Experience and Prospects," in *Asian Development: Present and Future*, ed. Robert Scalapino, Seizaburo Sato and Jusuf Wanandi. Berkeley: Institute of East Asian Studies, University of California.

Chen, Nai-ruenn (1967). *Chinese Economic Statistics*. Chicago: Aldine.

———— (1975). "China's Foreign Trade, 1950–74," in Joint Economic Committee of Congress, *China: A Reassessment of the Economy*. Washington: USGPO, pp. 617–52.

Chen, Yu-hsi (1976). "Rural Transformation in Mainland China and Taiwan: A Comparative Study," *Social Praxis* 5, 1–2:125–50.

Chen Yun (1955). "On the Question of the Unified Purchase and Distribution of Grain," *Current Background* 339.

Chen Zhong (1985). "Yanhai jingji fada qu de tudi jingying qushi" (The Trend of Land Management in More Developed Coastal Areas), *Jingjixue zhoubao* (Economic Studies Weekly), March 31.

Cheng, Chu-yuan (1974). *China's Allocation of Fixed Capital Investment, 1952–1957*. Ann Arbor: Center for Chinese Studies, University of Michigan.

Chossudovsky, Michel (1986). *Towards Capitalist Restoration? Chinese Socialism After Mao*. Hong Kong: Macmillan.

Chou, S. H. (1966). "Prices in Communist China," *The Journal of Asian Studies* 25, 4:645–63.

Chu Sze-te (1980). *Agricultural Problems in China, 1920s–1930s* (Chung-kuo nung-yeh wen-t'i). Taipei: Research Institute of China's Land Administration.

"Circular of the Central Committee of the Chinese Communist Party on Rural Work During 1984" (1985). *The China Quarterly* 101 (March): 132–42.

Clissold, Stephen, ed. (1975). *Yugoslavia and the Soviet Union 1939–1973. A Docu-

mentary Survey. London: Oxford University Press.

Cohen, Stephen (1971/1980). *Bukharin and the Bolshevik Revolution*. Oxford: Oxford University Press.

—————. (1985). *Rethinking the Soviet Experience. Politics and History Since 1917*. New York: Oxford University Press.

Commentary (1985a). "Accurately Understanding the Current Development of Specialized Households," *Zhuanyehu jingying bao* (Specialized Household Management Newspaper) November 19, 1985, in JPRS-CAG-86-008, March 14, 1986.

—————. (1985b). "Work Hard to Revitalize the Rural Economy," *Nongcun gongzuo tongcun* (Rural Work Newsletter) 10, October 5, in JPRS-CAG-86-004.

Council on International Economic Cooperation and Development (CIECD) (1970). *Taiwan Data Book*. Taipei.

—————. (1973). *Readings on the American-China Human Resource Conference*. Taipei.

Crook, Frederick (1985). "The Baogan Daohu System: Translation and Analysis of a Model Contract," *The China Quarterly* 102 (June): 291-303.

Davies, R. W. (1980a). *The Socialist Offensive: The Collectivization of Soviet Agriculture, 1929-30*. Cambridge: Harvard University Press.

—————. (1980b). *The Socialist Collective Farm*. Cambridge: Harvard University Press.

Davis (-Friedmann), Deborah (1985). "Intergenerational Inequalities and the Chinese Revolution. The Importance of Age-Specific Inequalities for the Creation and Maintenance of Social Strata Within a State-Socialist Society," *Modern China* 11, 2:177-201.

Davis, Deborah (forthcoming) "Retirement and the Urban Structure."

Davis, Kingsley (1972). *World Urbanization 1950-1970*. Vol. 2. Berkeley: Institute of International Studies.

Deng Zihui (1984). *Nongye wenti lun wen xuan* (Selected Essays on Agrarian Problems). Beijing: Zhongguo shehui kexueyuan Nongye jingji yanjiu suo.

Deng Zihui (1984). *Nongye wenti lun wen xuan* (Selected Essays on Agrarian Problems). Beijing: Zhongguo shehui kexueyuan nongye jingji yanjiu suo.

Deng Zihui (1954a). "Principles of Agrarian Socialist Transformation," *Current Background* 306.

Current Background, November 18, pp. 1-10.

—————. (1956). "Changes in China's Rural Economy and Problems in the Agriculture Cooperative Movement," in *New China Advances to Socialism*. Beijing: Foreign Languages Press.

Directorate of Intelligence, U.S. Central Intelligence Agency (1986). *Handbook of Economic Statistics 1986.*

Dong Fureng (1985). "Zailun wo guo shehuizhuyi suoyouzhi xingshi wenti" (Second Paper on the Forms of Our Country's Socialist Ownership), *Jingji yanjiu* (Economic Research) 4.

Donnithorne, Audrey (1976). "Centralization and Decentralization in China's Fiscal Management," *The China Quarterly* 66 (June): 328-29.

Draper, Hal (1978). *Karl Marx's Theory of Revolution*. Vol. 2. *The Politics of Social Classes*. New York: Monthly Review Press.

Duan Yingbi (1983). "Some Opinions on Farm Product Procurement," *Nongye jishu jingji* (Agricultural Technology Economics) 7, July, in JPRS CAG-84-002, January 26, 1984.

Eberstadt, Nick (1986). "Material Poverty in the People's Republic of China in International Perspective," in Joint Economic Committee of Congress, *China*

Looks Toward the Year 2000. Vol. 1. *The Four Modernizations.* Washington, D.C.: USGPO.

Eberstadt, Nick (1987). "Progress Against Poverty in Communist and Non-Communist Countries in the Postwar Era," in *Modern Capitalism,* vol. 2, ed. Peter Berger. Lanham, Md.: Hamilton Press.

Eckstein, Alexander, ed. (1968). *Economic Trends in Communist China.* Chicago: Aldine.

————. (1978). "The Chinese Development Model," in Joint Economic Committee of Congress, *Chinese Economy Post-Mao.* Washington, D.C.: USGPO, pp. 80–114.

————. (1980). *Quantitative Measures of China's Economic Output.* Ann Arbor: University of Michigan Press.

Economic Yearbook of China (1982).

Ellman, Michael (1975). "Did the Agricultural Surplus Provide the Resources for the Increase in Investment in the U.S.S.R. during the First Five Year Plan?" *The Economic Journal* (December).

————. (1979). *Socialist Planning.* Cambridge: Cambridge University Press.

Engels, Friederich (1969 [1894]). *The Peasant Question in France and Germany.* Vol. 3. Moscow: Progress Publishers.

Erlich, Alexander (1950). "Preobrazhenski and the Economics of Soviet Industrialization," *Quarterly Journal of Economics* 64, 1 (February).

————. (1960). *The Soviet Industrialization Debate 1924–1928.* Cambridge: Harvard University Press.

Fei, John, and Gustaf Ranis (1964). *Development of the Labour Supply Economy; Theory and Policy.* Chicago: Richard D. Irwin.

Fei, Xiaotong (1957/1979). "A Revisit to Kaihsienkung," in *Fei Hsiao-t'ung: The Dilemma of a Chinese Intellectual,* ed. James McGough. White Plains, N.Y.: M. E. Sharpe, pp. 39–74.

FGHP (Chung-hua jen-min kung-ho-kuo fa-kuei hui-p'ien) (1955). *Collection of Laws of the People's Republic of China.* 12 vols. Beijing: Guowuyuan.

Field, Robert (1982). "Growth and Structural Change in Chinese Industry: 1952–79," in U.S. Joint Economic Committee of Congress, *China Under the Four Modernizations.* Washington, D.C.: USGPO.

Friedman, Edward (1982). "Maoism, Titoism, Stalinism: Some Origins and Consequences of the Maoist Theory of the Socialist Transition," in *The Transition to Socialism in China,* ed. Mark Selden and Victor Lippit. Armonk, N.Y.: M. E. Sharpe, Inc., pp. 149–214.

Friedman, Edward, and Mark Selden (1987). "The Broadest Base. Some Lessons From the Success of Base Areas in North China in the Anti-Japanese Resistance," in *China's Revolutionary Base Areas in the Anti-Japanese Resistance,* ed. Wei Hongyun. (In Chinese.) Tianjin: Tianjin People's Publishing House.

————. (1984). "Maoism and Rural Misery," *Telos* (Spring): 196–99.

Friedman, Edward, Paul Pickowicz, and Mark Selden with Kay Johnson (forthcoming). *Chinese Village, Socialist State.* Berkeley: University of California Press.

Gartrell, John (1981). "Inequality Within Rural Communities of India," *American Sociological Review* 46.

Geraedts, Henry (1983). *The People's Republic of China: Foreign Economic Relations and Technology Acquisition 1972–1981.* Lund: Research Policy Institute.

Gerschenkron, A. (1962). *Economic Backwardness in Historical Perspective.* Cambridge: Belknap Press.

Gray, Jack (1970). "The High Tide of Socialism in the Chinese Countryside," in *Studies in the Social History of China and Southeast Asia,* ed. Jerome Ch'en and

Nicholas Tarling. Cambridge: Cambridge University Press.

————. (1975). "Mao Tse-tung's Strategy for the Collectivization of Chinese Agriculture: An Important Phase in the Development of Maoism," in *Sociology and Development*, ed. I. de Kadt and G. P. Williams. London: Tavistock.

Griffin, Keith (1979). *The Political Economy of Agrarian Change*. 2d ed. London: Macmillan.

————, ed. (1984). *Institutional Reform and Economic Development in the Chinese Countryside*. Armonk, N.Y.: M. E. Sharpe.

Griffin, Keith, and Ashwani Saith (1981). *Growth and Inequality in Rural China*. Geneva: ILO.

————. (1982). "The Pattern of Income Inequality in Rural China," *Oxford Economic Papers* 34, 1 (March): 175–79.

"Guoying qiye shixing laodong hetongzhi zhanxing guiding" (Temporary Regulations on the Labor Contract System in State Enterprises) (1986). *Guowuyuan gongbao* (State Council Bulletin), pp. 739–45.

Gurley, John (1976). *China's Economy and the Maoist Strategy*. New York: Monthly Review.

Harding, Harry (1987). *China's Second Revolution. Reform After Mao*. Washington, D.C.: Brookings Institution.

He Baogui (1985). "Nongye chengbao hetong fasheng jiufen zenma ban?' (What Should Be Done to Deal with Agricultural Contract Disputes?), *Nongcun gongzuo wenda* (Questions and Answers about Village Work). Beijing: People's Publishing House, 1985.

He Juan (1953). "On Distribution Relations in the Agricultural Producers' Cooperatives," *Xuexi* 1.

Hinton, William (1983). *Shenfan. The Continuing Revolution in a Chinese Village*. New York: Random House.

Hirschman, Albert (1958). *The Strategy of Economic Development*. New Haven: Yale University Press.

Ho, Samuel (1978). *Economic Development of Taiwan, 1860–1970*. New Haven: Yale University Press.

Horvat, Branko (1976). *The Yugoslav Economic System: The First Labor-Managed Economy in the Making*. White Plains, N.Y.: M. E. Sharpe.

Howard, Pat (1987). "Cooperation in a Market Context. The Impact of Recent Rural Economic Reforms in China," paper presented to the Association for Asian Studies annual meeting, Boston, April 10.

Hsiao, Hsin-huang Michael (1981). *Government Agricultural Strategies in Taiwan and South Korea: A Macrosociological Assessment*. Taipei: Institute of Ethnology, Academia Sinica.

Hsieh, S. C., and Teng-hui Lee (1960). "Agricultural Development and Its Contributions to Economic Growth in Taiwan," Chinese-American Joint Commission for Rural Reconstruction, *Economic Digest* series no. 17.

Hsu, Robert (1982). "Agricultural Financial Policies in China, 1949–79," *Asian Survey* 22, 7 (July): 638–58.

Hsu Wen-fu (1969). "Taiwan nung ch'an chia-ko shui-chun yu nung-yeh shuo-tei" (Agricultural Price Level and Income), *Taiwan t'u-ti chin-jung yueh-k'an* (Taiwan Land and Finance Monthly) 6, 4.

Hu Sheng-yi (1972). "Taiwan nung kung chiao-i t'iao-chien chih yen-chiu" (The Study of Terms of Trade Between Agriculture and Industry), *Taiwan yin-hang chih-k'an* (Taiwan Bank Quarterly) 23:1–25.

Huenemann, Ralph (1966). "Urban Rationing in Communist China," *The China Quarterly* 26 (April–June): 44–57.

Hussain, Athar, and Tribe, Keith (1981). *Russian Marxism and the Peasantry, 1861–1930*. London: Macmillan.

Ishikawa, Shigeru (1967a). *Economic Development in Asian Perspective*. Tokyo: Kinokuniya.

————. (1967b). "Resource Flow Between Agriculture and Industry—The Chinese Experience," *The Developing Economies* 5, 1-4:3-37.

————. (1983). "China's Economic Growth since 1959—An Assessment," *The China Quarterly* 94:242-82.

Jacoby, Neil (1966). *U.S. Aid to Taiwan*. New York: Praeger.

Jen Pe (1958). "A Preliminary Study of the Price Ratios Between Industrial and Agricultural Goods" *Economic Research* (Jingji yanjiu) (September).

Jiang Xuemo (1982). *Shehuizhuyi jingji shilun* (Ten Issues of Socialist Economy). Changsha: Hunan People's Publishing House.

Joint Economic Committee of Congress (1967). *An Economic Profile of Mainland China*. Washington, D.C.: USGPO.

Ka, Chih-ming, and Mark Selden (1986). "Original Accumulation, Equity and Late Industrialization: The Cases of Socialist China and Capitalist Taiwan," *World Development* 14, 10/11 (October-November): 1293-1310.

Kautsky, Karl (1970). *La Question agraire*. Paris: Maspero.

Kawano, Shigeto (1941, 1969). *The Rice Economy in Taiwan* (Taiwan beikoku keizai ron), trans. Lin Inn-Yen. Taipei: Taiwan Bank.

————. (1967). "Strategic Elements in the Rapid Economic Growth of Taiwan," *The Developing Economies* 5, 1-4:486-502.

Kerblay, Basile (1983). *Modern Soviet Society*. New York: Pantheon.

Kerr, George H. (1965). *Formosa Betrayed*. Boston: Houghton Mifflin.

Kirkby, R.J.R. (1985). *Urbanization in China: Town and Country in a Developing Economy 1949-2000 AD*. New York: Columbia University Press.

Kojima, Reiitsu (1975). *Chūgoku no keizai to gijutsu* (China's Economy and Technology). Tokyo: Keiso Shobo.

————. (1982). "Accumulation, Technology and China's Economic Development," in *The Transition to Socialism in China*, ed. Mark Selden and Victor Lippit. Armonk, N.Y.: M. E. Sharpe, pp. 238-65.

————. (1987). *Urbanization and Urban Problems in China*. Tokyo: Institute of Developing Economies.

Korzec, Michel, and Martin Whyte (1981). "Reading Notes: The Chinese Wage System," *The China Quarterly* 86 (June): 248-73.

Kreisberg, Louis (1979). *Social Inequality*. Englewood Cliffs, N.J.: Prentice Hall.

Kueh, Y. Y. (1985). "The Economics of the 'Second Land Reform' in China," *The China Quarterly* 101 (March): 122-31.

Kuo, Leslie (1972). *The Technical Transformation of Agriculture in Communist China*. New York: Praeger.

Kuznets, Simon (1963). "Quantitative Aspects of the Economic Growth of Nations: Distribution of Income by Size," *Economic Development and Cultural Change* 11, 2, part 2 (January): 1-80.

Lane, David (1982). *The End of Social Inequality? Class, Status and Power under State Socialism*. London: George Allen and Unwin.

————. (1985). *Soviet Economy and Society*. New York: New York University Press.

Lardy, Nicholas (1978). *Economic Growth and Distribution in China*. Cambridge: Cambridge University Press.

————. (1980). "Regional Growth and Income Distribution in China," in *China's*

Development Experience in Comparative Perspective, ed. Robert Dernberger. Cambridge: Harvard University Press.

————. (1982). "Intersectoral Resource Flows in Chinese Economic Development," in *Agricultural Development in China, Japan, and Korea*, ed. Ch'i-ming Hou and Tzong-sian Yu. Taipei.

————. (1983a). *Agriculture in China's Modern Economic Development*. Cambridge: Cambridge University Press.

————. (1983b). "Subsidies," *The China Business Review* 10, 6 (November-December): 21-23.

————. (1986). "Overview: Agricultural Reform and the Rural Economy," in Joint Economic Committee of Congress, *China Toward the Year 2000*. Vol. 1. *The Four Modernizations*. Washington, D.C.: USGPO.

————. (1987). "The Chinese Economy Under Stress, 1958-1965," in *The Cambridge History of China*. Vol. 14, *The People's Republic of China*, ed. Roderick MacFarquhar and John Fairbank. New York: Cambridge University Press.

Lee, Teng-hui [Li Denghui] (1971). *Intersectoral Capital Flow in the Economic Development of Taiwan, 1895-1960*. Ithaca: Cornell University Press.

————. (1972). *Taiwan nung kung pu men chieh chih tzu-pen liu-tung* (Intersectoral Capital Flow in the Economic Development of Taiwan). Taipei: Taiwan Bank.

Lenin, V. I. (1959a [1903]). "To the Rural Poor. An Explanation to Peasants: What the Social Democrats Want," *Alliance of the Working Class and the Peasantry.* Moscow: Foreign Languages Publishing House, pp. 20-91.

————. (1959b [1905]). "Socialism, Petty Bourgeois and Proletarian," *Alliance of the Working Class and the Peasantry.* Moscow: Foreign Languages Publishing House, pp. 122-30.

————. (1959c [1906]). "Revision of the Agrarian Program of the Workers' Party," *Alliance of the Working Class and the Peasantry.* Moscow: Foreign Languages Publishing House, pp. 135-41.

————. (1959d [1906]). "Concluding Speech on the Agrarian Question Delivered at the Fourth (Unity) Congress of the R.S.D.L.P.," *Alliance of the Working Class and the Peasantry.* Moscow: Foreign Languages Publishing House, pp. 142-52.

————. (1959e [1907]). "The Agrarian Program of Social-Democracy in the First Russian Revolution, 1905-07," *Alliance of the Working Class and the Peasantry.* Moscow: Foreign Languages Publishing House, pp. 166-74.

————. (1959f [1919]). "Economics and Politics in the Era of the Dictatorship of the Proletariat," *Alliance of the Working Class and the Peasantry.* Moscow: Foreign Languages Publishing House, pp. 313-23.

————. (1959g [1917]). "Resolution of the Seventh (April) All-Russian Conference of the R.S.D.L.P. (B.) on the Agrarian Question," *Alliance of the Working Class and the Peasantry.* Moscow: Foreign Languages Publishing House, pp. 188-91.

————. (1975 [1923]). "On Cooperation," in *The Lenin Anthology*, ed. Robert Tucker. New York: W. W. Norton, pp. 707-13.

————. (1977 [1899]). *The Development of Capitalism in Russia*. Moscow: Progress Publishers.

Lewin, Moshe (1968). *Russian Peasants and Soviet Power. A Study of Collectivization*. New York: W. W. Norton.

————. (1985). *The Making of the Soviet System. Essays in the Social History of Interwar Russia*. New York: Pantheon.

Li Bingkun (1985). "Exploration of Rural Tax System Reform," *Nongye jingji gongzuo wenti* 6 (June 23), pp. 17-22, in JPRS-CAG-85-029, October 24.

Li Bingkun and Tang Renjian (1986). "Some Thoughts on Reforming the Agricultural Tax System," *Nongye jingji wenti* 3, March 23, in JPRS-CAG-86-025, June 24.

Li Chengrui (1959). *Draft History of the Agricultural Tax in the People's Republic of China*. Beijing: Finance Publishing House.

————. (1985). "Economic Reform Brings a Better Life," *Beijing Review* 28, 29 (July).

Li Yining (1986). "Possibilities of China's Ownership Reforms," *Beijing Review*, December 29.

Li Youzheng and Li Shuzhong (1986). "A Turning Point in the History of China. Third-Line Regions," *Liaowang* 26 (June 30), in JPRS-CEA-86-096 August 18, 1986, pp. 9–16.

Li Zezhong (1986). *Shehuizhuyi suoyouzhi guanxi jiqi fazhan guiluxing wenti* (Socialist Ownership and Its Laws of Development). Shanghai: Shanghai People's Publishing House.

Liang Junqian (1986a). "Lianchan chengbao zerenzhi de jiben tezheng shi shenma?" (What Are the Basic Features of the Responsibility System?), in *Nongcun gongzuo wenda* (Questions and Answers on Rural Work), ed. Propaganda Bureaux of the Central Committee of the Chinese Communist Party and the Ministry of Agriculture, Animal Husbandry and Fishery, pp. 61–63.

————. (1986b). "Shixing lianchan chengbao zerenzhi shi bu shi fouding le nongye hezuohua?" (Is the Responsibility System a Negation of the Agricultural Collective?), in *Nongcun gongzuo wenda* (Questions and Answers on Rural Work), ed. Propaganda Bureaux of the Central Committee of the Chinese Communist Party and the Ministry of Agriculture, Animal Husbandry and Fishery.

Liao Luyan (1955). "Speech to the National People's Congress," *Renmin ribao* (People's Daily), July 26, in *Current Background* 352.

Lieberthal, Kenneth (1971). "Mao Versus Liu? Policy Toward Industry and Commerce: 1946–49," *The China Quarterly* 47:494–520.

Lim, Edwin, and Adrian Wood, eds. (1985). *China: Long-term Development Issues and Options*. Baltimore: Johns Hopkins University Press.

Lin, Ching-yuan (1973). *Industrialization in Taiwan, 1946–1972*. New York: Praeger.

Lippit, Victor (1974). *Land Reform and Economic Development in China*. White Plains, N.Y.: International Arts and Sciences Press.

Lipton, Michael (1977). *Why Poor People Stay Poor: A Study of Urban Bias in World Development*. London: Temple Smith.

Liu Jinjing (1975). *The Economic Analysis of Post-War Taiwan from 1945–1965* (Sengo Taiwan keizai bunseki). Tokyo: Tokyo University Press.

Liu Suinian (1984). "'Tiaozheng, gonggu, chongshi, tigao' ba zi fangzhen di tichu ji zhixing qingkuang" ("Adjust, Consolidate, Complete, and Raise": The Situation in Promulgating and Carrying Out the Eight-Character Principles), *Dangshi yanjiu* (Party History Research) 6.

Liu, Ta-chung, and Kung-chia Yeh (1965). *The Economy of the Chinese Mainland: National Income and Economic Development (1933–1959)*. Princeton: Princeton University Press.

Logan, John (1978). "Growth, Politics and Stratification of Places," *American Journal of Sociology* 84:404–16.

London, Miriam, and Ivan London (1970). "Hunger in China: The 'Norm of Truth,'" *Worldview* (March).

Lu Dong (1984). "China's Industry on the Upswing," *Beijing Review* 27, 35 (August 27).

Lu Shaoqing (1985). "The Problem of Child Labor in Rural Enterprises Calls for

Attention,'' in *Zhuanyehu jingying bao*, September 21, 1985, translated in JPRS-CEA—86–007, January 26, 1986.

Ma Hong, ed. (1982). *Xiandai zhongguo jingji shidian* (Encyclopedia of the Modern Chinese Economy). Beijing: Chinese Social Sciences Press, 1982.

MacFarquhar, Roderick (1974). *The Origins of the Cultural Revolution: Contradictions Among the People, 1956–57*. New York: Columbia University Press.

Mao Zedong, ed. (1956). *Socialist Upsurge in the Chinese Countryside*. Beijing: Foreign Languages Press.

————. (1957). "Talk at the Third Plenum of the Eight Central Committee," in *Miscellany of Mao Tse-tung Thought (1949–1968)*. Vol. 1, pp. 72–76.

————. (1965). *Selected Works*, vol. 3. Beijing: Foreign Languages Press.

————. (1965a). "Zuzhiqilai," in *Mao Zedong ji*, ed. Takeuchi Minoru.

————. (1977). "The Debate on the Cooperative Transformation of Agriculture and the Current Class Struggle," in *Selected Works of Mao Tse-tung*. Vol. 5. Beijing: Foreign Languages Press, pp. 211–34.

————. (1977a). "On the Cooperative Transformation of Agriculture," in *Selected Works*, vol. 5. Beijing: Foreign Languages Press, pp. 184–207.

————. (1977b). *A Critique of Soviet Economics*. New York: Monthly Review Press.

————. (1978). *Selected Works of Mao Tse-tung*. Vol. 5. Beijing: Foreign Languages Press.

————. (1979). "The Present Situation and Our Tasks," in *The People's Republic of China: A Documentary History of Revolutionary Change*, ed. Mark Selden. New York: Monthly Review Press, pp. 169–74.

Marx, Karl (1963). *The Poverty of Philosophy*. New York: International Publishers.

————. (1973). *Grundrisse: Foundations of the Critique of Political Economy.* New York: Vintage.

————. (1977 [1867]). *Capital. A Critique of Political Economy*. New York: Vintage.

Marx, Karl, and Friederich Engels (1972). "Manifesto of the Communist Party," in *The Marx-Engels Reader*, ed. Robert Tucker. New York: W. W. Norton, pp. 331–62.

McCoy, Al (1971). "Land Reform as Counter-revolution," *Bulletin of Concerned Asian Scholars* 3, 1:14–49.

Millar, James (1970). "Soviet Rapid Development and the Agricultural Surplus Hypothesis," *Soviet Studies* (July).

————. (1974). "Mass Collectivization and the Contribution of Soviet Agriculture During the First Five-Year Plan," *Slavic Review* (December).

————. (1980). "Bureaucracy and Soviet Rural Development: The City Boys and the Countryside," ms.

Model Regulations for Agricultural Producers' Cooperatives (1956). Beijing: Foreign Languages Press.

Moore, Barrington (1967). *The Social Origins of Dictatorship and Democracy. Lord and Peasant in the Making of the Modern World*. Boston: Beacon Press.

Myers, Ramon (1987). "How Can We Evaluate Communist China's Economic Development?" *Issues and Studies* 23, 2 (February):122–55.

Myrdal, Gunnar (1957). *Economic Theory and Underdeveloped Regions*. London: Duckworth.

Myrdal, Jan (1984). *Return to a Chinese Village*. New York: Pantheon.

"National Program for Agricultural Development 1956–1967" (1978), in *The People's Republic of China: A Documentary History of Revolutionary Change*, ed. Mark Selden. New York: Monthly Review Press, pp. 358–63.

Nee, Victor (1985). "Peasant Household Individualism," in *Chinese Rural Development: The Great Transformation*, ed. William Parish. Armonk, N.Y.: M. E. Sharpe, pp. 164–92.

1954 Quanguo geti shougongye diaocha ziliao (1954 National Investigation Materials on the Handicraft Industry) (1957). Beijing: Sanlian shudian.

Nolan, Peter (1976). "Collectivization in China: Some Comparisons with the USSR," *Journal of Peasant Studies* 3, 2 (January).

————. (1979). "Inequality of Income Between Town and Countryside in the People's Republic of China in the Mid–1950's," *World Development* 7.

Nolan, Peter, and Gordon White (1981). "Distribution and Development in China," *Bulletin of Concerned Asian Scholars* 13, 3.

Nove, Alec (1965). "Introduction" to E. Preobrazhensky, *The New Economics*. Oxford: Oxford University Press.

————. (1971). "The Decision to Collectivize," in *Agrarian Policies and Problems in Communist and Non-Communist Countries*, ed. W. A. D. Jackson. Seattle: University of Washington Press.

————. (1983). *The Economics of Feasible Socialism*. London: George Allen and Unwin.

Nurkse, Ragnar (1953). *Problems of Capital Formation in Underdeveloped Countries*. New York: Oxford University Press.

Oi, Jean (1983). "State and Peasant in Contemporary China. The Politics of Grain Procurement," Ph.D. dissertation, University of Michigan.

Ossowski, Stanislaw (1967). *Class Structure in the Social Consciousness*. London: Routledge and Kegan Paul.

Paine, Suzanne (1981). "Spatial Aspects of Chinese Development: Issues, Outcomes and Politics 1949–79," *Journal of Development Studies* 17.

Pan Wenhui, "Jianqing nongmin fudan" (Lighten the Burden on the Peasantry), *Zhongguo nongcun jingji* (Rural Economy of China) 3 (1986).

Parish, William (1984). "Destratification in China," in *Class and Social Stratification in Post-Revolution China*, ed. James Watson. Cambridge: Cambridge University Press, pp. 84–120.

Parish, William, and Martin Whyte (1978). *Village and Family in Contemporary China*. Chicago: University of Chicago Press.

Pepper, Suzanne (1986). "China's Special Economic Zones. The Current Rescue Bid for a Faltering Experiment," *UFSI Reports* 14, Asia.

Perkins, Dwight (1966). *Market Control and Planning in Communist China*. Cambridge: Harvard University Press.

————. (1978). "Meeting Basic Needs in the People's Republic of China," *World Development* 6.

Perkins, Dwight, and Shahid Yusuf (1984). *Rural Development in China.* Baltimore: Johns Hopkins University Press.

Petras, James, and Mark Selden (1981). "Social Classes, the State and the World System in the Transition to Socialism," *Journal of Contemporary Asia* 11, 2:189–207.

Piazza, Alan (1983). "Trends in Food and Nutrition Availability in China, 1950–1981," in *World Bank Staff Working Paper* 607. Washington, D.C.: World Bank.

Popovic, Svetolik (1964). *Agricultural Policy in Yugoslavia*. Beograd: Medunarodna Politika.

Potter, Sulamith (1983). "The Position of Peasants in Modern China's Social Order," *Modern China* 9, 4 (October): 465–99.

Preobrazhensky, E. (1965 [1926]). *The New Economics*. Oxford: Oxford University Press.

————. (1979). Selected essays in *The Crisis of Soviet Industrialization*, ed. Donald Filtzer. White Plains, N.Y.: M. E. Sharpe.

Rada, E. L., and T. H. Lee (1963). "Irrigation Investment in Taiwan," *JCRR* (February).

Rawski, Thomas (1970). *Economic Growth and Employment in China*. New York: Oxford University Press.

————. (1982). "The Simple Arithmetic of Chinese Income Distribution," *Keizai kenkyu* (Economic Research) 33, 1:12–26.

Renmin ribao editorial (1955). "Why Is It Necessary to Emphasize the Work of Consolidation of the Agricultural Producers' Cooperatives?" February 28.

"Resolution on Certain Questions in the History of Our Party since the Founding of the People's Republic of China" (1981). *Beijing Review* 27.

"Rice Review," *JCRR* (April 1964).

Reglar, Steve (1987). "Mao Zedong as a Marxist Political Economist." *Journal of Contemporary Asia*, 17, 3:208–33.

Reynolds, Bruce, ed. (1987). *Reform in China. Challenges and Choices*. Armonk, N.Y.: M. E. Sharpe.

Riskin, Carl (1975). "Surplus and Stagnation in Modern China," in *China's Modern Economy in Historical Perspective*, ed. Dwight Perkins. Stanford: Stanford University Press, pp. 49–84.

————. (1987). *China's Political Economy. The Quest For Development Since 1949*. Oxford: Oxford University Press.

Roll, Charles (1975). "Incentives and Motivation in China," paper presented at the annual meeting of the American Economic Association, December 28.

————. (1980). *The Distribution of Rural Incomes. A Comparison of the 1930s and the 1950s*. New York: Garland.

Rubin, Barnett (1986). "Journey to the East: Industrialization in India and the Chinese Experience," in *Social and Economic Development in India*, ed. Dilip Basu and Richard Sisson. New Delhi: Sage, pp. 67–88.

Rural Economic Survey Group (1983). "The Situation and Trends in Rural Reform," *Nongye jingji wenti* 6:4–13.

Sasamoto, Takeharu (1968). "A Salient Feature of Capital Accumulation in Taiwan— The System of Rice Collection by the Taiwan Provincial Food Bureau," *The Developing Economies* 6, 1: 27–39.

Schran, Peter (1969). *The Development of Chinese Agriculture, 1950–1959*. Urbana: University of Illinois Press.

Selden, Mark (1971). *The Yenan Way in Revolutionary China*. Cambridge: Harvard University Press.

————. (1978). *The People's Republic of China. A Documentary History of Revolutionary Change*. New York: Monthly Review Press.

————. (1982). "Cooperation and Conflict: Cooperatives and Collective Formation in China's Countryside," in *The Transition to Socialism in China*, ed. Mark Selden and Victor Lippit. Armonk, N.Y.: M. E. Sharpe, pp. 32–97.

————. (1983). "Imposed Collectivization and the Crisis of Agrarian Development in the Socialist States," in *Crises in the World-System*, ed. Albert Bergesen. Beverly Hills: Sage, pp. 227–52.

————. (1985a). "Income Inequality and the State," in *Chinese Rural Development: The Great Transformation*, ed. William Parish. Armonk, N.Y.: M. E. Sharpe, pp. 193–218.

————. (1985b). "State, Market, and Sectoral Inequality in Contemporary China," in *States vs. Markets in the World-System*, ed. Peter Evans et al. Beverly Hills: Sage, pp. 275–92.

Selden, Mark, and Victor Lippit, eds. (1982). *The Transition to Socialism in China*. Armonk, N.Y.: M. E. Sharpe.

Sen, Amartya (1986). "How Is India Doing?" in *Social and Economic Development in India*, ed. Dilip Basu and Richard Sisson. New Delhi: Sage, pp. 28–42.

Shanghai Labor Bureau, ed. *Chien-kuo i-lai an-lao fen-p'ei lun-wen suan* (The Debate on Distribution According to Work).

Shanin, Teodor, ed. (1983). *Late Marx and the Russian Road. Marx and the Peripheries of Capitalism*. New York: Monthly Review Press.

Shen, T. H., ed. (1974). *Agriculture's Place in the Strategy of Development: The Taiwan Experience*. Taipei: JCRR.

Shih, Chi-tseng (1969). "Taiwan nung-yeh chih-ching tui ching-chi fa-chan chih kung-hsien" (The Contribution of Agricultural Capital Outflow to the Economic Development of Taiwan), *Taiwan yin-hang chi-k'an* (Taiwan Bank Quarterly) 20, 2:60–75.

Shue, Vivienne (1980). *Peasant China in Transition. The Dynamics of Development Toward Socialism, 1949–1956*. Berkeley: University of California Press.

Solinger, Dorothy (1983). "Marxism and the Market in Socialist China," in *State and Society in Contemporary China*, ed. Victor Nee. Ithaca: Cornell University Press.

————. (1984). *Chinese Business Under Socialism. The Politics of Domestic Commerce, 1949–1980*. Berkeley: University of California Press.

————. (1984). *Three Visions of Chinese Socialism*. Boulder: Westview Press.

Su Shaozhi (forthcoming 1988). "Perspectives on Marxism Today," *Bulletin of Concerned Asian Scholars*.

Song Tingming (1986). "Review of Eight Years of Reform," *Beijing Review* 29, 51.

Stalin, Joseph (1955 [1929a]). "A Year of Great Change. On the Occasion of the Twelfth Anniversary of the October Revolution," in *J. V. Stalin Works*. Vol. 12. Moscow: Foreign Languages Publishing House, pp. 124–41.

————. (1929b). "Concerning Questions of Agrarian Policy in the U.S.S.R.," in *J. V. Stalin Works*. Vol. 12, pp. 147–78.

————. (1930). "Dizzy with Success," in *J. V. Stalin Works*. Vol. 12, pp. 197–205.

————. (1951). *Marxism and Linguistics*. New York: International Publishers.

Starr, John (1979). *Continuing the Revolution: The Political Thought of Mao*. Princeton: Princeton University Press.

State Statistical Bureau (1960). *Ten Great Years*. Beijing: Foreign Language Press.

————. (1982). *China Statistical Yearbook*. Beijing.

————. (1985). *Statistical Yearbook of China 1985*. Oxford: Oxford University Press.

————. (1986). *Statistical Yearbook of China*. Oxford: Oxford University Press.

Statistical Abstracts for the Past 51 Years (Taiwan-sheng wu-shih-i nien lai t'ung-chi ti-yao) (1946). Taiwan Province.

Stone, Bruce (1980). "China's 1985 Foodgrain Production Target: Issues and Prospects," in *Food Production in the People's Republic of China*, ed. Anthony Tang and Bruce Stone. Washington, D.C.: International Food Policy Research.

————. Szamuely, Laszlo (1974). *First Models of the Socialist Economic System— Principles and Theories*. Budapest: Akademiai Kiado.

Szymanski, Albert (1979). *Is the Red Flag Flying? The Political Economy of the Soviet Union*. London: Zed.

Taiwan Food Grain Bureau (1966). *Grain Statistics in Taiwan*. Taipei.

Taiwan Statistical Handbook (1965). Taipei.

Takahashi, Kamekichi (1937). *Gendai Taiwan keizai ron* (Essays on the Modern Taiwan Economy). Tokyo.

Tanaka, Kyoko (1978). "Mao and Liu in the 1947 Land Reform: Allies or Disputants?" *The China Quarterly* 75:566–93.

Taylor, Jeffrey (1986). "Labor Force Developments in the People's Republic of China, 1952–1983," in Joint Economic Committee of Congress, *China's Economy Looks Toward the Year 2000*. Vol. 1. *The Four Modernizations*. Washington, D.C.: USGPO.

Tian Yun (1980). "Handicraft Industry: Trends of Development," *Beijing Review* 37.

Tongji gongzuo (Statistical Work) (1957). 17.

Tucker, Robert (1973). *Stalin as Revolutionary, 1879–1929: A Study in History and Personality*. New York: W. W. Norton.

————. (1977). *Stalinism. Essays in Historical Interpretation*. New York: W. W. Norton.

Tung Talin (1959). *Agricultural Cooperation in China*. Beijing: Foreign Languages Press.

Unger, Jonathan (1982). *Education Under Mao: Class and Competition in Canton Schools, 1960–1980*. New York: Columbia University Press.

————. (1986). "A Survey of Twenty-eight Villages," *Pacific Affairs* 58, 5:585–600.

United Nations, Office of the Disaster Relief Organization (1981). *China, Case Report: Drought and Floods in the People's Republic of China*.

————. (1982). *China Case Report: Drought and Floods in Hebei/Hubei Provinces 1980/81*, Case Report no. 11 (May).

Vermeer, E. B. (1982a). "Income Differentials in Rural China," *The China Quarterly* 89 (March): 1–33.

————. (1982b). "Rural Economic Change and the Role of the State in China, 1962–78," *Asian Survey* 22, 9 (September): 823–42.

Vogel, Ezra (1968). *Canton Under Communism; Programs and Politics in a Provincial Capital 1949–1968*. Cambridge: Harvard University Press.

Wada, Haruki (1977). "Karl Marx and Revolutionary Russia," *Annals of the Institute of Social Science* 18. Tokyo: University of Tokyo.

Walder, Andrew (1986). *Communist Neo-Traditionalism. Work and Authority in Chinese Industry.* Berkeley: University of California.

Walder, Andrew (1987). "Wage Reform and the Web of Factory Interests," *The China Quarterly* 109 (March): 22–41.

Walker, Kenneth (1966). "Collectivisation in Retrospect: The 'Socialist High Tide' of Autumn 1955-Spring 1956," *The China Quarterly* 26 (April-June).

————. (1984). *Food Grain Procurement and Consumption in China*. Cambridge: Cambridge University Press.

Wang Haibo (1985). "The Ratio Between Accumulation and Consumption," in *Studies in the Problems of China's Economic Structure*, ed. Ma Hong and Sun Shaoqing.

Watson, Andrew (1980). *Mao Zedong and the Political Economy of the Border Region: A Translation of Mao's Economic Problems and Financial Problems*. Cambridge: Cambridge University Press.

————. (forthcoming). "The Family Farm, Land Use and Accumulation in Agriculture."

————. (forthcoming). "Investment Choices in the Chinese Countryside."

Wesson, Robert (1963). *Soviet Communes*. New Brunswick: Rutgers University Press.

White, Gordon (1983). "Revolutionary Socialist Development in the Third World," *Revolutionary Socialist Development in the Third World*, ed. Gordon White, Robin Murray, and Christine White. Lexington: University of Kentucky Press, pp. 1–34.

Whyte, Martin (1983). "Town and Country in Contemporary China," *Comparative Urban Research* 10, 1:9–20.

———. (1986). "Social Trends in China; The Triumph of Inequality?" in *Modernizing China: Post-Mao Reform and Development*, ed. A. Doak Barnett and Ralph Clough. Boulder: Westview, pp. 103–24.

Whyte, Martin, and William Parish (1984). *Urban Life in Contemporary China*. Chicago: University of Chicago Press.

Wiens, Thomas (1980). "Agricultural Statistics in the People's Republic of China," in *Quantitative Measures of China's Economic Output*, ed. Alexander Eckstein. Ann Arbor: University of Michigan Press, pp. 44–107.

Wilson, Duncan, ed. (1965). *Communist China 1955–1959. Policy Documents with Analysis*. Cambridge: Harvard University Press.

Wong, John (1973). *Land Reform in the People's Republic of China*. New York: Praeger.

World Bank (1983). *China: Socialist Economic Development*. 3 vols. Washington D.C.: The World Bank.

———. (1984). *China: The Health Sector.* Washington D.C.: The World Bank.

———. (1986). *World Development Report 1986*. New York: Oxford University Press.

———. (1987). *World Development Report 1987*. New York: Oxford University Press.

Wu, Hwei Ran (1970). "Economic Effect of Rice Control Policy in Post-war Taiwan," *The Developing Economies* 8, 1–4.

Wu, Rong-I (1971). *The Strategy of Economic Development: A Case Study of Taiwan*. Vander Louvalin.

Wu Xiang (1985). "Guanyu nongcun gaige he nongye wenti" (On Problems of Rural Reform and Agriculture), *Liaowang* 33 (August 18).

Wu Zhen (1954). "Fazhan nongye shengchan hezuoshe, bixu caiyong shuofu, shifan he guojia caizhu de fangfa" (To Develop Agricultural Producers' Cooperatives It Is Necessary to Use Persuasion Models and State Aid), *Xuexi* 8.

Xinhua News Agency (1985). "Peasants Move from Poverty Stricken Area," November 18, in JPRS-CAG–85–034.

———. (1986). "Village Enterprises Surpass Agriculture in Output," November 13, in JPRS-CAG–86–041, December 30.

Xu Weirong and Shi Xunru (1984). *Nongye jingji cankao ziliao* (References on Agricultural Economics) 6

———. (1985). "Shehuizhuyi dizu lilun zaitan" (Further Inquiry into Land Rent under Socialism," *Nongye jingji congcan* 5.

Xu Xu (1986). "Li Yining dui jingji gaige de sikao" (Li Yining's Thoughts on Economic Reform), in *Liaowang* (Outlook) 27 (July 7).

Xue Muqiao (1986). "Postscript to the Japanese Translation of the Revised Edition of *China's Socialist Economy*," *Jingji yanjiu* 10 (October 20): 31.

Xue Muqiao et al., eds. (1984) *Zhongguo jingji nianjian* (Economic Yearbook of China). Beijing: Jingji guanli chubanshe.

Yang Jianbai (1957). *The Internal Relationship of Proportions among Agriculture, Light Industry and Heavy Industry and Proportions Between Consumption and Accumulation* (Lun nung ch'ing chung pi-li ho hsiao-fei chi-lei pi-li chi chien te nei-tsai lien-hsi). Beijing.

Yang Jianbai and Li Xuezong (1980). "China's Historical Experience in Handling the Relations Between Agriculture, Light Industry and Heavy Industry," *Social Sciences in China* 1, 3: 19–40.

Yang Junshi (1981). "Zhongguo de nongye jitihua wenti" (Problems of China's

Agricultural Collectivization), *Dousou* (Awake) 39.

Yanowitch, Murray (1977) *Social and Economic Inequality in the Soviet Union*. White Plains, N.Y.: M. E. Sharpe.

Yeh, K. C. (1967). "Soviet and Communist Chinese Industrialization Strategies," in *Soviet and Chinese Communist Similarities and Differences*, ed. Donald Treadgold. Seattle: University of Washington Press.

Zhao Renwei (1986). "Problems of the Dual System in China's Economic Reform," *Jingji yanjiu* (Economic Research) 9, 20, in JPRS-CEA–122, December 22.

Zhao Zhanping (1985). "Guanyu shehuizhuyi tiaojian xia tudi youchang shiyong wenti de tantao" (An Inquiry into the Paid Use of Land under Socialism), *Nongye jingji wenti* 9.

Zhao Ziyang (1987). "Advance Along the Road of Socialism with Chinese Characteristics." Report Delivered at the 13th National Congress of the Communist Party of China, October 25, 1987. *Beijing Review* 30, 40 (November 9–15):23–49.

Zheng Jiaju and Ye Shaoqun (1985). "Dui gaige nongyeshui de shexiang" (Ideas on Reforming the Agricultural Tax), *Nongye jingji wenti* (Problems of Agricultural Economy) 4.

Zhongguo guodu shiqi guomin jingji de fenzi (An Analysis of China's National Economy During the Transition Period) (1959). Beijing: Science Press.

Zhongguo nongcun fazhan wenti yanjiuzu (Study Group on Chinese Rural Development) (1984). "Nongcun fenpei lingyu zhong de shenke biangeng" (The Deep Changes in the Realm of Distribution in the Rural Areas"), *Nongye jingji qingkuang* (The Situation in Agricultural Economics) 14 (December).

Zhongguo nongye nianjian 1983 (1983 Chinese Agricultural Yearbook) (1986). In JPRS-CAG-CEA–122, July 24.

Zhongguo shehui tongji ziliao (Chinese Social Statistics) (1984). Beijing: Zhongguo tongji chubanshe.

Zhou Qiren et al. (1986). "On the Transformation of National Economic Structure —Macroeconomic Environment of Rural Development in the New State, *Jingji yanjiu* (Economic Research), in JPRS-CEA–86–09), August 22.

INDEX